Have you ever dreamed of taking a journey
towards that faraway place of golden light and expanding horizons,
where the sun shines brightly on your biggest dreams?

Come with me, let's go.....

Saskia Rael

Praise For

A Suitcase Full of Faith

How One Woman Found Her Dream Trusting the Compass of Her Soul

"A Suitcase Full of Faith" is a beautifully-written, spell-binding story of one woman's journey of the Soul. Her journey is our journey. If you are ready to have your Soul awakened and uplifted, be sure to read this soul-on-fire, heart-warming, amazing book!

– **PEGGY MCCOLL**, New York Times Best-Selling Author of Your Destiny Switch, DESTINIES.COM

Saskia's angelic book presents a luminous encounter of radiant beauty, suspense, happiness and light. It is a captivating experience of compassion, oneness, healing and joy. Saskia, thank you for writing it. I love you and I love the readers reading it.

– **OREST BEDRIJ**, Author of Celebrate Your Divinity: The Nature of God and the Theory of Everything, CELEBRATEYOURDIVINITY.COM

In her creation of "A Suitcase Full of Faith" Saskia provides us with beautiful proof that the material we are teaching works! Living in the Now, listening to and trusting the message of the heart, allowing your inner truth to shine... empower all as the creator of their lives. Saskia teaches to focus on what one believes is possible by simply inviting you along for the ride as she shares her life story. Simply amazing! We want more!

– **JESHUA B. SWANSON,** Spiritual Channel and Author of Mastering the Grand Illusions, SHALALEA.COM

With the warp and woof of her soul, Saskia weaves a tale that takes readers around the world and into their own heart. A masterful storyteller, she not only weaves a brilliant cloth of many colors – in "A Suitcase Full of Faith" – Saskia reveals a pattern that beckons us to follow.

– **TONI SAR'H PETRINOVICH**, Author of The Call: Awakening the Angelic Human, SACREDSPACESWA.COM

The journey of our soul is a journey of reconnecting to the heart of ourselves. It is only by being true to our own heart that we truly walk the path of the soul. Thank you, Saskia, for sharing your journey and in this story helping all of us rediscover our own inner light.

– **JUDY SATORI**, Spiritual Channel and Light Language Sound Healer, THE-SOUNDOFLIGHT.COM

Saskia's honest and poignant account of her life forcefully yet gently reinforces what I know to be true: if we allow our Soul to guide us all will be well. This is a book to read when you need to remember what is possible, to trust in the process of life and of Spirit and to believe in a loving divinity. Pick up this book and feel the love and awakened energy. Enjoy every page. Let it open your heart, discovering the jewel that lives within.

– **MEREDITH YOUNG-SOWERS**, The Stillpoint School of Integrative Life Healing and Author of Spirit Heals, STILLPOINT.ORG

Saskia has written a remarkable book with more twists and turns than a Kasbah alley but the twists are good ones, and the turns make you wonder what lies around the bend. Here is a gem, of what quality, you decide but if exotic places, pleasing characters, and a mind crackling read is your cup of tea you may just find a diamond here.

– **BURT GOLDMAN**, The American Monk, GOLDMANMETHOD.COM

Weaving the Divine Thread of Your Soul

Second EDITION

Published by

Norvell Jefferson

ISBN **978-0-615-27247-4**

Printed in the United States of America

WWW.SUITCASEFULLOFFAITH.COM

A Suitcase Full of Faith

How One Woman Found Her Dream Trusting the Compass of Her Soul

SASKIA RÖELL

This book is lovingly dedicated

To all those who are a part of my weave –

You made the journey a golden thread.

To the friends I met along the way as

I traveled the continent of the Soul.

And to my family with love

Syb
Florian
Sytske
Shaffy
Sam
Gideon
Buddha
Mam and Pap

Acknowledgments

There are many I must express my deepest gratitude to for your role in inspiring the stories that created the joyful birthing of this Suitcase Full of Faith. You reside in my soul. There are a few who I will mention here:

My dear friend and soul sister, Sharon Lamm, who listened to her soul and told me it was time to put pen to paper. You impregnated my mind with the seed that it was my time to write. This book is the germination of that seed. I thank you from the bottom of my heart.

My writing coach, Tom Bird, who nourished my creative potential with your unwavering trust in my writer's voice. Though you never read a word of this book until it was finished, knowing you believed in me without a shadow of a doubt was the greatest gift. It taught me about the kind of trust that brings out the grandest expression of who we are. I embrace this example you embodied so passionately with my children and my clients.

My editor and soul sister, Susan Diamond Lethbridge. We 'met' when I gave you the Munay Ki rites; little did I know the future gifts we'd share. Your unstoppable flow of brilliant ideas and ability to pick up the thread where I left off made you the perfect midwife and nanny for 'Suitcase' and me. In the task of editing, you connected to my soul aligning the essence with words and love and care that shine so brightly.

My beloved husband, Syb Röell, for producing and publishing the first editions of printed copies and for so many other ways you are there for me, inspire me, trust me and love me so well. As the first copies rolled off the press, you gave 'Suitcase' her beautiful wings in which to fly out into the world. May she fly well into the hearts and homes of many special souls.

My 'spinning' teacher, Tricia Porter, who never knew I was spinning my stories full circle while I sat on my bike. During your class, I tuned up the Voice of my Soul as I spun my wheels faster and faster. These true stories are the magical result.

Thank you George Weinstein for the first proofing, Linda Lathrop for the last correction and Jacqueline Koopmans for taking a first peek at my newly-born book.

Through Heaven's Eyes

A single thread in a tapestry –
Though its color brightly shine –
Can never see its purpose
In the pattern of the grand design.

And the stone that sits on the very top
Of the mountain's mighty face –
Does it think it's more important
Than the stones that form the base?

So how can you see what your life is worth
Or where your value lies?
You can never see through the eyes of man –
You must look at your life,
Look at your life through heaven's eyes.

—Stephan Schwartz, *The Prince of Egypt*

CONTENTS

Be Still Thy Soul

Be still thy soul
Relinquish this hold
Make thee again whole
Be still thy mind
Let thee unwind
And seek out a shrine

Harvest the gold
That's planted around you
Strand by strand
You'll be somewhat more certain
Carve out your role
And reach for the heavens
All you can dream
What you can be
Know that the sky will deliver

Bestir thy heart
With journeys afar
And rivers of stars
Bestow thy love
On all that ye touch
On all that ye may

Hence, let it be told
That rhyme will be reason
Paint your world
With shades that will uplift you
And break, break from the mold
Shake off the illusions
Never again lost in dismay
All that you need is within you

Be still thy soul
And fix on the goal
Thy tale will be told
Be still thy mind
Make thee one
With the source of life.

—Bradfield

PART ONE

Prelude

There is more to life
than merely increasing its speed

—Ghandi

Spinning My Thread

The room is barely lit. The people next to me breathe heavily. Our bodies are in tune with the upbeat rhythm of the music. My legs are in sync with the song although they cry.

Still, I need to increase my speed and pedal faster. Destiny is luring me in the distance, seducing me to move beyond my limitations and push me to achieve my goal: The Finish Line.

"One more hill to climb and then it's over and you can race home," the teacher says.

I wonder why the *Finish* is called *Home...are there more parallels to spinning and life than we know? Or are they just the opposite?*

"If you haven't moved out of your comfort zone, no muscles or endurance are built," she continues. Sweat is dripping on the floor. *This ain't no smooth ride.*

I push harder. Her words resonate like echoes in my head, "Keep breathing and stay steady in the saddle; that's all we need to do today."

I guess it is the only requirement in this imaginary race. Soon our time is up and we cross the finish line and are home. *Are we*? In the end, having gone nowhere, we worked our bodies to become painfully aware that we are now *here.*

Gloria Gaynor sings, "I will survive…"

I catch my breath. *Yes, Gloria, me, too! What do we need in this earthy journey to stay alive?* Thoughts spin like circles in my head. Slowly and gently they fade to the background; the chatter silences itself. I am almost at the top of the hill when it happens…her words touch me so deeply, not only my legs, my eyes cry, too.

In a blur I see the teacher pointing at her belly button reminding us to spin from our core while she slowly emphasizes word for word, "Can you say: *'Here I am no matter what'* and take the baggage off your back and let the past be the past?"

Nobody seems to notice. I spin faster now, faster than I ever did before, spiraling out of my body, leaving the dark contours of the room behind, traveling light, no sweat, arriving at a place from where I can catch a glimpse of what my life is all about: my deep longing to be in tune with the rhythm of my heart, living in sync with the song of Soul. My unquenched thirst to unravel my weave is the intricate web I spun into the tapestry that's called the story of my life.

But where did I begin?

Karma Weaves

I sit behind my desk when the phone rings. It is 4:00 in the afternoon. Exactly twelve hours ago I began writing the first page of my book. I am still a bit dazzled at the courage it took. It was worth the confrontation with my Devil. I look at the fireplace where the last pieces of wood burn down. My office looks cozy at this hour.

I feel the urge to pick up the phone and still my curiosity to know who is on the other end. I almost never answer the phone. I am too lazy to run up and down the stairs a million times to hand the receiver to my kids.

My family and friends know me better. I carefully instructed them to always call my cell. I stare at the word OUT OF AREA. *Who is this?* It can't be for them.

My hand slowly moves to the receiver; this call is mine. I instantly recognize the voice when I put the receiver to my ear. Sandra, my Buddhist friend from Holland, is on the line.

Her timing is divine; today is my first writing day.

Sandra has never called me since we moved to Rockport. *Why is she calling me today?* It's been four years since I saw her last. We chat as if time stood still. Our strong connection doesn't need to bridge the gap of time; still, she doesn't tell me the reason for her call. I guess on a conscious level she wanted to reconnect; on a deeper level there was another reason.

We talk about our sweet memories together: how I met Dagpo Rimpoche, the great Buddhist teacher, at her house in Holland and how we both immersed ourselves in the Dalai Lama's Lam Rim teachings in Germany. Sandra introduced Buddhism to me in Taiwan. It is a gift that flowers till this day.

And then, out of the blue, she voices the most important Buddhist teaching. I write her words down on a piece of paper:

May all beings have happiness
and have all the causes for happiness.
May all beings be free of all causes of suffering.
Love is 'May you be happy.'
Compassion is 'May you be free of suffering.'

When I hang up the phone, it suddenly makes sense why she called today. *Was karma weaving my past into my future?*

The Compass of My Journey

Amazingly enough, it wasn't until the last page of this book that I could see how intricately my life's path was woven and laid out for me. Soul's companionship was undeniable.

From the moment I was born, she playfully trotted along by following my footsteps first and later by striding in front of me. In an *Ode to Soul*, the lessons she presented were daring; her trust in me was everlasting. She never failed in her promise that, if I followed her divine thread, the Universe would support my courage and save me *always*. I would *survive*; that was a stone-cold fact.

On my journey, the outer trail was my starting point; the inner trail brought me full circle.

What tools would I need in my knapsack for my Soul's journey? That would become obvious along the way.

PART TWO

Leaping on the Loom of Faith

The biggest adventure you can ever take
is to live the life of your dreams.

— Oprah

Whispers of My Soul

I turn the pages swiftly. I can't stop reading. My body, mind and spirit are immersed in the compelling story of *The Horse Whisperer*.

Suddenly my imagination comes alive: with eyes on fire, I stare outside the broken kitchen window of the desolated barn. I view the magnificent Colorado Mountains while my feet touch the land. My soles sense the raw emotions of the early Indians who walked the American earth. I breathe in the dust that spirals down from the hazy blue sky. I hear the horses cantering with the sound of freedom that stirs my Soul. *I need to go; that's all for now.*

I can't put the book down. The world I entered massages my heart's longing to listen and *leave*.

Within a few minutes, a bleak, rainy April morning transforms into an epiphany of '*pack up and go*.' My Soul takes flight . . .

I have the flu and my head is pounding. Nevertheless, my inner voice pushes me to get out of bed and walk to the window. I become still when I look outside. The view is different and I am back in my birth land.

Our back yard is fenced just like every other Dutch yard. In Holland, we have limited space for our 16,000,000 inhabitants; and so, we divide our flat land in little squares. We like the clean look of what belongs to us and what does not. Our yard is connected to five other yards.
I can view the whole neighborhood in the blink of an eye. Our yard looks like a postage stamp; one that is very playful and inviting.

There are small idyllic beds of wildflowers blossoming year round. Several pathways of old Dutch cobblestones were designed to accommodate our toddlers; they are 'roads' to practice riding their four-wheel bikes.

Above all, worth a try, is our famous swing. Its wooden structure towers high above the ground showing how creative we are with little space. Carefully, Syb freed the overgrown and weedy spot to create what became the most favored swing in the neighborhood. In one push forward, your feet can touch the window glass . . . and fly right through it if you jumped.

A few near-misses made it clear the challenge was more exciting than the risk it took to crash. The kids became masters in the art of '*bent-leg swinging.*' Usually I choose not to watch. A habit I think that is very wise.

I smile when I see the ridiculousness of how cramped we live our lives. My gut contracts as if I never realized this before. I long for *space*, endless fields of nothingness vibrating the freedom that is our birthright, swinging and floating up in the air, being able to touch the stars with the tips of my toes.

"It's time to leave," my Soul whispers, not wanting to disturb my contemplation. I nod silently. I know it's true. A deep shudder of fever runs over me. *What am I burning?*

I walk away from the window with a determined step. In my belly, I feel Soul's tickle. I don't want to go back to bed; the blankets will suffocate my spirit.

I decide to go downstairs and pick up the newspaper that was dropped on the doormat of our house.

With each step down, I dialogue with a different part of me. *Was I called to listen and leave Holland? Where would we go?*

One part still wants to go to Bali, manifesting the dream I've had for quite a while. I pictured us riding the Asian waves and tumbling ashore breathlessly, sunbathing for hours in the hot, white sand while I wiped the drizzle off my chin from savoring the overripe mangos.

I can easily see the seven of us living barefoot on a deserted, coconut palm beach, soundly asleep at night under a roof of twinkling stars. This would be an unforgettable, three-month experience for our family. This still appealed to me so.

Another part tickles me to take a step further now and explore the land of unlimited possibilities, to follow the trail of dust the horses left behind.

I am in a fast-forwarded dialogue with the two parts of me. When I reach the bottom landing, my head is foggy and confused. I pick up the newspaper and drag myself upstairs again.

Why for earth's sake did I go downstairs? I feel really sick now and long to snuggle under the duvet and drift into a dreamless sleep. The newspaper stuck in my hand is kindly asking to be opened.

I follow its lead and the paper's newness awakens me. Slowly the dizzy feeling in my head fades. One ad catches my eye. I read the announcement of the *American Green Card Lottery* and my heart beats into a gallop. Suddenly, I can't wait to enter our name in this race and *WIN*. I am so sure; *this* is our ticket. *America, here we come!*

I straighten my spine, lean back on the cushion and instantly feel the temperature of my fever drop as the temperature of my excitement rises. I pick up the phone from our bed stand and dial Syb's number. Suddenly it seems important my husband knows we are on the threshold of leaving for America. Not someday, but very soon . . .

Syb picks up the phone and patiently listens to my rambling story. He doesn't share my thrill. He wonders where the Bali idea went to. I don't blame him; however, for now, the navigation of my Soul holds the reigns.

"Syb, it's *America*," I say enthusiastically, trying to convince him with my tone of voice while knowing his mind is elsewhere. He silently assumes *time will tell* . . . truly hoping my idea will blow away with the soft whistle of the April wind.

What he doesn't know is this idea carries the force of a tornado. It will sweep us into an unstoppable swirl of synchronistic events. The book disappears under my bed; the lottery ad is clipped out. I don't need to read anymore. The horse's whisper is heard.

A week later, I bike with an elated feeling of success to the post office. As I drop our application letter into the tall red box, I blow a kiss on the envelope stamped for a trip to the United States.

I feel the spring wind will blow a breeze of good fortune against our backs. After all, it's only a matter of time until the spinning wheel of the lottery drops the 'green card' into our laps.

I ignore the red stop light as I pedal back home. In Holland, the light is always green; at least, that is the unspoken rule of the biker. My speed reflects my happy spirit; the world is at my feet.

"We are going to America," I sing to Sam and Gideon, who sit in the front and back seats of my old golden bike. They join my cheerful mood by waving their chubby hands to everyone we pass. We look like three happy campers in fantasy land; we are on a mission of 'no matter what it takes.' I dream on until three months later when the long-awaited answer is dropped on our doorstep.

When I open the envelope, I am stunned. I gasp for breath. *How can this be?* We are not the lucky winners!

The red light was not to be ignored apparently. I can only trace it back to a foreboding there was maybe…a little waiting time involved.

Still nothing can stop me now from touching down on American soil. I really feel we are meant to live there. The timing might be off but, before I give up on this dream, I know we have to explore all the possibilities, perhaps cross the Atlantic Ocean and touch the earth on the other side.

We also need to make sure the kids resonate with my outrageous plan. I will go to any length to investigate if our joyful life in Bussum, Holland, can be traded for a better life in America. If the kids are opposed, then, and only then, I will rest.

I hardly recognize the fierceness that drives me; my heart beats fast-paced. Something inside of me is stirred up *big time.*

One morning as I sit at our wooden Chinese kitchen table, Soul comes along for a personal chat. I sip my homemade cappuccino and drift off into a trance-like state of deep inner peace and presence. I have all the time in the world to enjoy this sacred moment. Gideon is asleep; the other four kids are at school; our Taiwanese dog Buddha snores at my feet.

Soul seizes a golden opportunity to grab my full attention. I am shown a picture of New Mexico. The red earth feels very familiar as if I recognize it from many lives lived. I am old and sit in my white adobe house. I glance over the stretches of prairie land where coyotes leave their footprints and birth their howling cubs.

The next moment I am surrounded by my most highly-admired gurus. They are my friends and I am one with them.

A moment later I see myself buried in the desert sand; my life has come to an end. I am ready to go to the light and I am deeply satisfied. My life purpose is fulfilled.

The phone rings, Buddha barks and, in a flash, I am back in the kitchen. The foam of my cappuccino is gone; the coffee is cold.

I don't care. I've seen the blueprint of my destiny. The inevitable will happen and the Universe will show us the way.

A few weeks later, it becomes clear that action is required.

The Yellow Bus

A seed is growing and many signs point in the direction we are heading for America.

Most weekends, while living in Holland, we picked a Saturday or Sunday to go on a scenic tour by car or bike to find the perfect place to enjoy a 'sacred coffee moment.' Usually all of the kids joined in but, on this particular Saturday, only the three youngest are part of the trip.

Instead of heading for the old part of the city, we decide to drive to Muiden, a little village 'under the smoke' of Amsterdam. It takes us only twenty minutes to reach this village.

We love the small winding roads that take us through the green meadows Holland is famous for. We drive slowly and take our time to watch cows and sheep tending to their week-old offspring. The calves and lambs are trying to escape their mom's watchful eyes with frivolous jumps and back flips. Our kids laugh joyfully at their attempts. Easily, we could watch for hours but our thirst reminds us it is '*coffee time.*'

As we settle down in one of the cozy corners of The Tea Garden, we wonder why we had never come here before. It is an oasis of peace so close to the big city. The place has a beautiful exotic garden with lush flowers overhanging red and yellow ceramic pots. Inside the teahouse, they sell home-baked goods made with freshly picked fruit from their orchard. I am reminded of the Italian countryside. The birds and people who flock here look like Mediterranean tourists. Apparently, the Dutch are busy elsewhere.

Only the coffee and the yellow school bus that enters the parking lot are a surprise. I've never seen an American school bus in Holland and neither has Syb.

"It's a sign," I exclaim as I grab a pen to write down the phone number displayed in large type on the back of the bus. "We need to be able to track them down *just in case,*" I explain to Syb.

"If we really do decide to leave Holland, we might want to rent this bus and drive all the neighborhood kids around for fun," I add.

It was something that just 'popped' in my head, a funny idea.

How little did we know then. Or *did we already know on a much deeper level our destiny was planned long ago?*

The note is kept and the number called. The same bus appears in front of our house less than a year later. This time it is there to pick up the youngest kids in our neighborhood and drop them off at our *farewell* party. July 1, 2001 is *celebration* time. And yet, before that happens, a whole life has to be lived.

Pilgrim, how you journey
on the road you chose
to find out why the winds die
and where the stories go.
All days come from one day
that much you must know,
you cannot change what's over
but only where you go.
One way leads to diamonds,
one way leads to gold
another leads you only
to everything you're told.
In your heart you wonder
which of these is true;
the road that leads to nowhere,
the road that leads to you.

— Enya, The Pilgrim

Where Do We Go from Here?

As usual on Sunday morning, we head to Amsterdam.

We take the famous world map called *The Dutch Bos Atlas* with us. I carry this map of the world under my arm because it doesn't fit in Gideon's stroller. It's too big and the table we place the map on is too small.

After two cappuccinos and a few apple pies with whipped cream, the time comes to open the book that holds the answer to our future. Our destiny depends upon the decision we make today.

Will we choose to go to the West or to the East of this huge country called America?

Slowly we count the pages, savoring our trepidation. The page of the United States comes into view. The country stares at us; its width is ENORMOUS.

"East or West is the question," I say. Both Syb and I look down and gaze from left to right at the fifty states of America. For a moment, we are both lost in our own world, not noticing the kids dropping the last crumbs of the apple pie on the floor for our dog Buddha. The scene above the table is as mouthwatering as under it.

"East," we blurt out at the same time. And right we are.

"To me the West is too laid-back . . . too much like a fantasy. East feels more like us. We are like the pilgrims," says Syb. I have the strong feeling, too, that East comes first, although my desire to go West is strong as well.

Life in the West feels like it would be mellow, more like our comfortable lifestyle in Bussum. Somehow, we both feel it is not the right time for us to live in California, later maybe.

We feel more like pilgrims bent on discovering new lands. We will work hard to plant our seeds in the fertile ground of American soil. We will harvest good crops that hold the potential to grow our *adventures* and *ventures* into all that we are, not only for Syb and me, but also to sprout in our kids, as well.

Where in the East will we go? This will be left to the One with the bigger picture. For sure, it is not for Syb and me to know; we have no clue.

It doesn't take long for the Universe to respond to our passionate quest. Two days later the phone rings and Annetine, our Dutch friend who lives in New York, is on the line inviting us to come and stay in her newly remodeled barn in South Hampton, Long Island, USA.

We figure the opportunity is too good to miss. Annetine's call settles it. Long Island is on the East Coast. That is the place to start.

Syb and I decide we will turn our visit into to a three-week vacation in the States to get a real taste of America. Our kids explode with excitement. What we don't tell them just yet is that our plan is for more than a vacation; it is to go and *feel* if this land is the place for us, a place for us to *live*. If we find it's not the place for them, Syb and I will go in a much distant future. Soul pinches me when she reads my mind: *I wonder if she knows more than I do.*

In two minutes through an invitation from a friend, the Universe moves us in the right direction and our life course is decided. The coast where we will spend our vacation in America is the coast we will come to live and make our home.

Deep down it feels as if our destiny was indeed designed long ago. Everything goes so easy in the flow.

A Holiday in America

This journey was unplanned, unexpected and absolutely held the promise of an outcome beyond our wildest dreams. Little do we know at the end of the three weeks, we will stand in awe of how unorganized but divinely orchestrated our trip was and how exhausted to the bone we will be when we arrive back in Holland.

It was going to be a daring adventure to travel to America with the dynamic crowd of our five kids. We had booked our tickets to New York last minute and there was hardly any waiting time between ticket arrival and travel departure. I packed little because we always travel light. When we finally are all strapped in our seatbelts and the plane is ready for takeoff, I see five happy faces totally oblivious to what the future has in store.

The plane ride is not easy. Gideon can't sleep and the stewardess tries to sedate him with too many bottles of apple juice; later we find out he is allergic to this. He falls asleep on Syb's shoulder after seven hours of walking up and down the aisle. Unfortunately, that is only ten minutes before we land.

Upon arrival at JFK in New York, some of our luggage is lost and one is ripped apart. My duffel bag arrives, zipped open on the conveyor belt; due to my hasty packing, I don't even know what is missing. Some of my clothing comes down the belt one by one and, when I see the Fool from the tarot card deck pass by, he gives me the impression he feels forlorn and out of place.

No other cards are in sight and it takes a little bit to realize he must be mine. Gosh, I can't remember that I brought a tarot deck for this journey, but the Fool— one of my favorite cards of the deck—doesn't need an explanation. His counsel is clear: "Jump, leap, don't look, go for your dreams, you are safe, the tools in my knapsack are all you need for your journey ..."

I pick him up and wish I had only brought his yellow knapsack instead of trying to guess how many bags we have. I set him in my purse missing the most significant meaning of his presence. I count my kids.

Patient as the kids are, we wait for two hours to finally have our lost bags returned and the ones that were ruined are replaced by a set of expensive new blue bags that are even better than the ones we owned.

It doesn't take us long to figure out that our "freestyle" traveling might work for trips around Europe but – certainly in America – it is not the way. We were warned frequently that "danger lurks in every corner" and we better use our eyes like hawks to guard our nest. This is a mindset that isn't ours and this form of management style is especially challenging on our kids.

They were raised the opposite way. They are free-spirited, friendly and trusting when talking to any stranger. Above all, they are interested and excited to explore the world on their own.

So far, this had always worked in our favor but not this time.

The only question is: *How we can manage this fear-based style with only two pairs of eyes, hands and legs?* It was an understatement to say we needed to be alert now.

Gideon the youngest is very skilled in his 18-month-old "walk and run" style, Florian the nine year old wants to be an entrepreneur on his own and the three others are in their hide-and-seek mode 24 hours a day. We are going to do our best.

We are still in great spirits when we leave the lost and found counter and, in the meantime, we need to find a cab to bring us to the Big Apple. The kids have played hide and seek behind the various, stranded suitcases and we can't wait to open the glass doors and experience the *real feel* of New York. The world of fast-driving cars, loud-honking horns and crazy cabdrivers who offer their service is presented all at once.

Their stubbornness and strictness of rules is a surprise to us and it takes a lot of persuasion to agree that the seven of us can ride together in the same cab. On this first day, we really want to be conscious of our budget. Had we known this is a skill we do not possess, we wouldn't have wasted our time explaining why we wanted one cab and not two.

We learn our lesson about rules in America: they are *to be followed.* We can no longer rely on our Dutch interpretation of rules as being *optional.* In the coming three weeks, we will have plenty of opportunity to practice patience and compassion. Perhaps we are as stubborn in our Dutch way as the Americans are with their rules.

The cabdriver regrets his 'deal' no matter what amount of money we offered. It is too late when he realizes his mistake.

Even if the cab was super-sized, a family of seven with three weeks worth of luggage and some camping gear is a set up for failure right from the start; little do we know the worst is yet to come. We squeeze ourselves in with laughs of flexibility, one upon the other in the back seat of his Ford. The luggage is handled the same way.

The trunk is overloaded but for us no challenge is too big. With Syb's well-practiced hands, a rope is tied from left to right and even the cab driver shakes his head in admiration when the trunk is finally closed and secure. Syb signals with his thumb that we are ready to go. The kids clap and I sigh. Then I smell an odor that means trouble.

Not now, I think. Gideon has severe diarrhea as thin as the many bottles of apple juice he drank. There is no stopping and the diapers are a faint attempt to halt this flow. A penetrating smell envelopes the small car quickly.

At every stop during this primetime hour of traffic, Syb jumps out of the car and kneels alongside the road where Gideon willingly allows him to wipe his butt with the spare sprigs of grass that have lost their green color. Unfortunately the wipes are long finished; they were all used above the Atlantic Ocean. Our new method doesn't relieve much but it certainly invites the stares of the stressed drivers passing us by.

The cabbie swears in Hindu and drives like he is back in Bombay, but there is no keeping up with Gideon's flow; the course of nature takes its turn. The traffic is slow but the cabbie pushes the pedal; the faster he drives the more noise the car makes. The back part of the car is overweight and it feels as if we scratch the ground at every turn. I hold my breath and wonder if our first day will be our last.

We arrive safely at Jan and Annetine's spacious apartment on the 19th floor of the Upper West. The apartment is designed with an eye for detail we can't grasp. Real art is on the walls and displayed in various places in the living room. The wooden floors are polished and shiny; they look like inviting ice skating rinks and it is obvious that young children were not part of this household yet.

I pray that Gideon will never come near a bottle of apple juice again and that the rest of us behave. But the kids are respectful and keep their hands behind their backs. They can't believe their eyes when Annetine shows them the 200 channels on TV. Holland seems far away with its six channels. Before we go to bed, we stand outside on the balcony and watch the big boats that cruise on the Hudson River at this late hour. We are mesmerized by the many lights that light the other side; New Jersey is like an arm's distance away.

It is hard to give in and go to bed. Our first day was phenomenal from sunrise to sundown and, if our whole trip will be like this, we had better get some rest.

The days in New York are the best; we take the kids everywhere and there is no difference in what we do with the five of them and what we would have done if there was only the two of us. On our first stroll through Central Park, Shaffy finds a KNIFE under a police car. We all shriek in delight: this can't be true, this is heavenly, what an adventure; a kid's dream has come true.

We fantasize that the knife belongs to a criminal who hastily hid it under the car when he got busted. Shaffy carries his trophy as a treasure worth his life; no one in the world can take it from him. He will be the hero of "*show and tell*" in class when he goes back to school—*how cool is that*?

Our expectation is confirmed: New York is a thrill. The kids find magic in everything they see, smell or touch. They widen their eyes at the sight of the heavy traffic when the seven of us race down Broadway; amazingly and without luggage, the Manhattan taxi drivers have no problem squeezing the seven of us in one car. We leisurely stroll along the windows of Bloomingdale's and FAO Schwartz. We visit the Sony building where we don't have hands enough to play the electronic devices. We almost buy fake gadgets from the vendors on 5th Avenue but we end up with popcorn instead.

When we take the touristy ride in a horse carriage around Central Park, we don't argue when only six of us are allowed. Syb waits patiently at the entrance of the park until we return. We learn fast. Rules are rules. Our adrenaline level is high. Indeed we have to keep our eyes open 24/7; the kids explore the new with a playful vigor that makes them disappear in a flash. A woman screams loudly when Sam, our four year old, mistakenly puts his hand on her stroller. After all, *he might have a deadly disease.* This is America; I almost forgot.

In Worchester, Massachusetts, we rent an RV for eleven days; it is a nine-person sleeper that can house our zoo. The challenge is beyond telling when we all hop into the enormous house on wheels and leave the safe parking lot of the rental company behind us. After few and sparse instructions, the owner wishes us luck and waves goodbye. We are on our way.

Syb has never driven a vehicle like this and I have never navigated the driver on an American highway. My biggest question: *Where do we go*? We have no planned destination and we need to trust our gut like we always did in Europe and Asia. But the American highways all look the same and our familiar way of following the sun suddenly doesn't seem to work. There is no sun, only rain in an unstoppable downpour. We need another navigation system. We need to have faith that an invisible trail of destiny will unfold our path for us.

The guy from the rental company had dropped a big book that feels like a bomb in my lap. "In here you can find every campground in America you're looking for," was all he said.

I wish I knew what I am looking for. Since our idea of camping without reservations is not an option, we have to believe in the luck the guy has wished us. The truth is the kids could have stayed on the parking lot of the RV terrain; for them this enormous car is a feast no matter where we land. It's the best vacation in the world and our first week isn't even over. I am glad I have strapped them tight in their seats, but nothing can spoil their fun. We drive fast because the one thing we have figured quickly is, when you don't know where you are heading, it's best to keep your speed "full pedal." Symbolically it must have meant there was no stopping us.

Syb asks me for directions and I browse like an idiot through the book that weighs at least a hundred pounds. "Uh, let's look," I mumble, trying to make Syb believe I know what I am doing.

The roads around Worchester are jammed at this peak hour and Syb needs all his attention behind the wheel, which looks like the steering wheel of the Holland America line. "We have hit the road, Jack," Syb says, but whoever Jack is he better help us in this fast-driving traffic maze that has no beginning nor foreseeable end.

The vehicle goes fast. I look through the manual on my lap and I am completely lost. The names of the places don't ring a bell. I have no idea where we are or where we are going. I wonder why I am assigned to this task and I guess Syb is wondering the same.

The Angels must have flapped their wings in the right direction because, after an hour drive, we pass a sign that leads us to a campground. It is not exactly the idyllic place we have in mind but we have to stop; it's getting dark.

We look around and conclude this place is horrific, nothing like the romantic pine tree campgrounds of France or Spain. All the RVs are parked on top of each other and I look in disbelief at the many long-bearded gnomes in front of every trailer. I take a breath—what a way to start our first camping day.

We are told we can only take a spot behind the washing quarters with no hook up, but that is fine to us. *Did we need a hook up anyway*?

All of a sudden we are aware that the policies in America are very different and we have to reserve in advance to get a hook up. For now we are all set. All we need is dinner. It's 7:00 PM and we have a raving appetite and our small fridge is empty. We hadn't thought that far ahead.

It's pretty obvious we can not go *out* for dinner with this *nine-sleeper-on-wheels*. We are glad to find there is a store in walking distance. For tonight it is bread and cheese from the convenience store.

The kids love the campground; for them it has its own idyllic nature. The many little stone men and the rusty slide behind the showers are good for at least an hour of fun. After dinner we go for an evening stroll along the cultivated footpaths that leads us through "*the land of the gnomes*."

The little figures look proud and polished in their cute, colorful costumes, their faces grim but satisfied in the shimmering evening light. They must have worked hard to make their owners' yards well manicured and neat.

The park is deserted at this hour. I ask myself why nobody is home to appraise their effort.

I read the kids a bedtime story but nothing can compete with their impressions of this first camping day. Right now I don't mind the *panoramic* view outside. The grey brick wall of the bathroom building doesn't matter anymore. The inside picture of being tucked in, bundled up and curled together in a *home-on-wheels* is *paradise* and perfect for us.

Our survival and improvisation skills come in handy; this is what we are good at. Each day we spend at a different campground.

The choice is easy; the kids love everything – they haven't inherited the pickiness of their parents. Since we have given up on finding the "perfect place," we just stop when we are ready for a break or when we pass a campground that has a swimming pool. How easy life becomes when we are in the flow instead of in a search for perfection. No reservations are needed; the Universe provides us every single time. Miraculously we always show up at the right time in the right place. Either someone has cancelled or there is a no show that reserved the perfect spot for us. Honesty requires me to say that parents and kids definitely have different tastes regarding camping in America.

The endless downpours can't spoil the fun. My daily trips to the laundry room become my sacred moments, time to sit and listen to the soothing sound of the tumbling dryers, nothing else to watch except the huge machines that do my work. Secretly I savor these moments of inner peace; it's worth the dirt magnetized to kids and clothes. I start to like the laundry for the first time in my life; it is a blessing in disguise.

We encounter bears in Canada, we swim and canoe in the different lakes, we watch the sunrise and sundown around our private campfire and we live on the simplest RV-cooked meals. Our fridge stays filled by the second week.

Now we don't need to drive downtown to shop. We even begin to like the Dunkin Donuts coffee; that says it all.

In Toronto, Syb shows his parking skills by parking in the midst of a glamorous street in this huge metropolis. The RV occupies three parking spots at once; we laugh till we can laugh no more as the kids take turns filling the meters one by one.

We keep on moving and, after two weeks, we are exhausted to the bone. We as parents are ready for some rest but it's not very likely to happen because of the divine design of this vacation. Although we have had a good practice in our daily survival instincts—finding food, fun and shelter—by now we have learned to do that with great verve. The timing is in accordance with the greater plan.

After 11 days we return the RV, we have had our share of rain, we long for the sun. When we look in the newspaper for a place where the sun shines, Rockport is the answer. *How could it not be*? Our bliss is in sight.

Throughout our journey, all of us are impressed and overwhelmed by the friendly nature of the Americans we meet. Wherever we go, we are welcomed as if we are old friends. The kids are loved and they can truly feel the genuine warmth and openness of the Americans.

One evening when we ask for a room in a Holiday Inn, the woman at the counter is so impressed with the number of blond-haired kids who stare at her at once she arranges the biggest suite for the cheapest price. But that is not all. On top of that she offers the kids free food and meals for as long as we stay. We are given the royal treatment. The kids are used to sharing their food and drinks when we go out for dinner; they never get their own soft drink. How their faces glow when the waitress takes their order one by one. Even a refill is reality here and Sam wonders, "How much better can life get?"

Then we are on the road again heading to our next destination. By now the time has come to ask THE question and, while driving and discussing the option of owning guns, I ask them if they can picture themselves living in the United States. In one breath a whole hearted YES is answered. The when and where is the only question.

The boys are all ears because they are wildly inspired by the idea of buying a gun. Numerous commercials piqued their interest and ignited a rambling fantasy to own one. Suddenly a gun is not an option but a necessity when living in the States. I ask myself, "Why are guns and America a match?" I am horrified at the thought of it and I start lecturing right away. "Absolutely no guns in my house," is my bold statement.

Syb is wiser and more relaxed. He does not take the words of a nine and a five-year-old too seriously. Instead he feeds their interest by exploring options about what kind of guns they could buy. Before I know it, Florian and Shaffy read only gun magazines. During the long hours in the car they are as immersed in their dream as I am in mine.

The Trail to Our Dream House

Rockport was to be our last stop before we head back to New York. We will end our trail where we started. We are invited at Frits and Joanna's house, which is on the ocean. Syb and I visited their lovely house in the fall and at that time nothing could stop us from falling head-over-heels in love with Rockport. The ocean smell, the small streets winding along the ocean, the numerous galleries downtown and the lobster boats moving in and out of the harbor were a feast for our eyes.

The one thing we didn't understand was how the people of this small town were able to make a living; everyone and everything reeked of relaxation. After we left there in the fall, we made up our minds that this town was for fishermen and vacationers. I couldn't imagine anyone in need of a life coach there. Life was already smooth and easy in this little town, the pace was slow, and problems belonged to another world. No wonder we were lead to Rockport as our final destination, our place to come to rest at last. Maybe life was a beach after all.

So, on the last leg of our vacation, a renewed spirit sweeps over us as we pass the sign *You have entered Rockport.* The speed slows down to 15 miles an hour and we can't wait to unwind at Frits and Joanna's house. Strangely enough, I only realize later that the days in Rockport were saved for last for good reason. The Universe knew her divine timing.

Our friends welcome us with open arms and it feels good to have a roof above our heads without need for a "hook up." No more calls to hotels or noisy swimming pools to watch, just an ocean view and wine on the outside deck with our friends. The sun shines bright and warm from the moment we arrive on Cape Ann and I gladly shake off the dampness and rain that has left my muscles sore. Instantly, I forget how wet we were when we pulled into Chapel Lane in Pigeon Cove.

The next morning, I wake up from the sound of crashing waves hitting the big rocks below their house. For a moment, I am confused as to where I am but, when I look around and see three heads of blond hair peaking out of the covers and still fast asleep, I remember we are in Rockport, Massachusetts.

I tiptoe downstairs, careful not to awake this sleeping house. The full-length window shows I am not the only early bird to sing her song. Florian, Shaffy and TJ are playing soccer outside. The sun is already high in the sky and I am magnetically drawn to go outside and walk to the edge of the cliffs that surround their yard. I climb down and slide my bare feet over the rocks slippery from the cold water splashed by the waves. The tide is high and I can touch the ice cold water with my toes.

For a moment I consider a courageous morning dip. Chicken as I am, I decide to save my ocean swim for later. I climb back up the rocks and walk towards the house. It is time to wake up Syb.

Our day has started but I have not seen what's written in the cloudless sky.

Joanna and Frits treat us to a lavish breakfast and, when I wipe the last crumbs of egg from Gideon's face, they urge us to take their yellow jeep and go for a tour. "Let's find our dream house," I exclaim loudly, but nobody listens to my heartfelt joke. I am unheard by them, but my call is answered minutes later.

Syb takes the driver's seat and the kids jump in the back. The jeep is a treat for us. With the top down and the wind blowing through our hair, off we go. The jeep leaves Chapel Lane with us inside for the ride and, at the end of the street, the blinker points automatically to the right. I must admit this was one of most crucial choices we made. We turn right as if we know where we are going. Determined to satisfy our priority of *first-things-first*, we trust our luck in finding the coffee place we are searching for.

Little do we know; the Universe has something else in mind. Had we turned left, the cozy coffee place would have been our end destination; apparently the Universe's order of first-things-first came on a different menu today.

Our jeep heads for a neighborhood in which there is no coffee house.

So, why were we driving around Pigeon Cove? Are we being magically pushed or pulled or did we make a mistake? Perhaps it doesn't matter. We are enjoying cruising through this beautiful neighborhood. As we drive through one of Pigeon Cove's quiet, spacious lanes, we spot a man walking a big white dog. "Any houses for sale around here?" Syb asks as a kind of a joke on me.

The man says, "Sure," as if he was waiting there for us to finally arrive. "Just drive a little farther down this street," he says pointing, "and look to your left. It's a big white house, a Victorian."

"Thank you," we say and, without taking the man too seriously, we drive off. The street is scenic; there are only a few houses on one side, woods on the other. The two things that amaze us most is the smell of the ocean and that we can view the sea from every angle.

The house rises majestically on our left just after the woods; the big trees shutter the view of the house from the road completely. The *For Sale* sign stands alone and lonely in the yard, overlooked by too many for too long. "This must be it," we are thinking, yet it looks like a magic castle from a fairytale more than a big, white Victorian. Syb doesn't need further instructions. He pulls the jeep neatly into the driveway. Before we stop, I am out of the car. The kids stay in the back of the jeep, thinking Syb and I will be back in a moment.

What drove me to head straight for the side door I don't know to this day. I run up the stairs that leads to the side door of the house as if I have been away too long. Easily the door slides open and I let myself in.

"Hey, you can't do that," Syb shouts to me in vain.

"I have to," I yell back, unconcerned about what will happen next. And then I am in the house. A sense of coming home overwhelms me and, when I close the door behind me, I whisper a shy, "Hello."

Instantly, I feel a delightful energy around me; the powerful inner presence of this house sparks with her joy.

I run upstairs, I run downstairs, I touch the walls. I know I have come home. The house puts her arms around me in a welcoming embrace. "I am yours," I hear. She beams and so do I. We have found each other and I am falling in love.

The ceilings are high and the sunlight caresses the walls, pretending to smooth out the cracks. I don't realize my pink glasses are on; I see only what I want to see.

I hear quick footsteps on the deck. Syb awakens me from my thoughts and, when he comes, I take him by the hand. It is like being kids again; sneaking in someone else's house is forbidden fruit, but we need to have a bite. We have a bite at last.

We run through the house; the many stairs create confusion as to where we are and how to get to each room. The kids will love this house; it is built for *Hide and Seek* although the game may turn into *Lost and Found.* The many secret hiding places are numerous. We wonder, "How long will it take to find one of them in this maze of rooms and stairs?"

We climb to the attic, the top floor. Via a wooden ladder, we reach the roof. Motionless we stand there, speechless; there is nothing more to say. The widow's walk gives us a view of the entire neighborhood. It shows the ocean from every direction; the mountains of New Hampshire glower in the distance. This house is surrounded by the sea and you can even hear the lulling sound of the waves, much louder than I thought.

Long ago, the women in this place must have gathered in the attic to climb the wooden stairs with leaden boots to reach the widow's walk, mustering their hope and prayers that the sea would be kind enough to bring their beloved husbands and lovers home. I look down and see the kids' hands waving from the yellow dot that is the jeep, parked as if it belonged here and never had to leave.

As fast as we ran into the house, we run out again. We praise the kids for their patient wait. "Let's get Joanna and Frits. They need to see our house," says Syb, and with that said, we race back to Chapel Lane as if our life depended on it.

Three minutes later, we are back at the house, but the scenery has changed. We are not the only visitors this time. A man with dark curly hair parks his car next to ours. "Hi, I am Michael, the owner," he introduces himself. He comes right to the point, "Are you interested in seeing the house?"

"Oh sure, we would love that," we answer politely, showing the most innocent faces in the world. He is happy and surprised to be in time for a tour; what a coincidence we all collided in his yard!

The whole clan follows his lead and like little ducklings we trod in line upstairs. We are nine in total now and I thank God on my bare knees that the timing was divine. *How embarrassed would we have been if we had welcomed the owner in his own house?* Our only option might have been to buy the house right on the spot, grateful to spare our shame. *How could it be that the house was empty for six months and the owner, who lived downtown, pulled in the driveway at exactly the same time? Was this meeting divinely arranged?*

The owner is friendly and shares all the details; he raves about the high ceilings and the two and a half baths (we have no idea what that is). I don't care about the details; I care about one thing: *When and how can we buy this house*? That is my only thought. The boys firmly decide upon their rooms at first glance; no doubt about a successful trade of countries. The rooms in the attic have guns displayed on the walls . . . so, *how difficult was their choice?*

I am wildly enthusiastic and deeply touched but I wisely keep my mouth shut. My face must have spoken more than words did; that much I couldn't hide. When we leave and close the door behind us, I know we won't see this house again until we are the owners. The Universe had kept her promise and brought us back to where our Souls belong.

102 Ocean Pines Avenue was for sale; to be marked *sold and owned*, it needed buyers.

Before we say goodbye to the owner, he hands me a picture of the house. I treasure it as if it is my newborn baby. I tuck it in my purse and, for the next year, it will not leave my side. We go back to Joanna and Frits's house and enjoy our last day of vacation on the beaches of Cape Ann. I can't think of anything else but THE HOUSE.

Unfortunately, Syb's mind is focused on business back home. There is tons of work ahead of him; his future focus is different than mine. He firmly declares *if the house is still for sale next year, we might give it a thought.*

The fact is we already decided during this trip that we were not going to buy a house and, for sure, not in Rockport. This village was way too leisurely and fun. *Hmmm*, all of a sudden I wasn't so sure.

We leave Rockport at sunset in the afternoon. We are sad and happy at the same time; we don't want our vacation to end but we are looking forward to going back home, too. We have some stories worth telling.

We wave to Frits, Joanna, TJ and Nico and turn left onto Granite Street. A slow-moving car drives in front of us. "Hey, that is the owner of the house," says Syb. His eyes and memory work well.

I don't recognize the car or the driver but it must be so. We all agree to follow him; we are wondering where he is going. "It's a sign," we blurt out—by now the kids are part of this game. *Was everything not perfectly orchestrated?* The guns were already hanging in "their" rooms and I can't care less at this point as long as we are all on the same page. The gun issue can be dealt with later. Boy, had I changed overnight!

The man in front of us knows where he is going; he never stops. We are glad the winding road is easy to follow. The speed in Rockport is 15 miles per hour—how could we forget. We are right on his tail.

After a while, he turns a corner and enters Gloucester. He halts at the stop sign right around the bend. As a good American, he knows the rules. *Stop* means *stop*! We beep our horn and he spots his followers when he turns his head.

He parks his car at the side of the road and walks toward us. "What a surprise," he says with a big smile on his face.

We tell him we followed him and ask if he is willing to give us his home phone number. We want to stay connected. "Just in case," we say, while I wave the card with the picture of the house up and down. "Yeah, right," I think to myself, "just in case." I know better. It feels like I'm on a treasure hunt like the one I had years ago when hoping to snatch Syb from the Tower of Taipei. *Would this be any easier*?

Our last two days will be spent in Greenwich and similar towns. We figure—in order to find work—we need people who are more in need of coaching than the Rockport beach bum who has already figured out that life is a beach.

To me it made sense that a city like New York needed to be at arm's length from where we came to live. I could imagine a lot of stressed-out New Yorkers in need of life coaching but, by the same token, I realized this idea was only my left brain talking. *What did I know of the greater plan?*

Truly our radius to find our dream house was as unlimited as water in the ocean. Basically we wanted to find a house on the East Coast of America, somewhere surrounded by nature. *How descriptive was that? Had the Universe responded to our passionate call and found the perfect match*?

Before we left Holland, Syb and I decided we would avoid the upset of driving around in an unfocussed way to find a house. We concluded we were not going to search for a place to live—instead, the place had to find us. Our focus was on the kids and vacation.

But now what? Our tour of Greenwich, Darian and towns like that was absolutely useless. Nothing compared with Our House in Rockport. My love was real.

A day later, I cement this thought when we are at the Greenwich country club. I summon the image of the tight-jawed faces of the bored women who watch their spoiled kids in the pool and entertained by dark-skinned nannies. Certainly there is lots and lots of coaching work here. I envision my practice in full bloom. Unfortunately, I found my place a day ago.

We fly back two days later, exhausted and fulfilled. Life gets back to normal as if we never left.

I am out of sync in Holland. Physically, I crossed the ocean; my heart and Soul are left behind. Day by day, the desire to be back in Rockport grows even though there is nothing I can do but pray and fantasize. Syb is busy with his new business, which is BIG. He needs all of his attention on the deals where his personal involvement is crucial.

I have placed the picture of the house on the mantel of our fireplace. Daily I say, "Hi," and I imagine myself taking a seat in one of the rocking chairs on the front porch. It brings me back to New England and for a few minutes I belong to the other side. In this sacred moment, my breath expands while my inhale easily finds the rhythm of the ocean's waves.

I drift away in resonance with the place my Soul belongs. When I drive over the highway to Amsterdam, I fantasize: I am on Route 128 to the North Shore Mall. Only the many cows along the road can distract my train of thought.

The kids are manifesting in an even bigger way. At night before they fall asleep, we talk about which room they'll get. Their imagination is vivid and in color. Their new rooms house lots of toys and, for the oldest boys, the guns hang loaded on the walls. I am thrilled because, when I switch off the light, they drift into sleep in *their rooms*. The manifestation process increases immeasurably by the fantasies of their lively minds.

Weeks pass by until mid October. I know it's NOW OR NEVER. I talk to Syb and share my feeling: we need to take action because someone is buying *Our House*!

We call Michael and ask him what is going on with the house. He confirms my suspicion. Yes, indeed, potential buyers are lurking nearby. The Universe makes her move. "Action" is the operating word. *But how do we proceed*? Michael's instructions are clear: if we are serious, we need to call a lawyer in Rockport and make a bid. The circus has begun. Suddenly, we need to increase the speed and pedal faster to get in on time. *How serious are we*?

The Universe is in step with our increased speed. We talk to lawyers and business is in full swing. Before we know it, we've hired a lawyer in Gloucester to make our bid. *What are we doing?* There is hardly time to think. We go faster than the speed of light. The bidding starts; the process is surreal. We go back and forth as if we are buying a car on the Taiwanese market. Although it seems like a game, we are in head-deep when one night the lawyer calls and asks for our final bid. *Showtime*!

Syb's face speaks more than words can say when he puts down the phone. I hold my breath. I sense the time has come to face reality. Syb hesitates from deep within. *Are we really buying an old Victorian house un-*

seen? Why leave our lovely life behind and make the leap? No jobs, no large bank account, no contacts, just a lot of faith we can make it work. *Is that all it takes?*

We talk briefly. Nothing in this plan makes sense; not a single thing is based on logic. We had never gone as far as we had now. This evening the reality and the consequences of this move are real. We savored the dream and, with one phone call, we are changed into potential buyers.

Syb's rational side speaks loud; he makes his point. Why don't we go later, sometime when we have it all figured out? We both have a booming business, we love our life so much, and after years of giving birth to our children and building our businesses, we should fully harvest our effort at this point. *Why now*? We are on a wave so high. *Were we out of our minds? Was there no other way?*

In a matter of minutes, I see my dream shatter in pieces. We are not going to America. I can't believe this doomed future fate of mine. I run upstairs, my Soul contracts, my life is over. I don't say much and put the blanket over my head.

Florian, who has listened to our conversation, runs to his room, crying loudly, "Why don't we go?" He has never been more upset. Somehow Florian's huge disappointment does the trick. It moves Syb's Soul to courageously stand up and speak. He reaches within himself and says the magic words, "OKAY, why not now! Why wait?"

That night, the lawyer calls back one minute before 12 PM. For the first time, we are seriously speaking about the terms. The speed is fast. It is as if the Universe wants to hurry up and finalize the deal, fearing we may back off. The lawyer explains that the owner is considering our bid; however, we need to increase our offer. Syb and I discuss the price and, after some intuitive play with numbers, we finalize our bid. Fifteen minutes later, we make a call to America and give our final price. The lawyer says he will call us back sometime on the weekend. So, until that time, we keep our fingers crossed. We don't have long to wait; as always, the timing is divine.

On Sunday afternoon when Syb is away at the hockey field and I am alone in the house with the younger kids, the lawyer calls. He asks for *the man* of the house; since *he* is not home, I am allowed to take the call. The question is, *are we okay with the final price the owner is offering*? In one blush, I say, "YES." I don't need time to think.

He asks if I have any conditions or if my answer is a full YES. He tells me my answer is considered a legal bid; we can't back off.

Was it my innocence or was it my stupidity or maybe my Soul was very wise? I say we are okay with the price, no conditions. I say, "Let's do it," as if buying a loaf of bread.

Oh, my God, I think to myself. I just bought a house over the phone. The receiver trembles in my hand.

I can't wait to tell Syb but I have to still my impatience until he comes back from the hockey field. A bottle of champagne is hidden behind my back and, when he opens the front door, I say, "I have good news . . . we bought The House." He lifts me up and swirls me through the living room until he asks, "You did say under condition of us getting our visas, right?" He puts me down and I look at him in shock. "Did I have to mention *that*?"

"I thought he would never sell to us with a condition like that. It's such a big risk for him; that can take six months. Who would go for that?" is my answer. The truth is I totally forgot; it never even crossed my mind and, perhaps, for a very good reason. Soul sedated my brain for the sake of the outcome. (We did hear later that Michael never would have sold the house to us with visa conditions.) Silently, I thanked God that Syb was away and I was the one to answer the phone. Syb looks at me in disbelief but sees the truth.

This whole situation is outside the threaded path. We have to pay the full amount on January 1st. The biggest question is: *How are we going to pay the full amount before we have sold our house?*

We need to solve this question within six weeks and there is no extra money in the bank.

That night, we sit down in front of our fireplace and rejoice. It is hard to grasp that we DID IT. We are the proud owners of 102 OCEAN PINES AVENUE, ROCKPORT, MA USA.

In the morning, I call a good friend and tell her we have bought a house in the States. She asks if we know what we have done and I honestly answer that we don't. This move is beyond explanation. It is a move of the Soul.

We pedal fast: we have to find a way to come up with the full amount to buy our new house in Rockport by Jan 1. Our Dutch house cannot be sold until spring; our savings account is empty.

"I know there are enough wealthy people in this world who could lend us the amount we need," I declare, passionately. The power with which I speak is felt in my spine; I shiver and believe my own words down to my core.

Eight hours later the exact amount of money is manifested. A friend calls early in the morning to ask us over for a drink. I tell him we have bought a house the night before. He is so very impressed and inspired by our story that he offers to lend us the amount we need. I look into the receiver to show him my smile. Without my asking or implying our need, the Universe has responded to our call. The money will be paid in full in January. *What was next*?

Weeks later we choose the bank for support instead of our friend as the lender. We want to protect our friendship and, amazingly, the bank transfers the full amount of money one minute before the closing time on the agreement. Our nerves are tested a bit.

My TRUST was anchored forever in a deep belief the Universe will support us when we live from the heart. Life becomes abundantly more satisfying when passion is our fuel. I had come to truly feel there was no other way; no matter how unpaved the road ahead of us, we have to listen to our inner voice. When we do, Soul *will* guide us with great wisdom ALWAYS.

It was clear to me that to ignite Syb's and my transformation process, we had to derail the train. We needed to let go of the structure around us that had become so comfortable. If we wanted to access our greatest potential, we had to take risks so we could discover new lands and explore the uncharted territories of our Soul. It was like the French poet Andre Gide said, “We can’t cross the sea by merely staring at the water.”

For sure, we were heading in a new direction. We were out of minds . . . and into our hearts. The story of “our big buy in America” goes quickly through the grapevine of Bussum.

Everyone seems to love the story while secretly thinking there is a big chance of failure we’ve overlooked. No visa, no jobs, little money, the kids don’t speak the language, to name a few. Our house wasn’t even sold yet. Through all this, our faith doesn’t waver. We just KNOW *all will be well.*

In January 2001, we fly to America. We must be there to personally sign the contract for our house. Finally, we will see the house we bought with our eyes closed. The inspection report was sent to us in December, providing us with the opportunity to back off. The ins and outs of the structure, the lead paint, the old pipes, and God knows what were explained in minute detail. I couldn’t face the task of reading and worrying. The house was solid and good; my Soul told me so and I believed it. The inspection report was studied only briefly by Syb. Even he couldn’t understand all of what was being said nor did he want to be bothered too much. We were not willing to give up the house. Intuitively, we knew all would be well.

Upon arrival in Boston, we drive straight to our new home. We can hardly remember how to get there. Nothing looks familiar because the season has changed. Now it is winter. After a few unplanned detours, we find ourselves in a “different” Rockport.

It had been snowing throughout New England, nothing unusual for the winter season there; however, a Dutch girl like me was not prepared for the American East Coast forces of nature. Holland has an intermediate climate with few highs or lows. Snow is a treat we don’t get very often. I am used to traveling light in every sense of the word. Dressy high-heel ankle boots on my bare feet and a fancy flitter-thin suede coat were enough for me and the dress of the day.

Ocean Pines Avenue looks beautiful with snow covering the high trees.

Most of the houses look celebrative; their Christmas lights still flicker in a welcoming mood. Our House looms in the distance, big and tall. The afternoon light casts a glow from the sun setting behind the New Hampshire hills far away. We park the car in our familiar spot and take a moment to still our minds and stare. This huge white Victorian is ours and we are hers.

The green shutters clatter in the wind and the red and white blossoming geraniums are gone. The porch looks very empty; my memory at a loss. We stand hand in hand while we gaze in silence at the front yard. We are only a few footsteps away from our newly-bought home. The path to the porch is covered with snow and slushy ice. A big wind gust seems to have formed piles of snow along the sides of the path. There is no apparent way to bridge the gap from where I am to where I want to go. Symbolically speaking, I need some help to get to the other side.

My fancy boots sink ankle deep in the soft snow, my bare feet inside are frozen. Gosh, how unprepared I am. I'll have to get my feet wet and I know it. Then, with one big scoop, Syb sweeps me off my feet and carries me over the threshold. The key turns and the two big doors swing open. We are ready to kick off our shoes and dance. Here we are, HOME!

The hallway we enter is icy cold and damp, the high window is cracked and the big mirror reflects in full length that winter has taken shelter within our house. It is visible that no one has lived in this once-so-lovely house for a long time.

The deserted atmosphere is audible by the chilling sound of the Northeastern wind echoing off the walls. The summer glow is gone. My rose-colored glasses fall off.

We start our tour and walk upstairs. The wall paper is crumbling and, indeed, this house is historic in every facet. The attic where all the kids plan to reside is in the worst shape; when Syb touches one wall, the paper cracks and, when he rips it off, the wall is badly cracked underneath. Even THE GUNS, which were crucial in this move for the kids, are GONE. *How will we ever explain*?

We are facing the real thing: *what have we done*? No word is spoken and we stay in silence; it is our comfort zone for now.

The only thing I can think of is: this house needs A LOT of work. Still, I don't regret the eyes we kept closed when we briefly viewed the inspection report. To me, it wasn't worth the worry; we were going to buy this house no matter what.

Now, the consequences are hitting us full in the face and we walk downstairs. The sunroom is below zero and we leave quickly. In my whole life, I had never experienced temperatures like this. We go on a journey through the yard, which is bigger than our whole neighborhood in Holland. My feet plow through the snow; I had better get used to it right away. A shack that neighbors the woods looks romantic; it gives us the homey feeling of our Dutch house, which is more comfortable to us right now than the enormous Victorian laughing loudly at our backs.

"*Hmmm*," we mutter. The holes in the walls of the small shack we can overlook but *how are we going to master the challenges of our new home?*

We blame our tiredness on jet lag and leave; we long for the cozy cottage of Frits and Joanna. The warmth of their fireplace and a glass of wine is what we need; we can always go back to our house later. *Was our enthusiasm dimming a little*? The overwhelming truth and consequences of "Project America" consumed our minds. We needed some sleep to come back to our heart and Soul. The shadow side of the coin was magnified; for some reason, we weren't fully aware of it yet.

The next day, we are invited to sign the papers; this evening, we are happy to enjoy the company of great friends and listen to the ocean storm above our heads. In the middle of the night, I wake up and listen to the waves. Listening to this sound is worth my jet lag and, yet, the memory of that night still gives me chills: Syb's breathing is heavy; *was he having nightmares about the house*? When he stirs, I ask hesitantly, "Are you awake, Syb?" He stirs. Bravely I continue on, "Do you think we would have bought the house if we had seen it a second time?" A long silence follows, outside the storm keeps thundering. I wait for his answer.

"Actually I was wondering the same thing," Syb answers, honestly. "Maybe that's why we never did." He's right; there was a reason why we never did. It's hard to imagine that we would have choose to move into this house with tons of work ahead, no kitchen, and a wind chill factor inside the house of below zero.

The truth was spoken and I felt a rush of adrenaline through my veins. It was freeing that we both acknowledged the same thing—that this move was beyond our wildest imagination—and we were both ok with it. We were free now. Mentally and emotionally, we were ready to "get to work." No mountain too high for us; Soul had blind faith in us.

We go back the next day and look with different eyes. We are able to face the cracks and, this time, we get belly laughs as we ridicule our idealism. When I am back in the yard and look up at the enormous façade of the house, I now know that extraordinary action gives extraordinary results but it also requires extraordinary effort and that means an extraordinary amount of work.

I was also aware I had better not get stuck on my *"winning formula"*: that I could do ANYTHING and do it all *alone*. Not this time. *How could I survive with that death sentence over my head?* I knew I wouldn't last long. Silently, I say to myself, "Please Universe, give us all the help you've got!"

And with that request, I gave my *"winning formula"* to the Nor'easter wind, blowing ferociously through the big trees.

Two days later, we wait in line at Logan Airport. We are ready for the next phase. We are in a reflective mood and ponder all the questions pressing on us: *Why must we follow the path of the Soul? Why are we giving up our warm nest in Holland and a social life that is blossoming and at its peak? Why are we giving up two businesses, both flourishing and in full bloom? Why now when every one of us is thriving? How will we cope with leaving our loved ones behind*?

There is no answer to the myriad of questions. In our hearts we know. The line is moving and we start walking; we can't turn back the clock. It's good to reflect but we need to continue through the birth canal, feel every push contraction and come out at the other side. The only way out is through. It is a tough but joyful process. We have to leave behind any pretense that we can do it all alone. We need a lot of help from the Universe—that is a fact. The plane takes off; the Boston skyline disappears quickly out of sight. The next time we see Boston, we will not be *tourists*; we will be *immigrants.* Butterflies tickle my stomach; they might have built a nest. For the next five years, I feel their joyful wings inside.

Our friends in Holland await us when we arrive back home, curious and eager to hear our stories. The fairytale is different though; to their utter surprise, they hear us say, "We were a little surprised to find the house in different shape than we thought." I can see the disbelief in their eyes. We let the shock fill-in the blank and quickly add, "*But* we L-O-V-E it!" This story is hard to explain, even for us.

From then on, we are unstoppable, full of enthusiasm, full steam ahead. We need to sell our house and apply for a visa. That is only the beginning of an endless list.

We are going to uproot everything; it is the only way to shoot our roots deeply into American soil.

"It is a move beyond human capability, but it can be done," the astrologer I consult says firmly. I take it in and believe her. Still, I wonder what it will take from us.

Looking back five years later, the question is: *Had we known that it took not only enormous amounts of faith, but also a big dose of tenacity, endurance, patience and trust, would we have done it?*

I answer, wholeheartedly, "Yes!"

Were these the qualities to be practiced in life and be brought as luggage for our journey?

The Magic 'Dwadle' from Hawaii

During lunch break the rumor spreads I am leaving with my family to live in the USA. When Adri, a blond-haired student, tells the group about our plans, silence falls. All eyes turn my way. Everyone has the same question and speaks at the same time, "You are leaving? But, why and how?" Some still gape in disbelief.

I explain, "We are going to reinvent our lives on the other side of the ocean. Although we have no job prospects, visas and little money, we bought a house in Rockport, Massachusetts on the East Coast of America. My Soul said it was time to go."

Again, silence falls until someone says, "You'll probably bring suitcases full of money."

I shake my head and answer, "No, a suitcase full of *faith*."

Before we leave for America, I hear about the work of the *American Monk*, Burt Goldman. He is offering training in Holland. I learn more about him on goldmanmethod.com and attend a lecture he gives in Amsterdam. I am really turned on by what he has to say and about the *results* of his work. I sign up to take Burt's first hypnotherapy training, and many more fascinating workshops follow. I am more than ready as a student and I'm sure I have found my teacher.

Burt becomes my inspiration. His life is a *true* demonstration of the principle we can manifest every dream we have. We simply need to access our subconscious mind and release all the blocks in the way of attaining them. According to Burt, we have an unlimited potential that is there for the taking. He lives what he teaches by example. From the moment I hear him speak, I drink in every word.

Burt's hypnotherapy class and his group of students are fun. I know many of them from former courses and trainings we shared. We will be together for a week in a village close to my home. I am very grateful I can drive home in twenty minutes and sleep in my own bed. Most of the students have to stay overnight.

This new course starts with a review of the basic hypnotherapy principles: *the subconscious mind rules our life without us realizing it consciously. If we are aware of our beliefs, we have the power to change our lives from the inside out*. For sure, I had experienced for myself how stunning the results could be when I let go of beliefs that didn't serve me.

By noontime, everyone is on the same page and we all know what we are here for. If we can take a close look at our beliefs, we can change our destiny. Everyone loves Burt's expertise; however, his personal stories are the icing on the cake.

The afternoon class starts and Burt bubbles over with excitement. He's been in Hawaii and has experienced the power of manifestation by holding an intention for 30 seconds and drawing something he calls a 'Dwadle.' We can't wait to hear more.

The trick is to think about your desire while drawing a type of doodle on a piece of paper and then keep circling it for a few seconds. When the 'Dwadle' is finished, you hold your intention on the *inner* lines and focus there for 30 seconds, then focus another 30 seconds on the *outer* lines.

Burt asks if one of us would like to be a 'guinea pig' – someone who has something BIG to manifest. The whole class points to me. "You go," they say, urging me to open my mouth.

I step forward and walk to the front of the classroom. My neighbor whispers "focus on a *really* big amount."

"Tell me what you want," says Burt. I share my wish to sell our house for the price it is worth. "Tell me how much you want for your house," he continues. I hear a whistle go through the audience. My price is high, very high; however, no money can beat my belief that our house is worth beyond what money can buy. My Heart and Soul agree; there is no greed, no guilt, no pain; the amount is right. I can feel it from my toes to the bottom of my heart. I close my eyes, hold my breath and state my intent.

Burt starts the 'Dwadle.' A drawing made with a fine blue marker on a large white sheet of paper and then circled will do the magic trick. Burt is focused yet relaxed; his hand effortlessly draws the thin blue lines on the paper. A strange form appears within seconds. "Now focus 30 seconds on the *inner* lines and hold your intent," he instructs me. I do as I am told. He continues, "Another 30 seconds and follow the *outer* lines of the drawing. Okay, it is a done deal," he says as a matter-of-fact, and I believe him.

I float back to my seat. I just "sold" our house for the price it is worth and, what is more important; it is bought by the people who LOVE our house from the inside out.

Yes, it is a done deal. I can feel it. The Universe will respond; the Law of Attraction is truly in action. Our house is sold a few months later for the EXACT amount I stated. The 'Dwadle' did its magic.

Syb wonders about it when he hears the amount of money I have in *mind* (really more of what I hold in *my heart*). "Ok," he says, "you are the one who is going to be in charge of selling this house because you truly believe this." He says this, fully trusting I can sell our house in whatever way I put my mind to. My experience in matters of business is zero; however, he knows my suitcase is full of faith.

When we are ready to put our home in Holland on the market, I declare with passion, "Our house is worth 'beyond pay'." I say it and believe every single word. I continue with a stipulation for the Universe: "Only the one who is head-over-heels in love with our house can buy it." I was so sure everybody wanted to buy our house; I even believed that, before we put it on the market, it would be sold. I felt our house was worth a million, no matter what price we asked.

This joyful, fertile energy was tangible in an extraordinary way. The renovation we did took place over a period of ten years; we molded the house into a reflection of who we were. We painted the walls in warm colors of orange, red and yellow; even though they were quite daring, it was the atmosphere that expressed us all. Our kitchen became the safe haven for us and the neighborhood's kids and friends who lived around us. Even my classes were held in this cozy kitchen with her walls in burgundy red and the cabinets in sunshine yellow.

Deep insights, laughter and learning served as sacred moments in the busy lives of all of us. Weekly dinners were part of our lifestyle and, fed not only our bellies, they fed our Souls, too. We had created the life we loved and, after ten years, we felt like we were totally in the flow. Ten years earlier, newly arrived from Taiwan with our first born child, Florian, we had no idea of how much we would become part of this community. I birthed four other kids in the bedroom of this house and survived the ten-year plan of renovation. I loved this house from the inside out.

Apparently though, Soul thought it was time to move; her timing was *Now, Not Later*. We would thrive as we moved forward, riding on this wonderful energy easily, and accomplish even more. What I didn't know was how well my rock solid belief in how much our house was worth would serve me.

The presale starts and it is crazy, more than crazy. I have no greed regarding the money I have in mind, not an inch. I am very detached and believe there are more buyers than we can ever dream of. The condition is already out there: ONLY the ones who *deeply* love our house may buy it.

Daily, people pass by and at least a few of them ask if they can see the house. From everywhere they flock to Bilderdijklaan 3. My Soul grins and says, "See?" I *do* see Soul was right and, when I ask a real estate agent to give us her estimate of what the house will sell for and she tells me the amount, I KNOW she is not connected to Soul, the place outside the comfort zone of the mind. *How can I tell her*? I feel I'd rather sell the house myself, but first she and I must walk the threaded path together for a bit.

She advises not to let anyone see the house yet, that it might start rumors. Sometimes strangers stand in the yard, their noses pressed against the window. We take her advice seriously and keep our doors closed.

A few days before the sale starts we change our minds. Finally, we give in to the outer world's advice to have a little common sense and not burn *all* our bridges behind our backs.

Why take the chance and have nothing left if the visa expires after one year? Or, a scenario we never even considered: *What if you don't get the visa after all because the Immigration office doesn't approve it? What would you do with your house in the USA?* It's amazing how many "*what if* scenarios" people have about the possibility of our dream falling through.

I still feel we needn't steer our boat in this direction and yet, on the other hand, it doesn't hurt to explore other options.

I thank God on my knees until this day that a doom scenario never ever, not even *once* crossed our minds. How blessed we were that we knew so little about procedures regarding visas and green cards; we had no idea it usually takes *years* not a matter of *months*. Our ignorance was truly bliss.

We give in and decide to rent our house. We figure that we can always sell it later.

In the same smooth flow the buyers came forward, that same evening the phone rings and the best possible renters call to ask for a tour. They are very interested and, what counts the most, the price and the length of rental time we have in mind is agreed upon. It *sounds* too good to be true; the Universe is working in harmony with our plan. However, the house keeps attracting buyers; her joyful, fertile energy radiates far and wide outside our neighborhood boundaries. I speak with every one of them while the little voice in the back of my mind keeps talking, telling me to ignore the "logical" advice of those recommending to rent instead of sell.

Day by day I am becoming more convinced that one needs to uproot completely in order to shoot one's roots and sprout in other soil. I am feeling, "*We better give it all we have because, as long as the energy of this house is still attached to us, it will hold some part of us back in the past. If we rent, we leave that back door open – yes, we'll have a way out— that's not what we are going to America for.*" We need to leap and leave everything behind. I know the *Truth* and so does Syb.

We decide to finalize the sale or rent in March; we have no doubt all will go as planned. We don't want to wait till the last minute, however, *what choice do we have*? In July we will be crossing the Atlantic. The plane tickets are ordered, the movers will be shipping our furniture in June. Our life in America is waiting. We are going, no matter what.

Syb hasn't even filed the application for our visa when we finalize the deal to sell our house. He plans to do this first thing in April … *I promise.* Knowing so much more now, after five years of living in the States, it must have been our 100% trust that made it all happen; it was a daring bet to assume we would obtain our visa in the mail in matters of weeks. However, our Faith is Strong; it doesn't waver. We believe we have plenty of time left. It's not to the outer world's liking, in fact, no one understands.

As if the Universe is in step with Doubt, her speed slows down, the lease contract lacks the signature and both we and the renters bide the next move. *Why is there a sudden halt from both sides? Has the Universe a better plan?*

A few days later, I receive phone call. The woman on the line is P, a friend of Wendy, a good friend of mine. She wants to let me know she is head-over-heels in love with our house. P's passed by it many times and even peeked through the window one day. She knows this is her house; *she loves it.* Her words ring a bell, as if I hear myself talking about our new house in Rockport.

I feel an instant liking for her. We chat for an hour like old friends. P tells me about her parents, who left Holland with their five children in tow to pursue her dad's entrepreneurial business in America on the East Coast. She loved growing up in America. I can't believe our stories match. I am astounded by the similarity of P's story and mine...I long to hear more and I am thrilled to meet her for coffee, even though our house is not officially for sale. However, she is in love with our house and I'd love to show it to her. We need to talk.

I chat with P over the phone a few times and I invite her and her family to come for coffee and a mini tour. Syb thinks I am crazy. "*Why ask them to come if we are going to rent the house*?"

I know it is a little strange but I also know P and I have to meet. The last phone conversation ends with, "Come on Sunday morning for cappuccino and I'll show you the house."

P and her husband come, the sun shines and we have a great time; they are wonderful people and we talk like we old friends. First, we drink coffee together with home-baked apple pie in our warm yellow kitchen; then Syb and I show them the house. I am so proud of our house and it shows. A couple of times they ask if it is for sale. "No, we are going to rent it," is our reply. Syb feels a little awkward; I don't.

When they drive away, I say to Syb, "If I were them, I would call and make a bid."

"Why on earth would they call?" asks Syb, and he is right. Still . . . if they really want it . . . they'll throw their principles overboard and call. That is what I would do, yet I know I am not them.

On Monday, I meet Wendy at school. She asks me how our coffee morning went. I tell her I had expected a phone call. She is on the same page as Syb. Still my reply is, "If I were them, I would call and make a bid. Dare us. You never know." I think to myself, if they love our house so much, perhaps it *should* be theirs.

The phone rings late in the afternoon and politely they ask if they can make an offer. I say *yes*, but first *do they want to come by one more time*? Yes, P says. She wants to see the area and I am excited to give her a tour. I will show her the house again, the schools and the neighborhood. We plan to go by bike and do a picnic in the field if weather permits.

As if I had orchestrated the "perfect timing," the Universe walks in line with my steps.

When P arrives, another young woman walks in the front yard and asks me if she can see the house. A woman with a child on the back seat of her bike stops, too. She tells me she and her husband are very interested. Inside, I smile. I welcome P and wave the others goodbye. I shake my head. "Everyone wants to buy this house; it's crazy," I say.

The look in P's eyes shows she is already in possession of the house that might be hers. It doesn't need much to ignite P's enthusiasm; everything is to her liking.

We bike through the small sand paths leading to the magnificent view of the Bussumer hei, a stretch of land with lots of wildflowers, sheep and endless pathways to invite lazy Sunday strolls. When she leaves, her heart knows all there is to know.

We are the perfect match because the price of our house is in their price range; it means we are all in for an easy ride. There is no hurry; it feels we are on the same wavelength.

On Sunday we get THE call and Syb answers the phone. He puts his hand over the receiver and whispers that their price offer is very good.

I wave to him. "I need to do the numbers," I whisper. I have to do the math. If this number is really what we want and if, according to numerology, it's okay, it's a deal.

"This is a very good offer," Syb mutters again.

I shake my head; it is not the amount of the 'Dwadle', although it is close. I need more time.

"Ok, *you* do the deal because you believe so much in what you are asking," he says and it is true. I need time to rethink the offer; we are going at a fast-pace these days.

In the meantime, the renters have not signed the contract and are hesitating. From one day to the next, Syb and I sink knee-deep in the deal. *Do we pursue it*? I feel thankful to the Universe for the perfect match of buyers and renters and it amazes me that the renters are backing off.

Syb leaves for his hockey game and wishes me luck.

I laugh and think of the other time he left for a hockey game. That was the afternoon I bought our house in America. *What will be waiting for him when he comes back home this time? Will I sell our house this afternoon?* I wave to him as he loads a bunch of kids from the neighborhood in his car. At least seven kids tumble into the van as usual; for Syb there is no group too big.

With a honking horn, he leaves. I go downstairs and vacuum the kitchen until the phone rings. I take the call. Within seconds a bid is made. We are almost there but not quite yet. We both agree the tango is not our dance. Funny that I feel so truthful knowing now in my gut that, if this conversation breaks the deal, it is simply not meant to be. He says he will call back later. I absolutely understand and vacuum some more. *Whose house am I cleaning, theirs or mine?*

It is an hour later when the phone rings again. This time I grab it on the first ring. When I answer with my name, it is silent for a moment and then I hear the single word, "Yes," followed by a loud scream in the background from P. We both have bought our dream house.

For the next hour, I keep peeking through the window to see if Syb is coming back as if that will bring him home faster. I am bursting with news. I distract myself with silly chores, but nothing can take the big smile off my face. At 6:30 PM, I hear screeching tires in front of our house. Syb unloads the car and walks in. He is sweaty and tired, one kid on his shoulder and the rest of the clan left in the yard. It is springtime and for them the day never ends.

Questioning eyes look at me. My cheeks are flushed and with one movement I reveal a bottle of champagne behind my back.

He screams, "You sold it!" My *yes* means celebration time, *oh yeah!* We are leaving in three months, now we *have to* get our visa. The U.S. Immigration and Naturalization Service called the INS for short had better approve it. We've sold our home in Bussum and already bought a house in Rockport even though officially we are not allowed to live there. We have already ordered the movers to collect our stuff in June. The goodbye party in Holland is planned for the 1st of July. We have every reason to celebrate!

However, a tremendous amount of work still has to be done. We come to the conclusion that our Rockport house is at least ten times bigger than our Holland house. Many trips to Ikea will need to be made. To leave, let go, buy more and detangle is a 24/7 job in every respect.

Syb applies for our one-year visa and it's cruel to watch how many details he has to cough up. I am surprised the INS doesn't need X-rays of our intestinal tracks. Our visa application is submitted in April and we fully trust it will arrive in our mailbox long before our departure date of July 6th. Whether or not our application will be approved is never a question.

We are rookies in the game of America's immigration law; however, beginner's luck is the fuel that moves the Universal pedals on this bike. We will be homeless in Holland from July 1st onward and homebound to the States. *Why worry? 102 Ocean Pines Avenue is waiting.*

Daily, friends and neighbors come to our door to ask if we have "news about the visa …" Everyone is concerned but us; our faith doesn't waver. The backup plan is to fly out on the 6th of July and pretend at the U.S. Customs check-in in Boston that we are on a vacation. They will believe us – no doubt about it – because we will be bringing bags packed only with beach towels. The rest will come by boat and, if all the five ducklings can keep their smiles inside, we will swim right through U.S. Customs with no eyebrows raised.

Our furniture will be shipped the first week of June. We are all looking forward to living in a completely empty house; that in itself is an adventure to us and I can't wait.

Syb and I go daily on shopping sprees. Everything we have is small and everything we need is big. It is symbolic of this move. Before the movers come to pack, we have bought the extra furniture we need and the containers will be a lot heavier than the movers expect. When we decide at the last-minute to design the hall, the porch and the sunroom with Portuguese floor tiles, Syb studies hours and hours to make a plan to design each floor. When the tiles are transported to the moving company, the final weight of our stuff blows them away. At our house, they made an estimate based on what we owned back then. After our Ikea trips and the tile purchase, the price for moving goes way up. No wonder, cartons upon cartons are carrying tons of tiles. The movers fully expect the ship to sink.

I swallow when the big trucks stop in front of our house. Our street is blocked for two days.

Our friends can't bear to look and I deeply understand. It is very emotional. The trucks silently leave our street late in the afternoon of the second day, no sound, no beep. The house is hollow and empty, everything is gone. Tears come to my eyes when I see them turn the corner. For a while, we will stay behind while our belongings are heading for America.

The closer we come to the departure date the more real our fantasy becomes. At the goodbye party at school, the children cry big tears. When they go to leave, they have their arms wrapped around each other and won't let go. It is heartbreaking to see how much love they share. To uproot them from the Dutch soil is tough for the parents and for their children.

"*Bye bye*, wonderful world." I take a deep breath.

Time goes by and our life is in full swing; we have hardly time to breathe now. No visa in sight, but there is a lot of other stuff to think about. The party we have planned on July 1st needs all our energy and attention.

We are having a kid's party and an adult's party. There will be a kids disco and an adult disco. The first one will be organized by the discotheque of our son Florian and friends and the other by a well-known guy who is supposed to rock the crowd in a big way. We have booked a line dancer who will teach everyone "*the real American thing*," a popcorn and snow cone machine and a huge jumping mattress for the young kids. A crew of teenagers is needed and they all need instruction in serving the food and drinks and in watching the younger kids; a caterer with all kinds of food and drink is booked.

We must arrange for the American school bus to bring all the kids to the party. There is enough to think about to keep our minds on Rock-n-Roll.

For a month we are invited to goodbye lunches, dinners and private parties, you name it. We say yes to all of them. Perhaps that was why I turn into a bit of a hermit upon arriving in the United States. I was still recovering. As the Dutch say, Syb and I were "walking on our eyebrows"; the focus on the present keeps us going. The future seems far away. Every moment is so intense it is effortless to stay in the here and now; we have no choice.

I am very happy the house is empty and that every piece of furniture is floating somewhere at sea. Daily the door bell rings at dinnertime and the only thing I have to do is open and stretch out my hands to receive the helping hands that provide us with everything we need. Our friends and family bring us food, blankets, basically everything we can wish for. We are wrapped in their love and attention much more than in the blankets. The

Universe hears our call.

How on earth can we leave all our loved ones behind?

Very late on a Friday night three weeks before our departure, Syb opens his email and there is a message on the screen, "You are allowed a *three-year* stay." Attached is a little note from our immigration lawyer expressing his amazement in regards to our case.

So far in his long career, it had never happened that someone who applied for a one-year visa is approved for a three-year visa!

Syb shows me the email and we jump up and down like kids. It's the ultimate proof the Universe is supporting our move.

The champagne in the fridge is waiting to be opened for one more bubbling feast. Celine is the one friend I dare call at this late-night hour; she doesn't need more than two minutes to scoot across the street and join in.

Mission Impossible: Paris

We wake the kids at 5:30 the next morning in order to undertake a fabric treasure hunt in Paris. We need fabric for every room of the house in Rockport, which is much more cloth than we can possibly imagine. Each room needs approximately three sets of curtains.

We want to decorate the house in the European style, which means it will be colorful and original. Given the fact that the kids are promised to choose what they want for themselves – we trust their unique and "well developed taste" – we are in for quite a ride.

After the sleepy kids tumble into the back of the American dark red van with wood panels on the side that is our luxury coach for this journey, we wake them up with the news that the visa has arrived. Our delight is much to their surprise. *Why did we make such a big fuss over a visa? Wasn't that guaranteed long ago*? We drive fast on the empty Dutch freeways. Saturdays are sleep-in days for the Dutch and the smart ones who are on the road are all on a mission, just like us. We drive fast.

Our first focus is a piping hot French *café au lait* with warm croissants at the *Place de la Montmartre*; the fabric for curtains can wait. We have no idea what is waiting there for us. The list we have with measurements is not quite exact; how many and how much fabric we need is the biggest question of all. In the midst of all the moving details, this seemed like a minor problem that we could easily conquer. *Or could we?*

Full of enthusiasm, we walk toward THE PLACE TO BE while enjoying the energy. This is *Paris*: the smell, the rapid French language, the beautiful stick-thin ladies who run elegantly on high heels to get fresh baguettes home before their kids wake up. We take it all in. With ease, we find the street where all the famous French designers are touted to buy their fabric for little money.

We slowly wander down the small street with even smaller shops. We are totally lost in the amount of fabric, choices, kids and our dog Buddha who pulls us in every direction. More often than not, Buddha becomes entangled between the ladies' legs, cloth and tables. *Why did nobody tell us Saturday is the worst shopping day in Paris?*

Buying fabric for a mansion with five young kids and a dog in tow was *Mission Impossible*. Whenever I see a fabric I like, Syb asks, "For which room?" followed by an even tougher question, "How much do we need?" I have no idea for which room or the amount we'll need. I just like it and know it will all work out.

It is a disaster. The kids are good sports; in every store, they show us passionately what they like. In chorus they express their favor, which means ten fingers pointing in ten different directions. They do their best.

Impatient chubby French clerks prefer to help other customers first. They look the other way. After a few hours, we leave the stores empty handed; we need a break. Aimlessly, we walk toward music playing a happy tune in the far distance. At first we can't picture where the music is coming from.

The trained ears of the kids have no difficulty in finding the "merry-go-round carrousel" within a minute.

While Syb and I drop exhausted on a bench, the kids hop on the shiny iron horses. We watch them go around in endless circles, our minds doing exactly the same. *Was this mission fruitless and insane*? The kids keep going around and around, yelling and screaming about their good fortune; they are riding for free! We wave, pretending to join in their delight and good fortune while really wondering about ours. *Had we underestimated this task?*

To buy huge amounts of fabric we needed to do some brain work; buying intuitively perhaps was not the way. However, we are not ready to give up and wonder how we can still choose what we need. We will not drive home without some fabric; that much we *do* know.

"Let me check the tulip fabric. We can decide later what room or which couch it is for," I say and, without waiting for an answer from Syb, I run off to the first store. The music has lifted my spirit; I am in the mood to get going. I have enough of watching the iron horses going nowhere.

Minutes later my clan follows and, in the meantime, five enthusiastic little French ladies have gathered who are willing to cut the many yards of cloth and not to forget the lining. The ladies enjoy listening to the little voices describing their heartfelt choice. Within moments, our indecisiveness is changed into action. In three hours, every child has what he or she wants for the bed and window and we have picked fabric for the uncountable number of windows as well as for all the many chairs and couches, too.

"Artsy and daring," is what the comments in America are years later. *Was it a taste of the 'House of Röell' style*? Every room has curtains in a different color; there is no logical match, just heartfelt choices that work to create an original *Röell.*

"We can start our own shop," is Syb's only comment when we leave the store. How we are going to load all these huge rolls of fabric in our car is the next challenge. As usual for Syb no task is too big; I still can't imagine how he did it and I was there. The seats are folded down and the many rolls are stacked on top of each other. The only way to fit all of us in is if the kids and Buddha lie on top of the rolls.

Of course, the kids think this is terrific; the car is not in agreement as it squeaks in complaint on its axis. I have the feeling we may crack through the bottom. On the way back home, it rains. It is miserable weather and the drive goes slow.

We haven't eaten and we all have ravenous appetites when the neon letters of MacDonald's shows up. "Well, if that is not a sign that we are heading for America, nothing else is," we say and pull into the drive-up. It is our first MacDonald's drive-thru experience; what a chance! Our Mission Impossible is complete and a grand success as we bite hungrily our first juicy Big Macs.

What a treat after being in Paris. I long for a glass of French wine and a warm goat cheese salad; the fare instead of a good French wine is *milkshake du jour* and it makes me laugh. Change is what is called for in every sense.

The next day we join the family tournament on the hockey field. The grapevine doesn't take long to give our friends a good laugh. "Tomorrow they will go to Budapest to buy carpet," Jan Willem, a good friend of ours jokes. We think it really might be a good idea.

Months later I unpack the 50 packets of fabric with the black printed name PARIS MONTMARTRE on top. It is a miracle that the endless yards of different fabric are exactly enough and fabulously match the interior of all the rooms of the house. Needless to say, the tulip fabric is still my favorite. Even though the fabric has faded five years after covering the couch in what we call the "tulip room", the tulips haven't lost their bloom.

The Web of Creation

"Every being is a unique thread in a galactic interwoven fabric. Each of us is not only a fiber in this tapestry; we are also embedded in its weave. And because we all long to experience our connection with one another, we feel if one thread of the tapestry is missing a hole exists in the whole. When we feel ourselves unraveling, we want to be reminded of our connection to something greater than our separate realities."

Where had I read these words of wisdom? Was overcoming my fear of spiders a crucial sign I was to be pulled into the mystery of the weaver and be able to unthread my weave? I must have known the answer. It was the thread that wove my life and this book.

When I was seven years old, I woke up one morning and decided this was the day to overcome my fear of spiders. I felt a determination so strong I couldn't resist the urge to face my fear.

I opened the back door and tiptoed outside. Everyone was still asleep and I wanted to keep it that way. It was still dark. I had made a plan and this morning I was my own coach. I knew how to overcome my fear and, with a quick jump, I stood in the back yard. My idea was to find a spider web and come as close as possible.

Because it was so early, the morning dew was fresh and the silver lining of the threads were glistering in the sun. I promised myself to stay there for a while and not to run away when a spider appeared. The next step was to hold my hand above the web and not run away when the spider touched or crawled upon my hand. Then I would take the spider out of the web and hold it for five seconds, slowly building up to one minute.

It was quite a daring task. An hour went by and I learned quickly. Of course, the first spiders were the worst. I was repulsed by their hairy legs yet I continued on. I became more skilled ready to let go of my fear completely. Triumphantly I held the spiders and let them crawl from my hand onto my arm. My scary predators were now my friends.

Proudly I stepped back inside; everyone was still asleep.

I giggled because now I was *Spider Woman*.

Was it then I became a weaver?

The sun came up.

That's how it happened. In that pivotal moment when the moon traded places with the sun, I became a weaver. For ages, the myths of weaving had existed in the world as metaphors for creation.

Now here I am creating a book by weaving the divine thread of my Soul with other souls from one story into another. I open my heart and become aware that my essence was spun from one golden strand.

Humankind has not woven the web of life.
We are but one thread within it.
Whatever we do to the web, we do to ourselves.
All things are bound together.
All Things Connect.

— Chief Seattle

Writer's Note

When I finally shed the Devil I had carried on my back and trusted my life to paper, I wrote and wrote; I was being rocked in the rhythm of Soul's song. After day 22, my pen came to a halt. *Had I crossed the finish line and reached my destiny*?

Not quite. Although the book was finished, my story was not. A new chapter began. I started a daring dialogue with Soul in search of the divine thread. *Could I unfurl my fabric and unravel the weave of my web? Would I be able to understand what my life was all about?*

Soul was creative beyond a doubt in showing me the answers I yearned to find. The thread I was to follow reflected like footprints in the sand.

Willingly I embarked on a breathtaking journey around my world in 22 days. I lit the torch and shone the light on my inner and outer trail.

I relived my life in reverse and realized that my spiritual quest began with the physical travels. I was amazed to see how my *Traveler Survival Kit* served as my faithful guide, leading me to the answers of *where I was to go and what was worth to see*. Although my restless Hopi nature loved the outer trail, something inside me yearned for more. The questions stayed the same.

I became courageous, and excavated the more remote and hidden sites; I descended to the unlit places of my emotional self. Learning to travel light, I shed the luggage from my back and let the past be the past. Fascinating encounters, detours and what not, came across my path; my journey was worth taking. Step by step, I followed the inner trail leading to the answers of my quest.

Then one day I found my faithful guide, patiently waiting, her torch divinely lit to shine the light on *where I was to go and what was worth seeing INSIDE.*

PART THREE

Weaving the Outer Trail

Who does not
believe in miracles
is not a realist.

— David Ben-Gurion
דָוִד בֶּן-גוּרְיוֹן

Israel

The smells of blossoming flowers and fruit still linger in my memory. The kibbutz was surrounded by flowering trees. During the different seasons you could pick your own peaches, mangos, avocados, and plums while you strolled lazily to the dining room. I felt so at home here and, the fact that this land was Holy, I had no doubt. After work I started to write poems in my journal about the discovery of my Soul. Despite the many hours of work, I felt like I had the all the time in the world. I read more books than their library could hold. I remember that the inner peace and joy I experienced was worth coming back to four years in a row.

I was caught in the country's spell. Living fearless and free; *carpe diem* was their credo and it didn't take me long to make it mine. I loved to be in the presence of the Israelis, who practiced the art of living each day as if it was their last in heart and soul. I couldn't get enough; I wanted to learn more.

The kibbutz experience taught me how to strengthen my mental, emotional and physical abilities to the max. It wasn't easy but it was the best "life skill" school I could have attended. I learned to work in jobs I hated, to show up when sick, to dance when sad, to clean the inside of 1,000 turkeys a day when heartbroken, to drive the tractor at 4:00 AM with a hangover, to pick hundreds of oranges by myself in the orchard in the pouring rain. The list was long but without regrets.

However, the best thing I learned was that the Universe saved and supported me *always*. I was safe no matter in what circumstance I found myself.

After months of working in the orange orchard, I deserved a rest and stayed in bed for a full day. It had been raining for weeks and I was fed up with my boring job. I thought I had enough; we, as volunteers, worked too hard. Days before I found myself stuck in the mud of the orchard too many times while pulling my ladder from tree to tree and I started to fantasize about a day off. Today the rain was pouring and my door stayed closed. It was *Heaven*.

The next day I was called to the office and told I can choose to either stay or go; they wanted my full commitment rain or shine. To me and ten others they are basically saying we can leave in a heartbeat. My mouth drops open. *How dare they say this to me*? I had worked without complaint for four months, six days a week. *Why couldn't I stay in bed just one rainy day?*

I wake up for the first time. Life is about commitment, you either go for it or not. They didn't want me if I did not give it my all.

They have no mercy for me when I close the office door behind me. With the door knob in my hand, I make up my mind.

Life is no picnic on the kibbutz and, if I don't change my attitude, I must leave. I want to stay because I love the life of hard physical work and the atmosphere of freedom brings me peace. I sit and think about their harsh words while I look at the sunset from the sandy porch. No way would I let go of what I had found.

From this moment on, I am on board and my life changes. I even consider living permanently on the kibbutz. I stay for a year. My dream job falls in my lap a few months after the encounter at the office. They assign me as a caretaker at the Baby House. It brings back sweet memories of my youth when I was my mother's helper with my brothers and sister when they were small.

In the kibbutz, the parents bring their babies and children to the baby and children's houses during the day in order to create the opportunity to work. They have no choice. Men and woman are equal and both have to work the same. Every person is assigned to the same jobs in a rotation system that is agreed upon by everyone who lives in the kibbutz. I bathe and feed the babies and play with them during the day. This job fits me like a wetsuit. For hours I sit on the grass and play with them. I walk around the kibbutz and visit my friends with all my 8 babies in the big square stroller.

I made many trips to Israel after my one-year stay. The second time I went with my friend Irene. We go on a two-month-long trail through Europe and finally reach Israel by boat. After eight weeks of island hopping, we arrive at the Port of Haifa. When the officials check our passports, they ask us if we expect to get any darker in Israel. Our hair is blonder than blond from the abundant rays of sunshine and our skin is deeply tanned from all the visits to the remote bounty islands in Greece. Arriving in the kibbutz makes us exchange sandals for working boots and say goodbye to the endless days of laziness.

When I go back to Israel the third time, I have to quit my job as a counselor in child psychiatry in order to stay for three months at the kibbutz *Givat Chaim*. It is a hard choice to quit but I can't resist the urge to go back to Israel again. I've been away for a year by then.

I hear P'dut's familiar voice when I call to ask if I can come. She is the volunteer manager. "Yes, Saskia, please come."

She is excited to hear from me because they need all the help they can get. The men are at war and there is hardly anyone left on the kibbutz to work. The number of volunteers is minimal. It is obvious that everyone is welcome.

My parents have no idea how serious the state of war is. It is even dangerous to stay on the kibbutz. The guards at the gate are gone, too. I hide this information from my parents and I pretend everything is great in Israel. I can't wait to go and I don't mind the state the country is in. The kibbutz is expecting me and I will arrive at night. The kibbutz is a few hours away from the airport. I trust everything will work out as meant to be. I think, if I follow my gut and give up my beloved job in order to stay in Israel, I am sure the Universe will support me. And so it is.

I fly out in the afternoon. My plane will arrive a little before midnight. P'dut has already informed me there is a possibility there are no buses at night because of the lack of men during this time of war. I may be stranded at the airport in Tel Aviv. I let go of this detail and excitedly take my seat. I dream of being back in the country I love so much. How I get there is not my concern.

Next to me sits a very friendly-looking Israeli guy. His name is David. We start to chat and he tells me he lives in Tel Aviv about one and a half hours away from the kibbutz. The first thing David mentions is there is no public transportation during the evening and at night. I take a deep breath when I hear this again. It unnerves me a bit this time. I answer, "I know," and leave it at that. When he asks me if I am to be picked up, my answer is "No."

"You want to come with me?" David asks. I look back at him and scan his face as if it will give me an answer about how to reply. *Do I trust my intuition that he is trustworthy*? Instantly I know the only thing to say is, "Yes, that would be great."

Upon arrival, David is met by a friend, the typical Israeli 'beau' with dark curly hair. He asks if I can come along and his friend doesn't mind. He doesn't question David as to where I come from. His old yellow car is parked at the far side of the parking lot and I hop in the back. David sits with his friend in the front seat. They talk in rapid Hebrew. I love the language but I don't understand a word of what they are saying. They laugh a lot and try to include me in their conversation.

We speed over the highway faster than my thoughts can track their meaning. I see myself from above. I notice the insanity of me driving on the highway with two total strangers at midnight. *Going where? Was I okay*?

My hand touches the doorknob, my physical idea of safety . . . to escape…*or was that an illusion*?

I relax and listen to the Hebrew language. It has a similarity to Dutch but has a sweeter melodic note.

About forty-five minutes later, we arrive in a dark neighborhood with a tall, eight-story building. I look around; the parking lot is full. I don't ask if this is where we are going. I stay silent. Right behind a container is a spot to park the car. As soon as I get out and plant my feet on the ground, I suddenly feel back home. The pitch black sky embraces me. I look up and think "Carpe diem, Israel, here I am."

David grabs me by the arm and says, "Hey, Saskia, are you a stargazer or what? Let's go." We walk up the stairs and I am very surprised when he rings the doorbell. *Aren't we going to his house?* The door swings open and an old lady in her evening gown shrieks when she sees him. An older man comes to the door too as soon as he hears the noise in the hallway. David introduces me to his parents; these oh-so-gentle people have faces cracked by their oh-so-many smiles. They welcome me as if I am their daughter. Although their language is only Hebrew, their body language speaks for itself.

David says, "I thought it best you stay at my parents' house." He turns around and, after a short Hebrew conversation; he blows a hand kiss to me and says he will be back tomorrow morning. I stand in the hallway; my luggage next to me suggests I stay. A moment later, his parents invite me to their kitchen table. David's mom starts pulling out the dishes from the shelves.

The stove is turned on and I figure she is going to cook us a meal. I look at my watch and realize it is half past one in the morning. Here I am sitting at the kitchen table of the most loving family I have ever met in Israel. The Universe guided me very well.

My body, mind and Soul are fed this evening with a better meal than I ever dreamed of. We talk with hands and feet and our conversation is as lively as if we are speaking Dutch.

When the old lady shows me my room, she first changes the sheets on the bed. The room is David's; he has apparently given his room up to me for this night. She takes my hand and leads me to the balcony that overlooks the neighborhood. I can see the contours of Tel Aviv. We both stand on the balcony.

When she feels it's time to close the door, she waits until I am in bed. She tucks me in. The sheets feel warm as if I am wrapped in a blanket of love. I can't sleep...*where am I and how did I get here*?

However, my body is tired. I take one last look at the sky—it is easy because the room has no curtains—and then I fall into a deep dreamless sleep. Before I wake up, David has arrived to join us for breakfast. His mom goes out of her way to care for her guest. The conversation is a bit easier now; David can translate his parent's many questions about Holland.

With a heavy heart and a stomach filled to the brim, I say goodbye to these lovely, loving beings. I realize we don't need biological ties or a long history together to be at home with one another. It's the shared connection of love that binds us. I have new friends overnight.

David drops me off at the main bus terminal. Slightly nervous, I find my way through the many buses and noises I recognize from the times before. I can take the bus to *Kvar Tikvah*, the crossing from where you can hitchhike to the kibbutz. I buy my ticket and, after an hour's wait, I take my seat. My excitement grows and I can't wait to go. From Kvar Tikvah, I hitchhike to the next crossing and from there can hitchhike to the kibbutz. The bus ride and the hitchhikes go smoothly and, within the estimated time, I am dropped off at the gate of the kibbutz.

The guard post is empty, which seems odd especially in this time of war. The atmosphere is different; it is quieter than I have ever experienced it, even on Sabbath.

The garbage belt is still there and the smell of rotten fruit is like baked apples on a rainy Sunday afternoon. I have always liked that. My heart skips a beat; I so appreciate to be back. I walk down the long lane and every step brings me closer to the heart of this small community. I first go to the office.

P'dut sees me coming and she walks toward me with her arms wide open. Tears stream down her face. For her, it is a sign of true love and commitment to come back in a time like this. In her broken accent, she explains why hardly anyone is here. She tells me that, even as an old-time volunteer, I have no special privileges. They will put me like all the others in the bullet factory.

I will clean bullets six days a week for eight hours a day. I stop for a moment and wonder *why did I come to Israel again*? I am challenged by the thought of cleaning bullets. As a pacifist in Heart and Soul, *how on earth can I do this*?

P'dut walks away without waiting for a reply. She is too busy with all the formalities of my arrival. I am supplied with sheets, a tea pot, a stove, work boots and two sets of blue baggy 'uniforms.' We all look the same. The latest style hasn't changed for the last ten years. Some more supplies like soap, coffee and other goodies pile on top of all my other stuff. My principles are tested. I walk over the quiet lanes; some sprinklers are turned on. I cool off as I walk right through them.

David O sees me coming when I enter the volunteer quarters. He is an old-timer just like me. I am so happy to see my old friend again. Some volunteers like David O and I return year after year and some even stay forever. The core group that keeps coming back calls themselves the *kibbutz freaks*. I am one of them.

The volunteer quarters are deserted. I have a room by myself, and I like that a lot. This time I won't need ear plugs to block out the noisy love sounds of my roommates at night. The next morning my alarm clock goes off at 6 o'clock and for a moment I don't know where I am. Outside I hear the tractors picking up the workers for the orchards and the fields. Slowly I rise and put on my working clothes. A big blue worn-out shirt and matching faded blue baggy shorts is my outfit. Everything is too big as usual. Only the brown army boots fit.

I glance over my body and feel satisfied with the uniform of alikeness with the others. Once I put on my hat, I am changed completely into a *kibbutznik.*

At breakfast everyone meets in the dining room and all the volunteers have certain tables where they sit. I like the breakfast; it is simple but there are a *lot* of choices. Eggs, fruit, porridge and bread; you can eat all you want. At home I eat a boring brown piece of bread with cheese, and here I can just pile up my plate. For us as volunteers the mealtimes are moments to relax and tell stories.

The atmosphere has changed; this time the dining room is empty; not only the men are gone, there are few volunteers. The ones who are here are assigned to the factory which is turned into a bullet factory for now. For eight long hours, I clean bullets while continuously wondering if I am doing the right thing. I thought I was a pacifist; *should I leave and go back home? Or should I support the Israelis no matter what*? Many questions go through my head. *Will someone be shot with one of the bullets I cleaned*? I wish I was as innocent as the first time; perhaps then I would refuse to do it and stay in bed.

After two days I decide to voice my thoughts to David O. He is the one to talk to because he represents the volunteers. We have a meeting and we discuss our work in the bullet factory.

I am not the only one who has doubts. We agree they should give us other work; we don't want to clean bullets anymore.

Our complaint is taken seriously and the next day I am working in "turkeys," which means I have to inject 800 turkeys a day. My big needle is attached to a reservoir that dangles around my neck. My first shot is the worst and certainly the most painful for the frightened bird. I don't push hard enough. "Harder and deeper," they say to me, and there I go.

The next shot is better. My needle disappears with more force in their mushy flesh. With that shot the chapter of eating turkey meat is closed. For eight hours in a row I give them their shots. I am horrified but I can't complain. I learn to have endurance and my way to cope is to switch off my mind. For months I patiently stand in the turkey cage and inject two turkeys at once. I have let my resistance go and bless each turkey I cause pain.

After 25 years, I have the chance to let my turkey trauma go. On Thanksgiving Day in America, I dutifully stuff an enormous 20 pounder in the oven. My kids want to celebrate this day the "*All-American Way*." As a good mom, I courageously get up at 6:00 AM and lock my early bird in the oven until sweat drips off his roasted chest. Six hours later, I take a leap of faith and taste the meat. I must admit I have done a darn good job!

The Sinai

My experiences in the desert set the tone for my spiritual quest. After I come back, I feel a yearning in my Heart and Soul; I want to feel THAT feeling of Oneness again. I was in my early twenties and, at that age, I couldn't pinpoint WHAT it precisely was I had experienced. I was totally in tune with God. I thought my blissful feelings had to do with traveling to new places, undoing myself from my past and my belongings and fearlessly following the voice of my Soul. This indeed was part of it yet, honestly, *what did I know*? I was still on the outer trail.

I meet Faith on one of my yearly visits to the kibbutz. She becomes my best friend for life – *how symbolic was that*? Besides, *what else could the name be of the one to hold my hand*?

Faith was the funniest girl I ever met. Her posh English accent made you assume she was the Queen Mother's daughter. The way she spoke was flawless. Faith was obsessed with her body; her tan and her looks meant everything to her. She was beautiful no matter how she looked; only she didn't know.

Our main interest was to have fun and try to escape our workload. Our small room contained two beds, a kettle for tea and a heater for French toast.

Every day after work, we brought white bread, milk and eggs from the dining room to make a divine meal. Months later I realized why we gained weight so easily despite the hard physical labor. At night we crossed the cotton fields and sneaked to the other side of the kibbutz .We liked to party on the other side of the road.

One Friday night, we cross the road and crash pub night at the kibbutz *Givat Chaim Ichud*. Their pub is bigger and more alive because of the number of volunteers they have. We dance until the music stops and when the last song is announced I look around and suddenly my eyes spot a blond-haired guy. *Who is this*? Our eyes meet for a split second, intense and powerful, and then the magic is over. The light goes on and I don't see him when I scan the room with my half-open eyes.

A week goes by and my heart stands still when he walks into our Friday pub night with a group of *Ichud* volunteers behind him. The roles are switched. It doesn't take him long to walk toward me and introduce himself, "Hi! Ik ben Tobias."

How does he know I'm Dutch? I can't believe he is, too. We talk a little bit and then we go "for tea" to my room.

I like everything about him. We kiss but nothing more; he is respectful and he leaves my room as the pub announces closing time. "I go," he whispers. I like him a lot.

As far as I can judge him, he is like-minded and I could fall for him completely. The kibbutz made everyone anonymous; we all walked around in the same clothes and did the same jobs.

No one shared their backgrounds. We were all alike. With Tobias I felt he was like me. No matter his blue outfit.

His voice was what really did it; he touched my Soul by the tone and timbre he spoke with. Something inside of me was stirred and I was attracted deeply to him. Years later in Holland, Tobias is a famous news reporter on national television. What is even weirder: he lives around the corner. His house is only five minutes from mine!

The butterflies in my stomach make me eager to find out more about him. I want to see Tobias again. One afternoon, I courageously walk over to the other side and when I am in kibbutz *Ichud* I wander around the volunteer quarters in order to find him. In a flash I see him with another girl but I dismiss the thought as quickly as it came. That can't be him.

"I think he lives with a Swedish girl," a woman says without much interest when I ask where he might be. I walk away more disappointed than I want to admit. *What did we have together anyway*? Basically it was only a kiss on a pub night. *Was it already a passé one-hour kibbutz fling*? I'm sad and I can't understand how that happened overnight.

By now I should know the kibbutz is THE place for heartbreak. The saying goes, "You are either heartbroken or in love." So far I had always been neither. Love affairs were very deep but usually short-lived. The variety of young people from the many different countries made it like a marketplace to shop. The Scandinavian girls were of great interest to the horny guys.

Herve, our famous French lover of the volunteer quarters, asks me one night if I want to sleep with him. My answer is "No, I don't even know you." "That's how you get to know me," is his clever reply. His accent is very cute and to hear him speak is a delight to every girl's ear. However sweet his voice is, my heart is occupied by someone else.

In the meantime, Tobias is kicked off the kibbutz. No one knows where he is. Many rumors about him go around. Some say he is in jail but, in the end, no one knows the truth. And neither do I. He is gone.

The following pub night I dance with Faith and when our most favorite song of the kibbutz, "I Will Survive," is played I sing so loud I lose my voice.

Indeed, I will survive. Faith and I dance till closing time and, when I go to bed, I let go of my feelings for Tobias. I shake off my sorrow and life has a different focus again.

As in every small community, a small story becomes a big story and my interest peaks when I hear about volunteers who live in the Sinai Desert. Little messages start dripping like water from an unclosed faucet on the kibbutz. One by one they form a pool that is big enough for me to dive into. It sounds fascinating to live in the Sinai Desert. I want to meet the Bedouins and sleep under the stars. I am bored of picking oranges every day.

I do feel sorry for Zachariah, the old pardess boss who loves Faith and me. Every Friday afternoon when Sabbath begins, Zachariah invites us to his house.

Fridays and Saturdays are very special days in the kibbutz. The ritual of celebration starts around 4:30 PM with tea, ice cream and cake. When you are lucky and are considered an *old* volunteer you are adopted by a kibbutz family. Sometimes by two families.

Zachariah asks me one day if I want him as a kibbutz father. This is a great honor and I couldn't be happier to come to his house on Sabbath. He calls me Ms. Rembrandt after the famous painter's wife Saskia.

Zachariah is old and wise and on Friday he enjoys telling us endless stories about his youth and how he came to Israel. I feel sad to tell him about our departure. Zachariah understands and waves our concerns about him away. I am not sure if I ever will see him again. "Bye bye, dear Ms. Rembrandt" are the last words he ever speaks to me.

Two day later Faith and I leave. We have little money and how to get to the Sinai and how to live there are questions we can't answer. We have faith and that is strong enough. We leave for an indefinite period to live in the desert.

At the end of the first day of travel, we arrive excitedly in the most civilized place in the South. The city of Eilat is full of tourists and entertainment; unfortunately, we can't stay there. We need to get to the desert as fast as we can. The idea of sleeping for free in the most majestic place on earth makes us move fast.

It takes us another whole day. We hop from bus to bus; we are in a hurry to get to Nueiba. And when we are close to our final destination we learn that the next bus will leave in two days.

I learn patience in Israel. We were building muscle in the knowing we had all the time in the world.

We wait one and a half days.

Upon arrival in Nueiba (which is now Egypt), we try to figure out where we need to go. After all the stories, we are very curious where *the* place to be is. In Nueiba, there is absolutely nothing but a kiosk to buy food; the rest is left to our imagination. Soon we find out that at the left side of the kiosk there is an area where they built a very small Club Med. Barbed wire divides the club from the rest of the desert. Basically it is the kiosk, Club Med and sand; endless stretches as far as one can see.

Now I stand glued to the ground. The scenery takes my breath away; the contours of the mountains in the background and the turquoise sea in the forefront are incredible. They are both translucent and look like an oasis of beauty.

Only this was not a deception of the eye. I tell Faith a million times this is the most beautiful place on earth; it is heaven on earth and so far I had never been there.

At Club Med they have volunteers from our kibbutz who are here called 'the workers'. The difference with being a kibbutz volunteer and this is that the workers are paid. We come to find out that some of our friends who left our kibbutz are working here.

Officially we are not allowed in the Club Med area so we need to climb under the barbed fence to get to their side. We want to speak to Ken; he is in charge of the workers.

Ken points out that some like us who just come to "hang" here are not allowed in the Club Med area; we better go somewhere else. People like us are living in the shade of the palm trees a few miles away. Ken lives with the other guys and girls in wooden huts.

Faith and I head for the place he describes. It sounds a little vague but when we start walking we assume that the area with the three palm trees is our spot. We find a bundle of clothes and a few sleeping bags. At least some people are living here. It doesn't take us long to unpack. I have brought my sleeping bag, two t-shirts, a skirt and a pair of shorts. It will be more than enough for the months to come.

The only thing I wished (later) was that I had shoes. Unfortunately, I did not. Upon arrival, I threw them away, which will almost cost me my right foot and Faith her both feet. We both develop severe infections from walking barefoot. The hot desert sand gives us many blisters and the pointy rocks hidden underneath the sand create open wounds that are very painful. We hit our toes an uncountable number of times, but it never really bothers us until we are back in the kibbutz.

We settle into our desert spot and we spread our sleeping bags next to one another. Satisfied we stretch ourselves in the sand and gaze out over the sea in front of us. Our first night is precious. We look at the dark sky; the trillions of stars twinkle like Christmas lights above our heads.

The mountains enclose us safely and the sea soothes us with the rolling waves. The breeze massages my face with her gentle touch.

I need nothing, absolutely nothing more. I love it here and it feels as if my Soul is bursting out of my skin.

The Star of David becomes my all-time lover of the night. I miss him deeply when I am in Holland again and sleep with a roof above my head. I come in rhythm with the night and day. We go to sleep when the sun goes down and we rise when the sun comes up. The Bedouins walk on top of our sleeping bodies before we stir. They try to sell us home-baked pita bread.

The dark-eyed girls are fascinated by my long, blond hair and often they sit around me in a circle and comb my hair. Each girl takes her turn.

After a while I become completely attuned to the Universe. I can manifest almost anything. At first I don't know that I can. Later I still don't know what I do, but I notice that miracles happen. We need them because we have no money and we start to get hungry.

"Let's find work" is my thought one morning when our bellies still make a rumbling sound after the pita bread we had for breakfast. A tractor with a long flat platform pulls up in front of us. The guy is looking for people who want to work in his melon factory in the desert. We jump on the offer and climb on the platform behind his tractor. He moves fast with his tractor when he drives off.

We almost roll off without him noticing that he has lost his workers within the first five minutes. The melon factory is about twenty minutes away from where we live. The job is arduous in its long boring hours; however it is easy to eat lots of melons and earn enough to eat something else, too.

I stand for eight hours on my bare feet behind a conveyor belt. My job is to catch the melons that roll down full speed and stack them in a box. I can't remember if I had fun but I do remember that the hours went fast.

Our melon boss picks us up at sunrise and we don't mind waiting because we watch the mountains turn from all shades of orange into pink and deep purple. Sometimes I am so hypnotized by the beauty of nature that our boss has to scream to get me going.

Our days pass quickly. Faith and I love this easy rhythm. After work, I can sit for hours and look out over the landscape and watch the camels walk by. An old guy tries to persuade me to come live as his concubine. He wants to SELL me to a tourist for a few horses and donkeys. I decline and choose the blissful state of living barefoot. By now many blisters and infections have formed but we can't do much except sneak in the workers quarters and wash our feet with clean water.

We've become good friends with the boys and girls who work in Club Med. At night we crawl under the barbed wire and crash the discotheque. Effortlessly we change from Bedouin hippies into the rich and the famous. We think no one can tell the difference between who is who. To find our way back through the dark night was a challenge at first, but we become experts in reading the stars to find the location of our sleeping bags. The trade of disco music for the sound of the crashing waves is night after night my lullaby to fall asleep.

Tobias is long forgotten. I am in love with nature and for once that was absolutely enough.

One Sunday morning when Faith and I are off from work, we plan to go on a long walk into the mountains. They've tempted us to explore them from the moment we arrived. We set off early without telling anyone. The sand is not too hot and our feet feel fine. We want to be back before noon.

We walk in a straight line toward the mountains and our nonstop talk is only interrupted by eagles that soar above our heads. They warn us we have to be able to trace our tracks. We don't listen because we walk and talk. We want to cross the sandy mountains and see what is on the other side. One mountain follows the other and there is no end in sight.

When we are out of breath, we stop for a moment and crash in the sand. "Oh, I am *sooo* thirsty," we say at the same time. The little bottle of water we brought for the two of us is empty and when I throw the bottle in the air and catch it we shake our heads in disbelief. How stupid we are not to bring food and water on this climb! I try to figure out the trail from where we came – there is none. We don't know where we came from and we don't know where we are going. The wind has blown away our footprints.

The desert has her magic and she is very seducing when you have no compass for direction. We see sand and similar mountains everywhere. We lay down and the only thing I can think of is to have fun by rolling off the mountain on our backs.

Breathless we lay at the bottom of the mountain, my hair is full of sand and, when I shake it off, I say jokingly, "We would be so thankful if we could quench our thirst. We need some melons." My mouth starts watering at the thought of the juicy melons we ate at the factory yesterday.

We stumble up and Faith and I have faith we will figure out how to get home. The time has passed faster than we thought and the sand is hot under our bare feet. In the distance, the sun reflects the heat. We understand how you can be sidetracked by following a trail that leads to an oasis that isn't there. Faith and I start walking although we don't know where we are going. Desert sand is all there is for now.

The heat is dancing in the air in front of me and I think I am hallucinating when I see a big brown canvas bag in the sand. We walk toward it. *Has someone lost this bag*? There is no road or path here. We carefully move the bag. It gives no sound. We open the bag and 3 big juicy melons stare us in the face.

We fall on our knees. *Who has heard my prayers*? We savor each bite and no drop is spilled. We continue our walk and effortlessly we find our way back. Our friends praise our luck but I don't believe in luck. In this timeless place the Universe supplied us; we were saved by the one with the Big Compass.

The next day I sit in the sand and for a moment my thoughts go back to the "unfinished business" with Tobias. I wonder if I will bump into him in Amsterdam someday.

It feels good to be detached; the magic I felt for him is gone. I close my eyes for a moment and when I open them I am hallucinating like yesterday. Tobias towers above the sand dune I am resting on. Before I open my mouth, a messenger comes running up the hill. "Saskia, Tobias is looking for you." I can see that but *how come he is here when I was just thinking of him*?

I invite him to sit next to me. He has changed and I can't relate to him anymore. He sells drugs and that business isn't of interest to me. I know he is still the same great person on the inside but outside he is on another track. The fact that he is here, however, is absolutely stunning. The law of attraction works whether I liked it or not. Tobias leaves after a few days. The next time I will meet him he has changed again and I like him a lot.

The time goes on and it never bores me to sit in the sand and watch the spectacular nature around me. The familiar routine of work, rest and sleep is fulfilling. It defies description. I look different after a few months. I am very much at peace, even more so than when I was on the kibbutz. The relentless sun and strong desert winds have given me a golden brown tan; unfortunately, the damage to my skin is done. No expensive cream can ever repair the cracks; at that point, I have no idea. I glow like the sun and that is exactly how I feel.

I write to my parents on little paper towels which I hand to strangers who are always willing to put them in an envelope and mail them. Later my parents tell me that every little note reached them and they were very grateful to get some news.

I was out of reach but deep in their hearts. They must have had a huge amount of trust in me.

To say goodbye and return to the kibbutz was the hardest thing I had to do. The desert had captured my heart. My return ticket to Holland was expiring and I had to go back. Faith was dealing with the same issue, too.

The last day I walk step by painful step because my feet are badly infected. It is obvious I need shoes for my painful feet and, not only that, the bus driver won't allow passengers without shoes on his bus .To get back is not as easy as it seems. First we need to find the right bus at the right time. The bus from Nueiba goes only when a driver and a bus are available at the same time. Usually it is a two-day wait if you are lucky. We don't mind waiting. We think that in the meantime we can find shoes.

After a few months we know there are no shops. The kiosk sells only food. "Sometimes in the trash," I hear a voice inside and, when I tell Faith, we agree this is our best bet. Indeed the trash can gifts us with flip flops in different sizes. It is the perfect solution for our wounded feet.

Faith's feet are in worse condition than mine. She can barely walk; her feet are swollen and she not only needs to get back to be on time for her flight, medical help is urgent. She limps and looks in bad shape. We wait two days and our ride to the kibbutz is as painful as our feet. We have left everything we love and forever will I seek to find the experience of Oneness, the harmony with the Universe I found in the desert.

Upon arrival in the kibbutz, the doctor is shocked when he sees Faith's feet. By now she has also developed a high fever and the antibiotics she needs are of the highest dose. The doctor is upset and tells her she might lose both feet; one foot is worse than the other. The thought of amputation drives her up the wall. I need antibiotics, too; my right big toe is in bad shape and very painful. For years I am not able to wear tight shoes. The spot stays sore even when my toe is cured.

I am sad, very sad to be back. The longing to be connected to nature sweeps me literally off my feet. I can't walk well and I sit in silence. I am aware of the many distractions that keep us from finding inner peace. To me it seems that the kibbutz has changed but, of course, it is me. I always felt so peaceful here – not anymore.

The normal world seems almost unbearable to me. The more distractions, the more distracted I am from who I am. In the desert, I felt fulfilled all the time. I had thought the kibbutz life was simple which is true. Now that is washed away by the Soulful episode in the Sinai. At night I lay awake and look at the wooden ceiling of my room. I am disconnected from my starry friends that granted my wishes and I miss the ocean's lullaby to fall asleep. I fly back home a week later.

My mom shrieks when she opens the door and sees my brown, cracked face. I had aged in wisdom inside and my outer skin looked a hundred years old. My hunger for travel was ravenous since the Sinai. However, everyone said I needed to get on with 'real' life and look for a job; they reminded me this would be very hard to find.

A week later I have a job I absolutely adore. I am the remedial teacher of the elementary school I love. The stars had never left me.

I said goodbye to Tobias in the Sinai but there is this nagging feeling I will meet him again. The thought of Tobias pops into my head again after I see someone who looks like him. I want to connect with him and I find his address in Amsterdam. My postcard reaches him but I forget to give him a return address and he cannot reply.

Three years later at New Year's Eve, I am in the Odeon, a popular theatre where the young people of Amsterdam gather to celebrate New Year's Eve. Many artists perform on the stage and, just a few minutes before the clock strikes midnight, I walk closer to the podium. The band is loud and jazzy and the crowd dances to the rhythm of the music. I am pushed forward but I don't mind. I can see the band better now.

In front of me stands a guy smoking a cigarette. Someone pushes me against his body but just in time I regain my balance and stand back on my own two feet. In shock I recognize the hair on the back of the neck of this guy. It is Tobias! I clearly remember his neck and, although it sounds crazy, I know it's him. I take a moment to recover and ask myself how to react.

I feel the familiar stirring and gently I touch him on his back and say, "*Tobias, how are you*?" He turns around and his mouth drops open when he sees my face. There is instant recognition. "I need to see you, let's meet," he says. We discover he lives around the corner from me. My street ends at his street. We shop at the same stores, we bike along the same street and we must have crossed paths a million times. And here we are; the timing is divine. He had changed again and now the timing is right.

We quickly make a date and set a time while his girlfriend, watches us, with wary eyes and my boyfriend is out of sight. Within three minutes, a 'play date' is arranged. The New Year had come to complete our karma and that was why we met again.

A week later, Tobias comes over for a Mexican dinner at my apartment. We eat, talk and drink too many strong margaritas. When he leaves the next day, I do not hear from him until a year later. I turn on the news and hear a familiar voice. He is well known, he looks wonderful and his spirit shines through with brilliance.

Egypt

I stare for a second at his Irish freckled face. When Eric arrives at the kibbutz and enters the dining room, I instantly know I will have a fling with him, not because of the way he looks, because my inner voice says so. I finish my lunch and don't give the inclination of my Soul much thought. Eric walks straight to my table and introduces himself to everyone. Before he shakes my hand, I get up to bring my dishes to the kitchen; our introduction can wait. A month later I travel to Egypt with him.

I go to Egypt with Brian, Eric and Peter and, at the end of the trip, the three of us say goodbye to Peter, who heads for Kenya. I still regret saying no to Peter's offer to visit his parent's farm in Kenya. Instead I choose to return to the kibbutz with Eric and Brian. Peter's infatuation with me made me hesitant. I didn't want to take advantage of him by accepting his invitation. However, as soon as he leaves, I wish I had told him what I felt and was open about my feeling that I would disappoint him. The way things turned out obviously was meant to be.

The borders are now open between Israel and Egypt and this makes it possible to enter Egypt via land. After a few months of picking oranges and working in the cotton field, I am bored and ready for a new adventure. We are warned about malaria in the area of the pyramids and we need to take malaria pills before we go.

At the pharmacy in Nathanya, we are instructed about the different options. There is a certain dosage you need to take before you go on your trip, a dosage for when you are there and a certain dosage for when you actually have malaria. We lose count and forget what we are told. We go home and try to figure out how many pills we need to take.

It is not surprising as to what happens as we haven't understood the instructions of the pharmacist well. I start my first dose of the pills and develop a high fever. I start hallucinating and I sleepwalk around the kibbutz. I am heavily drugged. The next day I find out that I have taken a double dose of the wrong pills. The instructions weren't crystal clear. From now on I am more careful. Brian has a similar experience although he doesn't walk around the kibbutz and his dreams are lucid; yet he still shakes when he wakes up. We count the days until our departure. We can't wait to finish our last task.

We leave the kibbutz with very little luggage. We won't be able to take much because of the way we are traveling.

After five hours on the bus, we arrive in Eilat. This is the place where our adventure begins. We have to take a taxi to cross the border. For the taxi drivers, this ride is new, too, and they try to get their best bargain. After a lot of back and forth talk with taxi drivers, we manage to find a taxi to take us to the border of Egypt. We are squeezed in between three Egyptian women. Two of them have baskets with fruit and vegetables on their lap. The other woman carries two live chickens.

Their body odor is horrific; I can hardly breathe. We need to change cabs two more times and it looks more like a secret mission than a drive to Egypt. Maybe this route wasn't allowed. I don't know and I don't mind. The windows of our last cab are covered with black plastic. It speaks to my imagination; it looks like we are part of a James Bond movie. When we exchange cabs, we have to run with our heads between our legs. We can't make noises; we have to be in total silence. I don't take it too seriously. I like this game and run as fast as I can.

After eight hours of little comfort we arrive in the most chaotic and noisy city I have been: Cairo, the capital of Egypt. *Had I expected Cairo to be like Israel*?

This city is similar to my travel experiences in other Arabic countries. Thousands of bikes, cars with honking horns, people screaming in harsh Arabic voices surround us as soon as we set foot on the street. I look around me when I step out of the taxi and I am almost run over with a bike. The cyclist scolds me with an angry face. The friendly atmosphere of Israel is the not the same here. Nothing feels friendly. It's hurry, hurry, *hassaha.*

In the late hour of our arrival, the lit buildings give the city an Arabic fairytale-like glow. We need a hotel. We ask a stranger if he knows of a cheap place to stay. He does and fifteen minutes later we arrive at a sleazy, dingy hotel in the middle of Cairo. Even inside the room, it feels as if we are standing in the middle of a traffic jam. We hear the hundred of cars honking; trying to push themselves through the little streets.

To close our window is not an option. The light breeze is the fresh air we need, even though it is highly polluted. I try to lock the door of our room but the lock is broken. I feel uncomfortable and unsafe and the company of these guys is not the most uplifting energy either.

Peter is the most gentle and most likeable but, because of his love for me, he is very shy. I lie down on the dirty bed and stare at the ceiling. *What was it that called me to Egypt*? I long for companions with whom I feel at ease. These guys are rather grim. I am bone-tired and think that maybe I need a rest to see the experience in a different light. I propose we go out for dinner.

We get up from our beds and leave our room a little later. On the dark streets the Arabic magic lurks in every corner. There is much to see and there are so many food stalls that look delicious.

We know we have to be careful and cannot eat meat or anything that is not thoroughly cooked. We make our pick and pay 25 cents for a bowl of rice with all kinds of vegetables. It's fascinating to walk down the streets but I need to stay close to my male friends.

My long, blond hair and bare legs are magnets for the Arabic guys. Openly, they not only whistle at me, they touch and squeeze me when they get a chance. The guys I am with don't notice it and they grin when I tell them.

I am glad when we are back in our hotel. The only surprise is that someone has gone through our luggage. Since there was nothing of value, nothing is missing.

At night I can't sleep; it is hot and, after being squeezed in between the women during the day, I am now in a room squeezed between three guys. The street noises and Brian's snoring keeps me awake. I might as well sleep in the middle of the street; noise-wise it doesn't make much difference.

I fall asleep until I hear a squeaking noise and sit right up in bed. I see the door knob turn slowly. Someone peeks around the door but, when I move, the man disappears quickly. I feel awkward and hope the pyramids are worth my stay in fear.

In the morning we go for breakfast on the roof of the hotel and the sleepless night is forgotten. The roof towers high above the center of Cairo and the cacophony of noises reaches us even this high. The view is magnificent and in the far-away distance we see vague contours of the pyramids.

The smell that comes from the streets is a mixture of jasmine, patchouli and burned wood. I am mesmerized by the street scene. The Egyptian world is at our feet. It is safe to watch it from above.

The city is very alive at 6:30 in the morning; apparently the traffic never stops. The Arabic men and women wear long dresses—they all look the same. Most of the women are fat, very fat, but that could be a deception of the eye. Their layered clothing doesn't accentuate their bodies. No curves are shown; what a waste of a woman's beautiful body we think. They dress according to the Arabic rules. I don't and that may be the reason I find myself almost 'eaten alive' within the next few hours.

We read in the newspaper that the Shah of Persia is to be buried today and the anticipation of excitement is already felt on top of the roof. We immediately decide to go there. What a chance to be part of it. According to the newspaper, the coffin will be carried through the streets of Cairo.

In the same moment we are reading this, the people start wailing. The high walls of the buildings echo their wails back and forth. I can't remember where we will find the place of the procession but I assume we should follow the crowd. We are determined to catch a glimpse of the coffin. It is too late in the end when I realize I should never be near this event.

As a blond, long-haired girl, I am live bait in a basin of hungry sharks. In Arabic countries, women do not mingle with men. So I am the only woman among thousands of highly aroused men.

The crowd we are part of grows bigger and bigger within the hour but it is too late to leave when I discover this event is only for the men. They are all dressed in long *djellabas* and their constant yelling and screaming seems to serve a purpose. It stirs more excitement in the atmosphere. I wonder what is going on. *Why is hysteria needed to bury the Shah*? It frightens me and, when I lose sight my friends, I am totally alone in a massive crowd of insanely-behaving men. I look around but my search is useless; my friends have disappeared and I need to pray out loud to be saved from those around me.

In the distance I can see the coffin accompanied by male figures coming my way. Somehow the sight of the coffin makes the men crazier and wilder. Whenever they bump into me, their hands are all over my body. Hurriedly they touch me everywhere, but my screaming is lost in the noise. It is a useless attempt; there is nothing to bring these men to stop. I slap them to no avail. I am in a sea of males pressing against me, swaying my body back and forth. I have nowhere to go, there is no escape.

I am terrified to be crushed to the ground. Hands keep touching me without respect. They are out of their heads, driven by lust. They must think they have arrived in Heaven. Allah has granted their prayers. To deserve such good fortune on a day like this is a gift from God.

I am happy to see the coffin is coming closer and I can almost touch it when they walk by. My disgust for the men is temporarily replaced with an eagerness to see this spectacle up close. I take pictures when the coffin is right next to me as I hit violent hands that touch me. How long this horrible play goes on I can't remember but suddenly it all stops. As if an invisible hand lifts me up, I am swept off my feet. For a moment I float directionless in the air and seconds later I land on the only platform that rises above the crowd. A television wagon is filming this event and is parked in the middle of the massive crowd.

I still don't know who swept me off my feet and onto the platform of the television wagon but I am grateful. I am safe.

As I look around, I see to my surprise Peter is sitting at the back of the wagon.

He smiles at me. He doesn't know what happened to me. "Hi, there you are," he says in his posh English accent. He sounds as if he has had great time. I feel a lot safer but I am still afraid to lose sight of Peter again.

I scan my body and see that it is battered and bruised. However, I have witnessed the funeral of the Shah and even captured a few pictures. *Why was I here*?

Peter and I stay on the wagon as long as possible and we ask the guys on the camera crew if they can give us a lift back to a more civilized part of the city. They wait till the crowd leaves. When most of the people are gone, amazingly we meet up with Brian and Eric.

I've had enough for today. I prefer the dirty hotel room. I want to sit on the roof and view the scenery from above. I tell my friends what happened but they aren't too impressed.

The next day we head out for our long-dreamed of visit to the Pyramids of Giza. We have to figure out a way to get there. A taxi driver approaches us when he sees the touristy look on our faces. He asks if we want to see the pyramids and, after a bit of bargaining, we agree upon his price and hop in the car.

He takes us through the traffic with great skill while honking his horn non-stop. Nobody listens anyway. We leave the city and take the back road to Giza. The pyramids tower high above the desert and their majestic presence sucks us in. A familiarity arises when I get a closer look. *Had I been here before*?

It crosses my mind I could easily tour us around. I was pretty sure I could still find my way.

"This is as far as I go," the driver says and stops somewhere in the sand. He tells us that he will pick us up again in the afternoon. We don't have much choice because there is no other way to get back to Cairo. Instantly we are enthralled by the energy and the height of the pyramids. They are unbelievable. I touch stones that are thousands years old. They are a hundred times bigger then I imagined. The sphinx is so big that only from a distance can you recognize the shape of it. None of us speaks. *What can we say*? I start to climb the giant stones of the pyramid. I want to reach the top. Exhausted, I arrive and, when I sit down, the view takes my breath away. I sit in silence while memories of past lives float through my third eye. I remember the eagles; as a little boy I could hear their messages. My third eye was trained to receive their wisdom. The memories are vivid and detailed as if I was here yesterday.

I get up and climb down to join the boys. The guys have been climbing the pyramids, too, and all of us gather at the bottom of the big stones. We gaze up when we hear a man talking Arabic. He invites us to see an undiscovered Pharaoh's tomb. Our eyes light up; of course, we'd like that. The man is secretive and whispers something we don't understand.

We need to follow him. His step is fast and he almost trips over his long dress in his hurried pace. He seems to follow an invisible trail that leads to a grave which is hidden between the pyramids.

After about 15 minutes he stops abruptly. *Are we there*? We don't see an entrance or shape that looks even slightly as that of a tomb. The man tells us to wait and, when he pushes aside some rocks, we can see the entrance. Now the rocks are removed and the entrance completely reveals it self. A very unpleasant feeling sweeps through my body. I don't recognize the significance and I don't understand what it means. *Why am I nervous to see something the world has not seen*? Months later I find out why. My premonition was a warning to *stay out* of this tomb.

We descend down a dark spiraling stairs that lead to the tomb. A minute later we stand in a candlelit room. Three famous Egyptian pharaohs are buried in this grave. I shiver; the atmosphere feels creepy and forbidden. I can feel it without a doubt. *Who were they and why were they never discovered after all the excavations they did at Giza*?

A wave of nausea washes over me. My inner voice tells me to get out NOW. I hesitate a moment. I want to take in the sacred opportunity to be in the presence of these important Kings. In contrast to the Museum of Cairo, we can touch the statues and the treasures, beautiful presents given to the pharaohs to be buried with them in their graves.

Eric is fascinated by the treasures within our reach. I want to take pictures to show to my friends yet my inner voice says firmly, "NO." She tells me again to leave NOW. I look around one more time. I see Eric gathering up some bones of the Pharaohs and other treasures, too.

It crosses my mind . . . wouldn't it be cool to have the BONES of a pharaoh king! Eric stuffs his treasures in his pockets. With no thought, he takes his finds – highly-valued belongings of the pharaohs – from the tomb.

Suddenly I run up the stairs as if my life depended on it. Out of breath, I lean against the entrance of the tomb, the sun shining brightly on the horizon. The heat leaves a streak of energy wavering above the desert sand. I look at the camels passing by; they seem undisturbed by the everlasting sun. In contrast, I am very hot; sweat drips off my body but I don't move. I wait. I don't even want to take a peek downstairs again.

Half an hour later Eric ascends triumphant, very satisfied with his catch. He doesn't realize the sleeping pharaoh is now wide awake. It's no wonder . . . Eric has stolen his sacred bones.

None of us is aware of the hand of fate delivered to Eric from stealing from a pharaoh's grave. Later we learn it is said to doom you until the seventh generation. Eric's future is grim yet we have no idea about this for now. Eric is happier than he has ever been.

We are all in good spirits when we leave the tomb. A man offers us a ride with his horses. We accept and, when I climb on the back of the smallest horse, I feel like I am back in my old Egyptian times. I gallop without a saddle. I am in my element. The horses are a bit wild but easy to lead. When we are whistled back by the old man, we are hungry and thirsty. It is time to go back to the city. We return to the cabdriver, who is overly friendly, most likely anticipating our hunger and thirst.

My neck hurts from turning around for a last look at the Great Sphinx. We come to a halt and the cab driver asks us to get out the car. We don't understand why but we do as we are told.

When he opens the trunk, the reason is clear. The back of the car is stacked with bottles of Coca-Cola, the most popular drink in Egypt. Surprised as we are by this friendly gesture, we accept and toast our "good" luck for the day!

After another few miles he stops again and the same ritual repeats itself. We get out the car and drink our Coca-Cola. Only this time the ending is a bit different than the first time. As soon as we get in the car, he locks the door and tells us we have to pay him not only for the fare but for the drinks, too. The amount he asks is outrageous; it is four times more than what the fare and the drinks are worth. Even if we had it, we wouldn't have given it to him.

He loses his temper and starts to scream at us. We offer a bargain which makes him even more upset. "You will pay what I ask, otherwise I will get my friends," he says. It sounds like a threat of a five-year-old who says he will get his older brothers to help him. I know he means it; he is outraged.

The man is a lunatic; we feel his energy gets worse by the minute. I am afraid he has no consciousness of right and wrong. He drives the cab wildly over the sandy road; we race around at a speed of 90 miles an hour. If I survived the funeral of the Shah and escaped the dark energy in the tomb, *what is my fate this time*? I must have faith.

We see the outskirts of Cairo; at least we are driving in the right direction but our doors are tightly locked. The man mumbles – I don't know if he prays or swears at us. We think the latter.

Eric hands the man the money for the ride but he yells and throws it on the floor. We ignore his decline and leave it there. We need to get out of this cab fast otherwise we will be smashed to pieces by this kamikaze driver. We silently signal to each other we have to unlock the doors and run when the cab lowers his speed.

Only when we leave the sandy road and hit the asphalt does he slow down to 50 miles an hour. He knows where he is going and I am sure he has made his plan; we are his prisoners and he is in charge. All of a sudden we enter the outskirts of the city and, as remote the desert was, the city brings us back to civilization. We almost feel safe. He sways the car to the left and without saying a word he stops and locks the doors of the car. He runs off. He is getting his friends to help him.

Brian, who was an expert in the army, doesn't lose a second and jumps forward in the driver's seat. He knows how to demolish the locks from the inside and with his magic hands he opens the front door. We run away and leave the car doors open. Moments later we disappear in the craze of the bazaar. We are safe!

Was this the first sign Eric's fate was doomed? My awareness did not stretch far enough to realize certain deeds create bad karma. I had no clue why things happened to Eric as they did. I would find that out much later.

The weeks that follow are a combination of adventure and magnificent experiences. We sail the Nile with ancient sailboats called feluccas at night. In the Museum of Cairo, we tour around and view the treasures of the pharaohs. We aren't allowed to touch anything but I am pinched, bruised and blue-legged by the guide's filthy hands. They can touch, but our hands have to be at our backs.

We have an extraordinary experience in the Valley of Kings, where we rent bikes and stay for hours in the graves where we are invited to excavate a site. My longing to become an anthropologist comes back full force. I have the feeling I know more about the sandy earth of Egypt than the "experts" there.

At the end of our journey we leave Peter behind; he will continue his trail to Kenya. When we wave him off at the main bus station in Cairo, my heart skips a beat. *Should I have joined him*? The answer is *No*, but as I write this down I think *Yes*. We would have had a great time.

Strangely enough I begin to be infatuated with Eric. He has an aura of authority around him and I admire his worldly travels. He has done it, been there; he has seen it all. I develop a weak spot for him during our last days in Egypt.

When we arrive back in Israel, we start a fling. We kiss a little but my sixth sense tells me to hold off. I can't explain why; he is a very attractive guy. Still I can't go any further than a kiss. "Don't go there," says my voice inside. I listen and just kiss. No more.

One night I hear a loud banging on my door and, when I open it, Eric is standing in front of me. He is very drunk.

"I want to sleep with you," he says bluntly.

I don't agree. I have a hard time pushing him out of my room but he leaves finally and tries his luck on the next door. He is very angry with me and the next day he immediately finds another girl friend, Kika, a beautiful thin English girl. My refusal the night before is to save me a LOT of trouble.

Bad things start to happen to Eric, one accident after another, sometimes with him, sometimes with someone very close to him. He accuses me of transmitting syphilis to him even though I never had sex with him. I am so glad now and I realize why I needed to hold off. It would have been impossible to prove I hadn't given it to him. Kika now has it, too, and every girl Eric has slept with has to be checked by the kibbutz doctor. His life is in a mess.

Bad luck seems to follow him wherever he goes. He almost gets killed when his tractor topples over in the cotton fields and it becomes obvious this isn't a series of coincidences. The worst is yet to come.

The kibbutz organizes day trips for the volunteers once a month. All the volunteers like the idea of going to the *Golan Heights* in the northern part of Israel because it is an overnight excursion.

Everyone is eager to add his or her name to the sign-up list. Hesitantly I put my name on the list. I want to go but part of me tells me not to. I cancel the day before we leave. I go to the office and cross my name off the list. I don't want to go after all.

Kika happens to be there and is beside herself over the opportunity because there are still a couple of spots open. Her sister Myra is going, too.

The group size is limited because they need enough guides to keep a close watch on everyone. The cliffs are steep and the mountains they are going to climb are challenging. However, in all the years the kibbutz climbed the Golan Heights, they never had a problem.

Kika is walking right behind or right in front of Eric when the accident happens. She takes a misstep while talking and falls deep down the cliffs. She comes to a halt on a platform that is impossible to reach. The group is aghast; they can see her body on the rocks. Her head is in a strange position from her body. Nobody can do anything. Myra is in shock. They can pick her body up only by helicopter. Kika is dead.

Although Eric had nothing to do with the accident, everything he touches seems to die or crumble.

What was going on? I am not the only one who starts to wonder. I don't know who sends Eric to Darlene; she is the one who can help him. She is a psychic and a psychologist.

Without any knowledge of his visit to Egypt, Darlene tells Eric: "You have shunned the holy graves and you are in possession of sacred materials; you are under the spell of the great Pharaohs. This carries on for seven generations when one steals from a tomb.

"You'll leave a trail of misfortune and the kibbutzniks are very concerned about this. You must know you simply can't just get rid of your treasures."

Eric wants to throw them in the garbage; he is scared out of his mind. He comes to my room right after speaking with her. With his familiar loud banging, he announces himself.

When I open the door, he quickly steps inside. He asks me what he was wearing that day we visited the grave. Since I have taken pictures, we know with one glimpse what outfit he wore.

He needs to burn these clothes and also the cupboard he has stored them in. It is a big wooden cupboard. Everything he has touched needs to go up in flames. Darlene spoke very clearly about how and what he needed to do to burn his "belongings." They had to be burned in a certain ritual.

I am in shock when I hear what he did might effect him until the seventh generation. I scan my mind if I have taken anything; I have not. I imagine what would have happened if I had ignored my inner voice.

Eric is willing to do anything to be released from the Pharaoh's spell. The only difficulty is he has to wait for the right wind and a specific moon in order to perform the burning ritual. Darlene described in vivid detail to him how he will find the right spot. The ritual includes Shamanic 'rules.'

He has to go alone and carry the big cupboard to the fields. A few days later the time has come. Eric leaves at daylight. Long after midnight he returns back to the kibbutz. He tells us that heavy thunder started as soon as he lit his match. The lightning lit the dark night sky. He felt an incredible power surge of energy flow through his body. He shivered and shook until everything was burned.

The thunder stopped when the fire died. Eric is exhausted and relieved when he tells us his story but he doesn't have proof the spell is lifted. Without notice, he leaves the kibbutz. Nobody knows where he goes; one day he just disappears.

Two years later I meet Eric in the kibbutz again. I don't recognize this bald guy who walks into the dining room where I am eating my lunch. He walks over to my table and this time I don't get up; I wait. He shares with us that he has a brain tumor. I am not hungry anymore. *Was his tumor a leftover from our visit to Egypt? Will he be haunted by his deed until the seventh generation*?

Africa

How dangerous the Cote d'Ivoire was for two Dutch girls escaped our attention. "Cook them in a pan" is the song the villagers sing to us as we pass by.

"Enjoy your stay" is the lifeline of the *Traveler Survival Kit* in this country. We trust the Universe will take care of us and so it does.

In my cozy loft in Amsterdam, I search the Saturday morning paper's travel section intensely. I look for an inexpensive airfare that flies as far away as possible. On weekends I check all the destinations from Africa to the North Pole. I am an expert in travel prices. In my fantasy I have traveled the world and visited every country on the earth. Today I spot an airfare that flies to Abidjan for little money. I have no idea where Abidjan is located. I look at the world map. Abidjan is the capital of the Cote d'Ivoire. My plan is made; the country sounds appealing. I have never been to this part of Africa.

Wendela, a French-speaking friend of mine, decides to join me in a heartbeat. *Why not go to Africa*? And so it happens that on a snowy winter day we exchange our wet country for the warm African sun. We arrive at the airport of Abidjan without delay; that is the only part of the trip that goes as planned. The airport is a mess; it looks like a filthy garage where people shuffle papers behind their wooden desks.

They look bored and they throw passports and luggage around with an equal lack of interest. We see our passports disappear in the hands of a young boy and we wait eagerly to get them back. Half an hour later they tell us our passports are lost. Absolutely no one knows where they are. We wait an hour; someone finds our passports on the floor. We can leave.

It's dark by the time we walk outside. We are like magnets for the many taxi drivers. They scream and pull at us. We have no plan of where to go and what to do. A cheap hotel close to the coast is our mission but *how do we get there*? The wild dark guys are only interested in two snow white girls who probably have lots of money. To get us where we wanted to go was the least of their interest.

We choose a guy with a friendly face although we can hardly see his eyes. His white teeth give us a smile and that is enough to pick him as our driver. He drives off and speeds into nowhere land and we regret our choice. We don't trust him but we can't leave his taxi; we are in the middle of nowhere.

The poverty scares us at first sight. The streets are of sand and the traffic is chaos. The king of the jungle rules: the bigger the car, the fewer dents. After 45 minutes of driving we urge him to either stop or drop us off at the nearest hotel. He says he knows where he is going, but we don't. A little later we stop at a place with neon lights on the side and we guess this is a hotel. When we get out of the car, we hear the sounds of waving palm trees; they surround the small *Hotel Griffon.*

A guy limps on one leg and slides himself towards our taxi. I wonder if we should stay; he looks so creepy. We have not much choice than to spend the night in his hotel. The strangest thing is that we have never seen people with such dark skin before and I am blown away by the fact that I need to get used to it. In Amsterdam we live in a multi-racial city but the men here look different. They must think the same of us—we are whiter than white.

The one-legged guy shows us our room and closes the door with the warning that it is very dangerous for two white girls to travel alone. We are the only guests in this hotel. We are too tired to figure out where we are. Within half an hour we are fast asleep until an enormous loud bang wakes us up. We scream; it sounds if the hotel roof is breaking in half. I sit straight up in bed and try to switch on the light. The electricity is out. We are in the pitch dark.

Wendela asks me to lock the door but I can't find my way. I am disoriented and can't see much. When we hear some shuffling behind our door, we don't know what to do. *Who can we call for help*? We certainly don't want to call the creepy guy at the front desk. We huddle together on Wendela's bed and wait till the morning comes.

Half asleep we wait till the sun starts rising and immediately we forget what happened to us the night before. We run outside. Our balcony doors give access to a patio that leads to the sand. We are on a magnificent beach with waving palm trees. The coconuts are big and ripe. They hang right above our heads. We sit down and absorb the view. Women stroll by so elegant in the way they walk.

With each step they sway their hips from side to side. Their back and head stand straight on top of their spine. Their bodies are wrapped in the most colorful clothes. We are in Africa!

Enormous waves crash ashore and in a matter of seconds we get into our bikinis and unroll our towels on the sandy beach. The smell, the wind and the beach are out of the catalog of Dream Vacations. This must be undiscovered land. We are the only foreigners here. Soon we will find out why but for now there is only the ocean to greet us.

Fearlessly Wendela and I jump into the waves; immediately we feel the undertow sucking us into the ocean. On the beach a young boy comes running toward us. We can't hear what he says, but he keeps screaming at us. The African French language is hard to understand. We wave back but I lose touch with the ground under my feet. The current is very strong. More people gather and join his screaming. They look concerned. We understand they want us out of the water as soon as possible.

But it is hard to swim against the current, especially for me; I am not that good a swimmer. We manage to get out. We haven't seen the signs that say it is forbidden to swim at this beach. Either the sharks or the strong undercurrent will kill you. We get the message and run out of the water. Diving in was easier.

Breathless we rest on the white sand. The boy points to a sign of a dead body. That says enough. He tells us a week ago someone from the other side of the street died at this beach; he was eaten by a shark. What a story to come home with.

In the dark of night, we overlooked this sign and I am so glad we didn't go for the night swim as we had fantasized. It was too late and the darkness and trip had frightened us. Maybe the delay caused by our passport disappearance had saved the sharks from a tasty meal.

We go back to our room and study the hotel map. Last night we were dropped off in a remote area. There are no buses from here to the city and the only way to get to a bank and change our money is to hitchhike to a village nearby. We decide to walk and hitchhike. We ask the creepy guy what had happened last night. He can't answer our question because he wasn't there. He warns us that it is very dangerous for white girls to hitchhike. He makes his point but we have other plans; we won't spend our vacation at his gorgeous beach hotel.

We leave the next day and follow our plan to go north. It means we have to cross the jungle by bus and cross our fingers to arrive in one piece. The bus station looks like a 24/7 marketplace. Food stalls are everywhere, animals are for sale and music from ghetto blasters is turned up full blast. We have the feeling we are alive. Everyone is selling something and everyone is going somewhere.

Our bus is the cheapest because we're taking the jungle route. It says a lot that even the local Africans shake their heads when we ask about the jungle route. Don't do it is their heartfelt advice. Still we discard caution and choose cheap transport over comfort and safety. The ticket seller says our bus driver plans to escape the endless number of land posts.

The country is so corrupt everyone who wears a uniform can stop you and demand money. This bus driver is skilled in the jungle route and I believe what they say. The most dangerous part of the trip is that he wants to drive at night. This "secret route" is for the pros we learn later. Another lesson we learn is to never risk your life for money.

We arrive early in order to claim our seats but after five hours we find out that the bus driver has some more passengers in mind. The bus fills up with as many people and animals as possible. Chickens, goats and all kind of livestock are part of the gang. We are a lively bunch and our claimed seats are shared with four other passengers. With a loud blowing horn the bus driver announces his departure, I wonder why all of us have waited for so long because the bus was full for hours; not an extra soul could fit in this doubtful vehicle. The bus almost topples over to one side when it begins to move.

The roof is packed with boxes and some boxes fall off right away. The weight is not evenly divided; everyone has bundled up their stuff. We watch the owners of these boxes gasp. The bus driver comes to an immediate stop which is so sudden more luggage falls off. The livestock inside the bus screams and some chickens escape from their owners. It takes another 30 minutes to get ready and finally he blows the horn again.

We leave and drive toward the jungle. Above the hills we see the dark clouds hanging overhead. It doesn't look good; the forecast predicts heavy rain and thunder. We need to hurry, says my neighbor who sits half on my lap.

We are not even an hour on the road when the bus takes a sharp turn and continues on a sandy path that leads to the jungle. With a loud bang the bus sways to the right, and it takes the driver all his strength to keep the bus on the road. We have a flat tire and everyone needs to get out. Rain starts to fall.

Most of the passengers are Muslim and the first thing they do is roll out their mats and pray. Allah is called to help and I pray that he listens well. The road to Khorogho is long and bumpy and Allah's help is more than welcome. As time passes by the sky is getting darker and darker, not only from the clouds, but as the evening comes. The driver is impatient and with a lot of swearing he finally fixes the tire within an hour.

When he is done, everyone hurries to get in the bus. "*Allez, allez*," the people yell to the driver. To us it doesn't make much difference, time is on our side. We'll head north and when and where we will end up is not up to us it seems. We drive off and we hear a loud scream of anger. The driver bangs with his fists on the steering wheel and screams again. The lights won't work.

I am guessing it's hard to drive in the jungle without lights. The bus stops again, everyone gets out, the mats are rolled on the muddy sand and prayer starts. We wait. The rain starts to pour but the praying crowd is oblivious to the big silver drops. The driver must be some kind of magical handy man because he is able to fix one of the little lights. Unfortunately, this light is the size of a flashlight but it works. He is satisfied for now.

Wendela holds up a page of the *Traveler Survival Kit*: "enjoy your stay." We do enjoy while we bump up and down in our seats.

Time after time we are stopped by young guys in army clothes. We have to pay at these roadblocks; that is what they are for: money. Otherwise they are a dead end and we might be, too.

The guys that stop the bus don't look older than 16, but their guns give them the authority to do as they like. We pass little remote villages where children run around naked. Women stir big pots that hang with an iron rope above the fire. Life is simple here; the western world is far away.

The ghetto blasters in our bus blast loud and the sounds seem unreal to the people we pass. We come from another world. The passengers keep themselves busy with eating and I must say that the food everyone brought smells delicious. We live on water and dry biscuits. It is safe and boring but it stills our hunger. It starts raining heavier and the driver is a nut; he races through the dense jungle with only a flashlight as his guide.

Thunder starts in the distance as we drive toward the storm and everyone stops speaking when the lightning strikes through the dark trees. It's a miracle the bus escapes the fiery arrows shooting right above us. I hear the thunder roar and it feels as if we are in the middle of a battle in the jungle world. The lightning is accompanied by crashing sounds.

We watch as elephants run for their lives.

This is scary, uncanny and our bus driver is in a hurry. He speeds as if he is behind the wheel of an Indy race car. The bus sways from left to right. The bus has no glass windows and the dust and dirt spits up in our faces. It makes us as dark as our fellow passengers.

We keep our faith until we are stopped by a lot of gunfire. We have hit another land post in the middle of the jungle. We are in nowhere land where survival depends on money. A uniform and a gun are the magic tools that bring our bus to a halt. This land post seems a serious matter; everyone is dead silent and the music is turned off; the ghetto blasters vanish under the seats. People put their hands in front of their eyes. A sense of deep fear is felt through the bus. What now?

I spot a wooden shack on the left side of our bus. There are many guys in uniform who smoke cigarettes. They all point their guns toward the bus. Everyone needs to be searched and all of us must hand over our identity papers.

We have to give up our passports, which disappear in the hands of the foreman with two guns. I am not too happy with what happens. We would rather hide our white bodies for these angry, vigilant men. All of a sudden I see how the Dutch newspaper headline will read: "Two Dutch girls vanish in the African jungle." I understand how easy that is. If they keep us here, no one will ever know and no one will ever tell our tale.

I pray and pray and I don't care who hears my words.

The luggage is taken off the roof while the rain falls heavily and it feels like we are in the middle of a military coup. We have no choice; we must obey. Like a herd of sheep, we stand in the mud; thunder crashes through the trees.

The dark African night is suddenly not as romantic as I foresaw in my cozy den in Amsterdam. *Were we innocent or just plain stupid to go on this trip*?

We are called forward and they search us, we have tied our $900 in a wash cloth around our waist. They can't find anything on us and let us go but we don't know if it means we are free. They keep the bus detained; everything has to be unpacked. The people don't protest but do as they are told. Nobody speaks and we don't know what this means. We realize this is dangerous beyond imagination. The guy at the front desk of the hotel was right; he warned us many times. He doesn't seem so creepy now.

After many hours, the military guys seem to get bored of their soaking search. They let us go and watch us pack. We vow to each other to never again take the cheapest route. This adventure is not worth my life. My eyes are filled with orange dust. I try to close them and thank our saviors from above. Allah was good to us. My mouth is dry and my ears are filled with red earth but my heart is filled with thankfulness beyond belief.

The bus leaves and heads for more puddles and thunder. Only God knows where we are going. At 5:00 AM we arrive on the other side of the jungle.

As if this was planned before we left, we are greeted by a blond-haired woman who walks toward us. "Hi, I am Madame Chatelaine," she says. "Come to my place and I will show you around." *How did she know we were traveling on this bus? Why had she walked the sandy dirt roads to meet us at this hour*? We assume she is taking us to her hotel; instead she brings us to her home. Without an explanation, she shows us our room.

Hours later we wake up. Sand is everywhere in my ears, my eyes and even the roots of my hair are orange. We look as if we survived a sand storm. I take a shower and an orange trail seeps down the drain in the bathroom floor. After I dry myself, the towel wears orange stains.

Where were we? Her house is decorated in the simple African style; the tile floor and wooden statues make us feel as if we are in a museum.

We are treated like long-lost friends. She feeds us breakfast and takes us for a tour in her jeep. We drive down the rolling hills; the landscape is incomparable to anything I have seen before. The orange earth is wet and moist. I can't take my eyes off the fields where we spot the shapes of wild animals. It's hard to see what herd is taking flight.

Madame Chatelaine is delighted with our visit; she is an angel and perhaps we bring the breath of fresh air she was waiting for. She is thrilled to drive us around and give us a look behind the scenes of her life. She volunteers at a leper village.

The people are happy with a visit from us white strangers; it's unnerving to know many of them will die.

After two days of being bathed in the comfort, safety and warmth of Madame Chatelaine's, we leave. She is concerned about our safety and her fear is heartwarming. Before we leave, she invites us into her bedroom and sits us down on her high bed. She asks us to close our eyes and open our hands. I feel a hard object is placed in my palm. Each of us is given two pure gold rings.

"Take them and keep them, you might need them," is all she would say with tears in her eyes. We don't want to accept these but our attempt to refuse her gift is waved away. "I have plenty," and with that she opens the door and says goodbye. We are sad and excited to leave the safety of her farm. As soon we hit the road, we are occupied with finding the right bus to the right destination. Despite warnings, we feel very safe and protected from above.

Our first stop will be a local gold market in a village farther north. We are curious and hope we can sell our wares. *Will they trust two white girls*? We find the market easily; it is nothing like a normal market. There are no women; only men who act very arrogant; everyone is important here. We realize we have to play this game according to their rules. The marketplace is huge and each seller has a tent. When we enter the first tent, we are invited to sit and drink tea first. Our plan is to visit several shops and get an idea what our rings are worth and then sell them to the best bidder. It is really my cup of tea; I like to bargain and bid back and forth.

In every shop we drink tea and eagerly the men show us their treasures. They weigh every piece of jewelry on small gold scales and with loud voices appraise how much their gold is worth. Each one has, of course, the best and finest quality gold. We are most interested in the expensive shops. It comes down to three dealers we are interested in. They offer high quality and their prices are alike. In one of the shops, the dealer has the exact same copies of our rings.

When we ask him what they are worth, he mentions his price. We pull out our rings and show them to him. He knows he can't bargain anymore. I don't know why but the guy is fixated on the rings and he weighs them many times.

We play the game as if we know what we are talking about. We drink one cup of tea after the other. He calls one of his friends and a moment later a circle of guys gathers around us. It is scary in one way and hilarious in another. We have nothing to lose. If he doesn't pay what we have in mind, we will go to someone else; he knows that. The rings must be worth a lot because he pays what we ask. We leave the market with the first bus that stops at the market; we don't care where it takes us. We have enough money to extend our stay and go farther north.

The simplicity of how the Africans live is impressive. In some ways life seems a lot easier when lived in tune with Nature. The villages have sandy roads and everyone walks barefoot.

The kids run around with very little clothes. At each village we visit, we are welcomed with open arms and sing their favorite welcome song, "Cook the white ones in our pot."

Needless to say, it is not our favorite song and we are glad they aren't hungry enough for such a hearty meal.

We come across a Catholic missionary with nuns from France. They take us in and ask if we want room and board in exchange for our help. We tend to and help care for the sick people. We sleep in bunk beds in a barrack behind the main entrance. When our shift is over we walk through the village, which has only one shop and a post office. We then sit at the village circle until we go to bed. We feel we can easily stay here and work for a few years, but we want to see more of the country and so we pack up and go.

By now we've been warned too often not to walk or travel at night; there are too many "crazy guys" who'll murder for a penny, according to the nuns. They instruct us to hide our valuables. Our money is tied to our waist and our luggage is not more than one tote bag holding one pair of clean clothes. I can't imagine we will be of interest to anyone.

One day we land in a small village. The bus drops us off at a marketplace famous for its cloth. When we get off the bus for a moment we are confused by all the ghetto blasters and millions of people. *Why had the Traveler Survival Kit guided us here*?

We discover soon enough that the marketplace is worth a visit. It is a two-story building and from the many lines of people it looks like there must be good bargains. *Was it our bewildered look or was it the same helping hand that sent Madame Chatelaine*?

We don't know but, again, in this remote part of Africa, we are approached by a blond-haired woman.

She looks out of place in the chaotic market place and signals to us to come and talk with her. "What are you doing here?" is her first question. We tell her about our adventure and how far north we want to go and come back full circle to Abidjan.

"You can't stay here; this village is not for girls like you. Come with me. I invite you to my home." She walks and talks at the same time and we follow her to her car. Wendela and I look at each other and we both think the same thing: the Universe is watching over us, we are safe no matter what.

Catherine welcomes us to her home as if we are part of her family. The guest room is ours and, after a week of cold showers and beds full of cockroaches, we are beside ourselves with joy. Our bedroom overlooks a corral of horses and high mountains. The view brings me the inner peace I long for. The journey was quite hectic so far. We throw our luggage in a corner and stretch out on our beds. "What have we done to deserve *all this*?" I ask Wendela.

It would be heaven if we had not caught a stomach virus. The same afternoon both of us become very sick and we couldn't be happier we are in a clean room with our own bathroom. We travel back and forth to it a million times.

Catherine's husband Patrick is a veterinarian and they've lived in this village for the last five years. They are familiar with this stomach flu and reassure us it will pass within two days. We feel guilty for being sick and staying in their house but it seems Catherine is happy to accommodate us.

She makes us eager to get well because she has a great number of trips in mind for us. If Catherine keeps her plan, it will take her at least a week to tour us around. We don't have that much time if we stick to *our* original plan.

Catherine and Patrick go out of their way to show us around. They share their life's work with us and take us on trips to the nearby villages. One morning we get up at 4:00 AM to climb one of the highest mountains. The climb is steep but the flock of exotic birds we see is incredible.

Every step we take is worthwhile because Patrick's trained eye spots every animal big and small. Big snakes, monkeys and animals I have never heard of pass in front of our eyes. The top is far away and, if we want to reach it at sunrise, we need to hurry our steps. I am out of breath, not only from the shape I am in, even more so from all the unfamiliar early morning jungle sounds.

We reach the summit in time. There is no way my camera can capture what I see and feel. I sit there in silence while I take in this eternal moment on top of a mountain on the Ivory Coast.

Patrick shares with us that he teaches the Africans how to care for their animals and how to irrigate their land. He is very inspired and his passion is to educate the locals how to run their farms in a more efficient way. Many farmers improved tremendously over the years through Patrick's guidance and that makes him want to stay much longer. There is such a need for education, he says. He takes us on many tours to show us all the projects he is working on.

It is very hard to say goodbye to Patrick and Catherine, who have become good friends by now. They say we can stay longer but we don't want to take advantage of their hospitality. They have done so much for us; it's time to go.

We extend our stay in Africa an extra week with the money we earned from the rings. After another week of living on maniocs and rice, we are glad to leave and fly home. Because of the enormous hassle to change our flights, we can only get on a plane that goes to Belgium. We don't care. However, when we arrive in the snow in our flip flops, we realize we have no money to take the train to Amsterdam. To hitchhike is our answer. *How else would two suntanned girls from Africa with orange-colored tote bags and bare feet come home? Was the Universe still on our side*?

We walk toward the exit road outside the airport. The roads are quiet because it is Sunday. The second car that stops asks us where we are heading.

"Amsterdam" is our answer.

"Hop in, that is precisely where I am going." The friendly guy speaks in Dutch and smiles at us. His car is warm and cozy.

Two and a half hours later, he drops me off at my front doorstep. I am home, safe. I pick up the Saturday newspaper dropped at the door mat. *What country is next?*

Japan

The old lady in our bedroom closet is dying; her death is just a breath away. *Were we supposed to help her or was she working her way to the other side alone*? We are warned not to come near the closet. It is not easy to fall asleep.

Why Japan? My plans were often made without much thought. They were born out of a desire to connect to a deeper understanding of myself through other cultures. I kept playing a game with the Universe (or God if you will). I continuously challenged the Universe to check on the waterproofing of my belief that, if I followed the voice of my Soul, I would not get wet, I would be rewarded. Usually it didn't take the Universe long to respond. Nevertheless, I was the one to make the first move. *Synchronicity* would describe this pattern best and everything worked out far better than if my mind was the tour leader. That became a stone-cold fact.

Not long after my initial idea of going to Japan, I receive a phone call from a friend who was my best buddy for the first seven years of my life. Jessica and I were inseparable from the moment we were born until the moment I moved to another town. Her mother was mine and the other way around; we fantasized that we were sisters. It's funny that we lose contact as soon as I leave my birth town. We never speak again until I pick up the phone when she calls. It takes me a while to recognize her voice; the strong bond of sisterhood is still intact.

After a little chit chat, she asks me if I like to come and visit her in the west part of Holland. I tell her I am planning a trip to Japan.

"You're going to Japan?"

"Yes I am," is my reply.

"Who with?" she asks.

"Alone. Me, myself and I," I say. The conversation goes back and forth like a ping pong ball.

"Can I come?"

"Of course! Absolutely."

And so it is decided we will go together. My only concern is that she might not like to go on the cheapest fare. I want to grab the chance of as many stopover places as possible. Jessica fully agrees we need to experience as many countries as we can. We book our tickets to Japan without delay the next day.

We are not prepared for the Pakistan Airlines experience. We get what we wanted: as many exotic stopover countries as possible. One of the places we land in is Islamabad, which is the worst country to visit for a blond-haired girl since Egypt. Everywhere we walk we are harassed by the Arabic men. I don't get their disrespect for women. I greatly admire them for their disciplined and devoted prayer sessions but *what did they discuss with Allah*?

We can't walk on the streets and we need to be careful where we go. Because of our cheap ticket, there is a rumor we will have to stay another week in Pakistan because the plane is defective.

I pray to Allah and he listens. We leave after three long days of hiding in our filthy hotel room. After Japan and on the way back home, our plane breaks down on the runway. We raise hell and are transferred back to Amsterdam via Alaska, first-class mind you! We come to understand what *PA Airlines* really meant. P was for *Prone* and A for *Accidents*.

Japan is a complete culture *shock* in a good sense. We step into a world of fast-moving puppets; it looks surreal. I am glad Jessica is with me. The noise, the smells have no comparison with any other country. The people are well-dressed and look impeccable. We tower high above the tiny Japanese. We learn to nod and bow and do our best to adjust to their ways. We need to, because we are the big foreigners who can only communicate with their big hands and big feet. The metro stations are packed with people but never is there the faintest smell of sweat. They look fresh and clean, as if they showered just a minute before.

A metro chief with white gloves pushes the last persons into the cabin before the train leaves; always trying to fit in as many people as possible. We don't mind being squeezed in between the other bodies. Everyone smells like white lilies. I can't imagine myself enjoying this in the same way being sandwiched in a New York subway train.

Even at night, Japan is safe for us. Fearless and free we explore the small towns with their myriad of little streets. The metro connects the different districts and the system is flawless. The train arrives and departs on the dot. In Japan you can't get lost. Life is meticulously planned here. You know exactly where you are and where you need to go. It is the 180 degrees opposite of the Arabic countries I've visited.

We decide to visit the famous temples and shrines the country is rich with. We choose to travel the "old fashioned way." We hitchhike. In Europe this way of traveling is common but in Japan they think we are from outer space. Carefully, we copy the Japanese signs from the map and we draw them on big pieces of paper. We make sure our copy is exactly like the drawing on the map, otherwise we'll end up somewhere else. The first time we try our experiment we feel confident that all will go well. But, within 10 minutes, we have caused an accident. Every driver passing by turns his head; it is very frightening to watch them speed to the wrong side of the road.

After 15 minutes a car stops and the driver asks us in half English and half Japanese where we want to go. He asks us why we are standing on the side of the highway instead of taking a bus or a train. With a lot of effort, he explains that we better not use our thumbs again; it might mislead the Japanese guys. To hold your thumb up in Japan means something quite different. It makes sense. This man helps bring us to our destiny though we are not sure if he completely goes out of his way just to please us.

The Japanese have no word for "no," which makes it hard for any driver to refuse us a ride. There is an abundant supply of drivers who at times fight with each other to be the lucky one. If we ask them if they are heading a certain direction, they say yes, no matter where they are going. It seems they have no other option. It is a wonderful way of traveling. We meet the nicest people and we see a lot of the beautiful countryside. The people who give us a ride often open their homes and feed us, while we can hardly communicate with more than a smile. That is enough.

It's good our trip doesn't have a predestined trail except to experience the "Japanese feel."

In Kyoto, we sleep in our first temple. When we arrive at the gate, we have to knock for an hour until the monks hear us and open the big wooden doors. The monks love foreign visitors and they proudly show us their place. We feel like intruders and tiptoe through the temple. We are in awe of how endlessly they sweep the wooden floors.

At 4.00 AM the huge temple bells wake us up. The morning meditation begins. The Zen culture immerses us in total peace. We visit many temples and each experience is kind of similar in the sense that the Zen culture gets under our skin.

After exploring the temples, we want to stay in a real Japanese home: a *ryokan*.

The *ryokan* we pick from the *Traveler Survival Kit* is situated on a tiny little street, which is so narrow the windows from one side to the other almost touch each other .

The woman who owns the place opens the door after she observes us a bit from behind the rice paper window.

She hardly speaks English but, with a nod, invites us in and asks us to take off our shoes. She points to a basket to leave them in. Our size 8 and 9 shoes don't fit in the tiny basket. *What now*? We put them on the floor. Her dress is tightly wrapped around her frail body and with her small feet, most likely a size 3, she shuffles in front of us.

She looks like a Geisha; her face is painted white and the cloth of her dress is made out of the purest embroidered silk. When she looks behind her to see if we are following, she must have been afraid that we were bumping into the delicate marble Buddha statues displayed on either side of the hallway.

The atmosphere is out of a book and I can't fathom how this world exists behind the rice paper walls. *Why don't we know how to create stillness in our western world of hurry and worry*? The silence is almost deafening. We tiptoe up the stairs. The rooms are separated by sliding doors made out of rice paper. No other foreigners stay here but us.

She brings us to a room in the attic of her small house. On the left side of our door, we see a big cupboard, which opens in our room and is also an access to the room next door. She talks rapidly and points at the closet; her finger goes up and down. We don't know what she is saying but we understand we are not supposed to open that closet.

She makes that *very* clear somehow. We get the message; we will not touch that door. Of course, we are totally curious and wonder why.

If we had known that a death ceremony was planned, we might have left right away. After the mini tour, the rice-paper-thin lady looks at us from head to toe and says in broken but clear English, "You need a bath."

We agree. We put our backpacks on the floor and unpack our stuff. There are no chairs or beds; everything is on the floor. We will sleep on *tatami* mats.

"First bath, then bed," she says in her broken English; she talks like a mom.

Outside we hear kids screaming in Japanese. I look out of the window but I can't see much. Our room is facing a wall at the back of the house. We go downstairs for our bath and we do as the lady tells us. On the ground floor is a bathroom with two big Japanese bath tubs. Both are filled with water to the top. She points to the first and then at the next one. We need to soak in the first one and then go into the second one afterwards.

We nod and pretend to understand. A moment later, I wish I could turn back the clock. If we had studied the bathing rituals in Japan better, we would not have made such a huge mistake. Oblivious to the rules, we plunge with our fully soaped bodies into the first tub.

The moment we sit and soak we know we have done something very wrong. We stare at the Japanese bath rules on the wall.

We can't read it but I have the unnerving feeling we have done something immensely stupid. The clean water in the first tub is now a bubble bath. I ask Jessica what to do but her eyes tell me what she really thinks. We burst into laughter. We get out and aren't sure if we will get spanked with the bamboo stick of the old lady. Maybe we had better leave the place.

We do our best to clean up the bubbles but, unfortunately, the more we try the more they multiply. At least we are clean, *very* clean.

We go out for dessert that night; it is our usual ritual that serves as our dinner. This time it takes 90 minutes to decide what to pick. We stroll from window to window to make our choice. They all look like little pieces of fine art. "The making of" must take more time than the "eating of." We walk back through the lantern-lit village. The old people sit in front of their shops and keep a lively conversation with each other. We wish we knew what the gossip was about; in a look behind the scenes of these people, *what would that reveal*?

When we come back, we are tired and gratefully stretch our clean bodies on the *tatami* floor. Funny enough, as much as we looked forward to the stillness, the silence is gone. We listen to a light cough coming from the forbidden closet. For a while the cough stops and then we hear lots of talking on the other side. Something is going on in the room next to us. We look at the closed closet and remember the stern look on the old lady's face when she made it clear that we were not to go in there.

Again we hear coughing and it sounds like someone can barely breathe. I try to sleep with the knowledge that people are aware of what is going on in the closet. According to the loud talking, we assume they are discussing what to do about the person's cough. It becomes impossible to sleep; the coughing is loud and sounds deadly to my ears. I hear vomiting and gasping noises. I am ready to break the lady's rule. I want to help. Her gasping breath gets worse by the minute. *Could there really be a person in that closet*?

I walk foot by foot to the closet. I don't want to make any noise. I have to see what is going on. I carefully slide the bamboo door a jar, adjusting my eyes to the dark. My hand covers my mouth to protect me from shrieking. It is obvious that someone is dying.

I see an old woman coughing and almost suffocating in her own mucus. But I can see that the closet has access to the other room. A crack in the closet door shows that a few women in the other room are lighting candles.

I back away and close the door at our side.

"Jessica, what do we do?" We ponder and come to the conclusion that it is not up to us to intrude in perhaps an ancient ritual of death.

We lay back and I try to sleep. I pray for the person in the closet and, after a few hours, the coughing stops abruptly. The lady has died; she has passed over to the other side.

In the other room there is a bit of noise, then silence. We go to sleep. The next morning the old lady in the closet is gone and our ancient geisha shuffles around as if nothing had happened.

I want to ask her about it but she reads my mind. Her eyes lock into mine for a second saying, *no questions . . . death is okay . . . however, your bubble bath was a SIN.*

PART FOUR

Weaving the Inner Trail

I no longer believed
there was such a thing
as an accident.
Everything that happened
was a result of some form
of cause and effect
and therefore had
an underlying reason.

—Shirley MacLaine,
Dancing in the Light

Spoonfuls of Spirituality

On April 24th I open the first page of Shirley MacLaine's book *Dancing in the Light*. From then on Shirley becomes my spiritual teacher. I follow her lead by tracing her tracks. As determined as I was, I place my first footstep on the trail of my spiritual quest.

Shirley writes, "On the morning of April 24th…" and continues, "I couldn't accept the synchronicity of my personal event as merely accidental. As I had told everybody I knew, I no longer believed there was such a thing as an *accident*. Everything that happened was a result of some form of cause and effect and therefore had an underlying reason."

The sun sets when I start reading and the sun rises when I look up and turn the last page. My world has changed overnight. It feels as if I am struck by lightning. So is my heart. My Soul's light is turned ON, my torch is lit and there is a new chapter of my life: *The Inner Journey begins*. The book hadn't landed in my lap merely *by accident*. Oh, how I was ready to *dance in the light*! I vibrate now at another frequency. *How come I never knew all this*? I dance and swirl around my small room. I want to tell the world we are eternal beings, we are made and molded out of love and we never die. It all makes sense. Of course, there is karma and life after death. The law of cause and effect says there are no accidents. We design our own destiny and I can't wait to start right away.

Suddenly, I am given the insight we are the creators of our own life. We can make any dream come true. I understand we attract every experience into our reality. I keep shaking my head in disbelief of how asleep I was. Shirley's words were very clear and I resonated with every word she wrote.

Synchronicity is at my side and OF COURSE the timing of this book was divine. Everything falls in place. Instantly my world becomes round instead of flat. The Dutch land birthed me and housed my Soul. Now it was time to journey and explore the inner world so I may come full circle. Perhaps it was symbolic. I left the flat land soon after I finished the book.

The direction I was to follow was lit up, bright and shiny. I couldn't miss the light.

Despite my lack of sleep, I am wide awake when I bike a few hours later to the Salad Garden, my favorite restaurant. I meet Jacqueline for a Dutch *café au lait*, served in big white soup bowls. My cheeks are flushed as I enter the restaurant.

My 'holy bible' is tucked under my arm. I can't lose sight of Shirley right now. My birth mother needs to be at my side. I walk to the table and show Jacqueline the book.

I want to share it all. I start to lecture her about how logical it is that reincarnation is our Soul's way to learn and evolve. It makes sense we are reborn many times. We are slow learners. I can't stop talking and I hardly take the time to taste the fresh baked pie. Jacqueline listens but can't catch up. My speech goes faster than I can explain.

For the first time I feel my life is validated and my life purpose is clear. I want to include my best friend in all these life-changing insights. Jacqueline is lost in my new trail—she wonders where I am going with this.

I leave the Salad Garden and feel vibrant and full of life. My look at life has changed. I race home to read some parts of the book again. I wish I could visit America and trace Shirley's steps. I want to visit the gurus she met and I long to learn everything about spirituality. My fire is ignited and there is nothing that can hold me back. I am more than curious. And now that my torch is lit, I want to find my answers to *what was worth seeing and where I am to go*. The Universe takes me by the hand.

My boyfriend Josh calls me a few days later and asks if I want to go out for dinner. "We need to talk about something," is all he says. I frown. Josh is never serious and not especially much of a talker. *What is this going to be about*? The subject of marriage doesn't cross my mind; how little did I know of what was coming.

I arrive in time and take a seat at the little table of *our* Greek restaurant across the street from his house. Josh doesn't need many words to explain; he has been offered a job in Houston, starting at the beginning of June. His uncle owns a company there and they need an energetic young guy. Josh is the perfect candidate. The oil business is booming and without a doubt Josh is the one who can smoothly move into the position they offer. *What do I think*?

I have the dream job: I am a counselor in family therapy in Tulpenburg. *Will I drop that in a heartbeat and go with Josh*?

The world is spinning around me. *What did he just say*? This offer was not a coincidence. The Greek owner stands at our table ready to take our order. I glance at the menu. "Give me today's special," I say. There was enough on my plate already.

I love the idea of moving to Texas; what a chance! However, Josh explains, I can't join him if we are not married. The problem is with the visa; it means I can't come, he can only go alone. We were faced with a dilemma I wasn't quite ready for. To break our relationship was not an option and to marry him was an idea of a different world. I certainly had ordered the today's special.

Josh asks me to marry him. He is a man of few words. His best friend Bart had always joked, "If you want to marry Saskia, you'll have to move to a faraway country and no doubt she will follow."

And here I am about to witness his joke coming true! *What was true love? What is the definition of a husband and how does that feel*? I loved Josh; he was such a wonderful, energetic, kind and generous person. I couldn't find fault. *But was Josh my true partner in life*?

No one could answer my questions. My conclusion was perhaps I was afraid of commitment. To be honest that sounded odd but *how well did I know myself* I asked. Lots of questions passed through my heart and mind; I couldn't come up with a solid answer.

Josh is sure. "You are the woman of my life," he says with a big grin on his funny face.

I say, "Yes." Today's Special is my choice.

Later that night I wonder what would have happened if I said *no*. We were having a wonderful LAT (living apart together) relationship and *to break that apart*? No, that seemed very odd. I feel relief knowing life is meant to be experienced and I can't think of a more wonderful, nice person than Josh. *Were there a certain amount of butterflies I needed or was the feeling of being totally at ease with each other enough*? Maybe I read too many Danielle Steele books. Maybe I was trapped in the fairytale that I still had to blush at Josh's touch.

We marry May 28th in the Salad Garden and it is a glorious day. Deep in my heart, there is a tiny bit of doubt because my questions remain unanswered. Still, I love him and I am THE woman of Josh's life; that feels really good. The only one to advise me was Soul; she didn't say much. The one word she said was, "*GO*." A few weeks later, we leave for America unaware I will fall head over heels in love with the earth of that country.

I look up at the sky when my feet touch the American soil for the first time. The sun shines abundantly behind the clouds the plane has just slit in halves like ripe peaches. I feel it in my gut; life is juicy on this side of the Atlantic Ocean. I widen my eyes when I see a rainbow appear. I know that promise; this must be Soul's invitation I am to *dance in the light*.

Life is WUNDERLICH

WUNDERLICH is the name of the complex Josh and I live in and truly the name says it all. The small complex is built in a rural area outside the 610 Loop of Houston. By car it is "only" an hour and twenty minutes away from the city. Surprisingly to us and probably because it was our first time in America, it seemed the same distance as the one we drove to the border of Holland. I have no problem with this trip; easily I go back and forth, a few times a day. I am hungry, almost starved. My spiritual appetite needs to be fed.

Arriving in America was one thing but choosing where to live was another. Fortunately Josh and I had no set idea about where to live. The American maxim *location, location, location* means nothing to us; everything seems wonderful. The real estate agent has a ball. We *Ohhh* and *Ahhh* at every condo she shows. Compared to our small apartment in Amsterdam, we can't believe our good luck. We can rent in a certain price range and we have free reign to choose. With her slow Southern drawl, she says, "Pick anything y'all like, honey. Just lemme know."

As soon as we drive through the gate of WUNDERLICH, we know we have found our place. Indeed it is wonderful; our small condo has two floors, a living room and kitchen with the biggest fridge I have ever seen in my life. I wasn't used to the American standard size; big is BIG in this country.

Each condo mirrors the other. Only the furniture gives you a hint if you have walked into your own home or your neighbor's.

We have no furniture; everything is in storage. Two days after our arrival Josh's uncle calls us with the message that our furniture will stay in storage for another year. "Something with the visa; Immigration won't approve it," is his explanation. For us, no problem; I feel as if I have entered *Heaven's Gate*.

We rent furniture and I enjoy how simple life is without a single item from the past. My wardrobe reflects this simplicity even more. My white canvas tote bag holds a pair of sneakers, a pair of pumps, a pair of jeans and a red pair of sweatpants and a few tops. That's all. I become creative with what I have. Our budget doesn't allow me to buy new clothes but I don't care. When we go out for dinner, I combine my red sweatpants with my high-heeled pumps; the shoes make me feel like a star.

Looking back, I am glad we were in America; it spared me the stares of the *haute couture* ladies of Europe. Nobody here cared; I didn't look different from anybody else. After all we were in *Texas*.

The complex has a small swimming pool with three lounge chairs and when I tour around for the first time I picture myself reading books in the middle of the day. I have no doubt how easy it will be to ignore the chores of the day for the simple reason there were no chores anyway. My days stretched from six in the morning to twelve at night. There was plenty of time to be lazy and immerse myself in hours of nothingness.

I didn't realize then that the Universe had other plans. I would become bored *sooner* rather than *later*.

The first months I know nobody except Josh; he is off to work at 6 AM and is there till 7 PM. I want to get in shape and decide to swim every morning; I think *the earlier the better*. My idea seems great at first but I soon give up after realizing my day after 6.30 AM is quite long. I had a lot of time on my hands. No work, no conversations by phone; basically there is no one to talk to. If the phone rang, it usually was someone who dialed the wrong number: I kept picking it up because you *just never know*.

The silence isn't uncomfortable. Life is exciting because everything is *new*. I feel so free. My adventurous nature is ready to explode and for weeks I go on endless rounds in the car. I drive around in the nearby neighborhoods and uncover several American habits after making many mistakes. In stores, I browse for hours without buying anything. I entertain myself and quiet my appetite in the huge supermarkets during lunch where I am often offered new foods to try.

The most hilarious moment is when I realize that the question "*How are you*?" is always answered by me in vivid detail as if my most intimate buddy really wants to know my state of mind. I tell them where I am from, who I am and how I feel that moment. What an insight I have when I discover *months later* that I could have spared my in-depth tale with the simplest of answers "*Fine*." Yet I never regret the many friendly encounters I experienced; they were the highlights of my first "lonely" days.

It doesn't take me too long to figure out I need to make better use of my time than just *adventuring* around. After awhile the "*How are you*" chats no longer satisfy me. I long for *nourishment* of my Soul. A search in the newspaper and a few phone calls lead me to a job in a child care center. It seems easy; I go for an interview and get the job. But when they call back to confirm my coming, they ask me for my Social Security number. I have none and I know I am in trouble. I give them my Dutch phone number. They tell me to start a week from now.

The next day I call them back to confess my sin; we couldn't risk our visa for such a mistake. It is painful at first; I wasn't ready to retire at age 26 and go back to the pool at 6.00 AM. *What was I to do if I couldn't work*?

I ask myself if I want work or if there is something else I need to look at. I *do* see an interesting thread. I had never realized my identity was hung up on my profession as a counselor in family therapy and child psychiatry. Until now it gave me prestige and I always had a handful of stories about *my kids*. The entertainment level of my stories was high because the work was tremendously interesting and I loved it more then anything in the world. My work was my passion and the other way around.

Now I had to figure out my life in WUNDERLICH if I couldn't work. I was sure there were more options than to swim in the pool or just drive around.

Was the Universe giving me a chance to study instead of work? I start searching and visit several different universities. I think about going to Tulane and becoming a social worker.

I ask my Soul to show me the way: *where was I to go and what was worth seeing*? Only a day later the phone rings, and I am surprised when I answer and hear a very warm voice with a Southern accent at the other end. She introduces herself with, "I am Amy. I am the wife of Bert." Bert is a Dutch colleague of Josh's. She asks me out for lunch and I still remember how thrilled I was to meet a new friend. We hit it off right away because our interest in spirituality is alike.

The first lunch is the beginning of my spiritual adventure in Houston. From that first lunch onwards, many more lunches follow and we start to meet weekly. I look forward to the lunches more than anything. Every Thursday her big American car honks the horn and within a second I slide into the front seat and I become part of another world. We chat nonstop until we reach the downtown area of Houston. My heart becomes alive when I see the skyline rise. The polished buildings are a feast for my eyes.

What has a tremendous impact on my life is Amy's suggestion to do a weeklong course called *Silva Mind Control.* In the course you learn to control your mind and how to function on another, more powerful level of the mind: the *Alpha* level. On this level you have access to your unlimited possibilities.

Josh joins us and every night the three of us drive downtown and enjoy our four–hour-long seminar. He sleeps through the entire evening. I am glad to hear and Josh is, too, that even if you fall asleep you "get it" anyway.

I am just the opposite. I sit on the edge of my chair and drink in the information. I intend to not miss a word. Josh is much rested after the seven days and I am flying sky high.

On the last day we learn how to read each other's energy fields. We are instructed to go to Alpha level and gather information about an assigned client who is ill. I am dumbstruck when I can make a complete scan of an unknown client. In detail I describe the body of a woman who limps with one leg. She has a left hip problem. I diagnose her as if I am looking at an x-ray. I pass the *Silva* test.

I am fascinated about this aspect of the training and, after certification, I sign up to become one of the volunteer "healers" who will send healing energy to the sick. For hours and hours I sit at my kitchen table calling forth the people from the list in my imaginary healing office. Each and every one of them I send my healing light. I have found a calling and the Universe responds. My days are filled with "work"; my little kitchen is "my office." I feel wonderful in WUNDERLICH.

From one thing comes the other. A few weeks later, Amy shows me a flyer of *The Excalibur School* in Houston. This school offers classes on *Soul exploration*. One glance at the flyer is enough. The same afternoon I drive to downtown Houston and look for the school. When I enter the building, I sign up for every class I like. It feels like I have found the study I was searching for.

My daily schedule is filled now, every morning I drive two and a half hours to the school and at night I do the same to home again. Each day I spend five hours or more in the car.

However, every minute of class is worth the drive. I take classes in *Soul Exploration, Past Life Regression*, *Soul Mate* classes; you name it, I am there. My passion is aroused as never before, and my Soul jumps up and down with glee.

We have mandatory meditations and every morning and night I do my best. It is not easy for me to quiet my mind and have no thoughts. However, I am determined and disciplined to make it work. I think of Shirley MacLaine and remember her stern advice to *practice, practice, practice.*

One night a man suddenly appears in my meditation. He is distinctive with his black moustache and dark hair. His posture and energy are powerful. He stares at me with a big smile. I have no idea who he is. *What was he here for? What does he want*? I don't know what to think when he doesn't leave but stays in my meditation until I open my eyes.

When I walk into the school the next morning, Tom stares at me; he has made his entrée into the school. He sits silently on the sofa facing the door. It's his first day teaching at the school.

I stop dead in my tracks and look at him; he gives no sign of recognition; I know it is *him*. I have no time to talk because I can't be late in my *Soul Exploration* class. I ask Lorna, my teacher, who he is and tell her about my nightly encounter.

"That's what he does all the time; he knows which students are ready," she says. As soon as class is over, I can't wait to talk to him. I sign up for his *Tarot* and *past life* classes. I know I am ready to be his student.

What I don't know is that he will become one of my greatest teachers and that, for twenty years, I will teach everything I learn from him and from this great school.

Josh and I love our life in Texas. In my spare time during the day, I learn and read everything about spirituality I can get my hands on. Even at night I don't leave a stone unturned. Next to my bed lies the big purple book *Dream Interpretation.*

Every symbol has a meaning my teacher says…and dutifully I unravel my subconscious mind. I am thrilled to be so close to the source. I feed my passion day and night; I hunger still for more.

The months pass by smoothly, and visits from our family and friends are an uplifting change. I confide in them about my new world and, when my mom comes for a visit, it sparks her Soul, too. She leaves inspired by the world of spirituality and arrives home, not only with a heart filled to the brim, also with a suitcase bursting full of books.

Born to Be Free

Josh and I plan a trip to Guatemala. *Why there*? Soul must have led us, because not only does the trip have a great impact on my subconscious mind about how to birth my babies, there is much more.

The *Traveler Survival Kit* serves as our faithful guide and as expected we are transported to places with a rich history. Eloquently, the book describes details about the Mayan culture, the rituals, the traditions and the sites worth taking a look. Passionately, we follow the map we have in mind.

Today the menu is a little different; we are literally transported back into the natural ebb and flow the Mayan culture is rich with. Her deep connection with nature doesn't come from a book. *What did I know*? As a tourist, you are supposed to want to *get somewhere.*

For more than three hours we sit and wait on a wooden bench along side the road. The departure time is delayed by the hour and, according to our Dutch need for punctuality, we are very late. Our expectation to leave and arrive at a specific time is not being met today.

The *Traveler Survival Kit* had informed us very well. We knew that our attitude would be the key to a relaxed and joyful journey . . . or not. Letting go of expectations was a lesson we received by the dozens in this amazing country.

Sometimes we wait a full day only to find out our bus driver had called in sick because of a party he went to the night before. Hangovers are the excuse *du jour* in this place and I really can't blame them.

There is enough to see and be entertained right where we are; however, this morning we are eager to get on the road. I don't know why. I quickly learned time doesn't exist in this part of the world. *Why do I feel so anxious to get on the bus and go?* Perhaps I picked up on someone else's hurry, not mine. *Why worry, why hurry*? There is always a *mañana. Why not today?*

A few hours later, I will understand why. There is someone who needs to get someplace fast.

Josh and I travel light which makes us free to come and go wherever we like. We have two very small tote bags which we carry by hand. When the bus driver signals he is ready for departure, we hop on the bus in less than a minute. I wonder if there are two more buses coming. I count three times the number of passengers than available seats. Caged animals, chickens, goats, lots of baskets with vegetables and fruits are carried in the bus and stacked under and above the seats.

The beautiful, colorfully-dressed people talk and laugh nonstop. Nobody is concerned; there is enough room for everyone. We share our seats.

Before we leave, the bus driver asks us to carry several big, heavy stones and pieces of wood into the bus.

There was a lot of rain recently and deep puddles on the road are waiting for us. The bus driver was forewarned. As happy as everyone was to climb IN the bus, everyone climbs OUT again. We all pitch in and go on a stone hunt and leave another hour later. I am curious to see how this old bus will carry us all.

We take our seats after the rocks are loaded. Josh and I are squashed between an animal cage and local goods; we enjoy being close to this lively scene. The bus begins to move with a loud cheer from all the passengers. We are in this together. We are a team. We are ready to go! The Christmas lights and electric statues of Jesus and Maria are switched on by the driver. It is a familiar ritual for everyone; they will guard us as we go. The muddy dirt road is bumpy, *very* bumpy, and we need to hold onto each other and sit tight in our seats.

It doesn't take long for the driver to stop again and usher everyone out of the bus. An enormous puddle, as big as a pond, lies in front of us. We need to get to work and build a bridge. The men don't hesitate about the *how to's* or *what's*; they get to work right away. No thinking or strategizing or planning like people from the West do; just action instead. The women cheer them on while they work. I join in their chorus; I like this job.

When the bridge is built, the men push the bus to the other side.

We all cheer! All are one in our mission to get the bus to the other side. We are a happy bunch. The *Temple of Tulum* we were dreaming about is long forgotten; we are in the here and now.

Josh and I enjoy the ride and the bridge building and the clapping as if we belong here.

Every time there is a puddle, the same ritual is performed. The whole bus begins cheering when we see one coming. The bumps in the road cause someone to scream in the back. Before I know it, there are people walking up and down the aisle. They hand cloths and towels to a woman in the backseat. I turn my head but I can't see what the commotion is all about.

A Spanish-speaking man points at someone in the back of the bus and explains the upheaval. "This is very good, is okay," and eloquently he describes what happened, "Woman gets baby." We keep driving; the road is still bumpy.

"Oh," I say and turn my head back to face the front of the bus. Nobody seems to mind. Life goes on; our journey continues. The bus driver stops in a small village after another half an hour.

An elderly woman helps the woman and the baby off the bus. She helps the mother carry her child into a house. I'm not sure it is *her* house; however, someone waits for her at the door. We all wave, clap, and yell, "Happy *birth* day to your child." The bus continues on to our next adventure.

No book, no guide, no *Traveler Survival Kit* can ever compete with learning by example. The pure energetic transmission from this Mayan mother impregnated my subconscious mind with the seed that to give birth was easy; after all, it can be done in a bus. I was never going to be contaminated with horror stories about birth.

I understand *what was worth seeing today* and *where I was to go from here*. It was my initiation into *Mother Nature's way*.

Years later, I come to understand when and where my body's wisdom was triggered. My five children are all born in a matter of minutes, instead of hours. I never forgot this pivotal moment of *birthing in a bus*. I was like her. That experience was my past and my future. I was free; from this woman, I learned a lesson about my birthright. Her beliefs planted seeds in my DNA.

The strangest thing happens the day after we arrive back in Houston from our trip. Bart, the best man at our wedding, asks me to send information about Guatemala to his best friend: *where to go* and *what is* worth seeing.

Who is this friend of Bart's and why should I take the time? With great reluctance, I drive to the post office and mail a number of pages copied from my trip diary to Bart's anonymous friend in the south of Holland. *Why do this*? I ask myself again. I'm a little angry with this guy I am sending these to. The stamps are too costly. I am *really* annoyed at myself for giving in to this odd, ridiculous request.

An eagle circles above my head as I drop my memoirs into the post box. *What was he seeing? Did he know something of my future?* A more intriguing question is *how is it possible that these pages copied from my trip diary, still in their stamped envelope, drop into my lap two years later in Taiwan?*

A year after our arrival in Houston, Josh is transferred to Singapore. All our belongings and furniture are still packed and in storage in Holland. The departure is effortless, just like the change of countries. We only have to call the rental company to pick up our furniture and I pack my white canvas bag. After a year, that is all I have. We are ready to go. We only carry hand luggage when we hop on the plane to Asia. Most of my luggage is inside of me; my heart is "overweight." I have learned so much.

Was it symbolic that our past was in storage? Or was this the best way to explore and venture with the new? I am curious to see what the Universe has in store for us.

Setting Foot in Singapore

How was I supposed to entertain myself in this foreign country where I didn't know anyone but the mailman? Josh leaves a few days after our arrival. I am completely alone and our new house is as empty as dust in the air following a rain. The day counts many lonely hours. *Where was I to go? What was worth seeing?*

It only takes a week for Josh to go on a business trip for ten days. And here I am. I must enjoy the company of *myself*, as if put to the test. *Can I survive my fear*? The iron fence around our property doesn't give me the safety I long for. This morning I finally accepted I had no choice but to close my eyes and doze off in my lounge chair by the pool; I was exhausted and happy to make up for my sleepless hours.

I put some suntan lotion on my body and counted myself fortunate that we were members of the *Dutch Club*. The club is situated in the lush countryside of Singapore; obviously, the location was picked for good reason. The palm trees bring shade to the white-skinned expatriates who look for cover from the sizzling tropical sun. Singapore is smack on top of the equator. The sun shines year around; there are no seasons in this part of the world.

The way this bothers me is that my blue jeans now belong to a long lost object of the past. I face my new life without long pants; shorts are my future and I hope my legs are ok with this. They definitely need some color.

The pool area is almost empty except for a dark-haired woman who looks the same age as me. She sits on the other side of the pool and reads a book. Every now and then she looks up and our eyes meet. After spying on her for a while, I gather my courage and walk toward her. I introduce myself by telling her my name and asking hers. I have learned from living abroad to *always* make the first move; don't wait for others to do so to have a good time. *Nobody* comes knocking on your door.

At the *Dutch Club* I don't have to worry about a language barrier; everyone at the club speaks Dutch. Aimee tells me her name and invites me to take a seat in a lounge chair next to hers. We hit it off right away; we are buddies from the first moment we talk. *Was it luck, good karma or were we just old friends*?

Both of our husbands are away for a week and time is on our side. We can play without curfew; nobody is expecting us home at a certain time. Aimee arrived in Singapore only two months before I did; she hadn't explored much of Singapore either. Aimee asks me if I'd like to stay at her place while Josh is gone, and so it happens that our friendship is cemented three minutes after I get up from my lazy chair.

I am overjoyed to meet Aimee, especially because the nights alone were tough enough. To trade continents and own nothing more than a t-shirt and a pair of shorts and sneakers were minor in comparison with my fear of burglars. During the day, I would already dread the night. I would try to keep my fearful mind at ease by being busy but, of course, "the elephant grew bigger and never left the room."

What happened at the moment of surrender? The Universe surprised me with the best company I could have wished for.

Suddenly life in Singapore was offering more than fearful nights home alone. After a few swims together, we want some action and Aimee drives me back to my house to pack. From then on, our "girls' trip" begins. Most afternoons that week, we pretend to live in colonial times when ladies were supposed do nothing else than stroll down the lane with their umbrellas in the palm tree parks.

Aimee and I enjoy ourselves by exploring "Chinatown." Each small and narrow street is decorated with Chinese red paper lanterns above our heads. In front of the shops the main tourist attraction is the row of snakes hanging there, dripping blood; they are highly favored by the Chinese men. The shop owners know how to brew a hefty potion to "uplift a man's *potential*." No shame for them; everyone is invited to watch the ritual where their clients gulp down the warm blood *and* smile. Quite some sacrifice for the *promised* outcome.

One afternoon we have a true English *afternoon tea* in the famous colonial Goodwood Park Hotel on Scott's Road. The hotel was restored over the years and turned into a work of art that truly reflects the era of the 1930's. High arches and decorative hallways with marble floors make us feel we may meet the Duke of Windsor face to face that day. I can understand why it was his favorite place to *hang out.* I feel very much at home.

We indulge ourselves with an irresistible Durian Puff and the Chinese Moon Cake. The hotel's "eat as much as you like" policy is quite a gift for our curious taste buds. We can't stop *trying*; we simply indulge in *everything.* It all looks and tastes so good. Our mouths water from bite to the next bite. As we sit back in our lounge chairs, we admire the wealthy people who enjoy the place, too. A jazz band plays softly in the background; the whole ambiance takes us back to the rich colonial style. When the last song is played, we get up and decide to head home. We have a hard time walking back—we have eaten *a lot.*

At home we recover from our feast of *over* abundance. We throw our tight skirts on the floor and exchange them for loose-fitting shorts; we want to fully enjoy the after glow of our banquet.

Aimee and I stay together until our men check in again. Their arrival home doesn't change our friendship. In the daytime we discover every hidden treasure the island offers and, at night, we go back to our men.

A few weeks later, I meet Inge, who also becomes a *friend for life.* She is Dutch, too, and the same age as me, born only a day later on March 17th. Inge and I have a lot in common.

When I leave a year later for Taiwan, she follows in my footsteps. We both give birth to our first child in the same hospital, only she is due three weeks before my *due* date. We both leave Taiwan after a year and move to Holland where our first children grow up together.

Most of our time in Holland is spent together at the zoo. We meet three times a week at the monkey cages.

Inge, Aimee and I are like the three musketeers. Inge loves to shop and has a knack for spotting expensive clothes for less. In this city every brand is copied and most of the fakes are so good that an expert can not tell the difference.

We spend days bargaining *in the basement* and sometimes we stay for hours and end up paying a price for something that is less than the cost of a satay stick. It is well worth the fun.

Josh loves everything about the Asian culture. Unfortunately, he spends more time *out* of the country than *in*. It takes me a while to get used to his busy travel schedule; I'd rather have him home. My fear at night never dissipates; I simply live with it. I know our "guard dog" Spuds is too fast asleep to get up and check out a stranger in the middle of the night. He sleeps soundly all during my wakeful vigilance. I know the iron fence is a farce.

After about two months the right job comes along. When I hear that the Dutch school is looking for a teacher, I jump on it. It doesn't take much effort to get an interview with Jeremy the headmaster of the school and, after a short talk, I am onboard. Jeremy is the friendliest man I have ever met. He is experienced and very capable to run this school. The job is perfect for me, although diploma-wise I am overqualified.

For Jeremy and me, it is no problem. For Marie, my colleague, it is; she hates me at first.

The minute I make my entrance into the school, a mantel of jealousy falls around Marie's shoulders. Marie, who has worked at the school for two years, is the Kindergarten teacher and she reigns over her domain *alone*. Because the number of students has increased, Marie's class is too big. She can't handle all the kids anymore, and the school's need to find another teacher creates my job. "Evenly" she divides the class: the bottom 2/3 and the top 1/3; she takes the latter. Her students are a year older and she says *thus more difficult*.

In her eyes, I was a big threat with my "light-hearted" ideas and "child-like" approach to teaching Kindergarten; *how dare I think it was joyful and easy to teach*? I didn't think teaching Kindergarten was *that* different from teaching older kids. I felt confident in my skills; my attitude of trust and joy seemed to push a button in her. The job she found so hard to do, I didn't take seriously enough in her eyes. I *loved* to teach and I wanted this job with *all* my Heart and Soul. It turns out that Marie's jealousy teaches me a lot more than learning to work with these wonderful, young children.

The first morning I arrive in my old red MG – maybe it was the car or maybe was me –the kids like me instantly. I am in love with them. Over time, each kid is invited for a ride with me *alone*. What an unthinkable thing to do in 2008, especially in America where teachers are not allowed to say the word *poop*. In Singapore, we were free; lawsuits and signed papers are waiting in a future era.

The children are a delight. Their innocence and their eagerness to learn makes me enjoy my job the very first day.

I pull out every creative idea I have. My grandmother "Oma Tuynman" must be proud to see me use everything she taught me when I was young. "My children" create artwork inspired by Oma. Their originality blows Marie off her chair. It takes me awhile to recognize a pattern.

She starts to pull tricks on me like not reminding me of the upcoming holidays. Even though she is supposed to let me know, she never does. At the end of one day, she asks with a big smile on her face in a voice dripping with honey about what my kids have made for their mothers. I look at her and gasp for breath. *Mother's Day*! Oh, my Gawd! This is the most important day of the year. *How could I not have known?* I wasn't a mom nor was either of my two friends, so it wasn't something we talked about.

Strangely enough the school doesn't have a calendar with these important events marked on it and Jeremy assumes Marie will give me the heads up. She does not.

I answer, "Nothing yet" and go to work. That evening I drive to the wood factory and ask the men to saw rectangular pieces of wood. Until midnight I paint polish on top of them so all have a beautiful shiny glow. In the morning the kids decorate them with dried flowers which they glue on the wood. Their presents look shiny and glorious and I see Oma smile in pride from far above. My grandmother taught me an endless repertoire of creative skills that came in handy at "last moments" like this.

Next to many other things, Marie doesn't want to share the school's

Dutch songbooks with me.

I call my friends at home and ask them to sing to me and teach me songs they remember from when they were young. They send me their books after a while; the singing "classes" by phone were too hilarious and we often laughed more than I learned.

In spite of all this, Marie's attempts to create havoc are overruled by my love for my work and for my students. The parents are very happy and so are the kids. I've learned my lesson; I stay *on guard* and keep my eyes and ears open to make sure I never miss an important holiday again.

After a while I feel it is too difficult for me to be relaxed and watch my back at the same time. My intention was never to outshine her. We both have our own class and I don't see why I am in her way. My flair to teach from the heart and not hurry and worry is what feeds her fear and dislike. She is very organized and punctual and I think we could be a wonderful team and complement each other. The angels must have felt sorry about this, too, because I always was made aware of what I needed to know, sometimes at the last minute.

Despite my passion to teach, I feel there is a possibility she may ruin my year in the end. This behavior needed to stop; I wanted to be friends and end her sneaky way of attacking me. I wondered *how*.

One night, when Josh is traveling and I am alone in the house, I decide to do a meditation for this. I need to forgive her and I wrap her in pink light.

For about half an hour, I send her love and light. I think about the good things and good qualities she possesses; I sum up everything I like about her.

My ego is quiet and I feel at peace; I am ready to move with her into a phase of *friendship*. The next morning when I walk into the school, Marie runs towards me. "Let me show you something you can do with the children today," she says while looking at me with the friendliest eyes I had ever seen. "I want to help you and give you some of my books. Here is a Dutch song book I really like."

I cannot believe what I am hearing! *Was this the same Marie who spoke to me yesterday? Was this the effect of the healing visualization from last night*? From that day onward, we become very good friends. I never tell Marie what I did and I let go of the first episode of my teaching there. My step is lighter; I am very grateful for this change.

Marie and I become close and I find I truly like her a lot. I discover a side of her that is fun and, even after school, we not only go out *for business*, we have lunch and laughs at her house. She confides in me about her "side business" which is selling fake watches to her friends in Holland.

In Singapore, the market is hot. Down in the basement of the shopping malls are racks and stands with huge displays of fake watches for very small amounts of money. Exact copies of *Gucci, Dior, Rolex,* you name it, are available for anyone who pays their price. The business is very lucrative.

Most of the expatriates and tourists are able to find their way through this maze of shops. However, Marie and her husband are *pros*. They know where the cheapest watches are sold and how to sell them for a good profit.

I like the excitement a lot and, even though I buy some for my family and friends, I don't have the time or energy to make this business mine. I am an outsider on the inside.

Little do I know that, when I sign up with Aimee for the upcoming *South East Asia Field Hockey Tournament* in Jakarta, Indonesia, my life will become a *roller coaster*. The easygoing teacher with nothing else on her mind than her adorable kids and classroom is in for *quite* a ride.

It is only with one's heart
that one can see clearly.
What is essential is invisible
to the eye.

— Antoine de Saint-Exupéry,
The Little Prince

Meeting Syb

How much fun! We are going to compete for the "South East Asia Field Hockey Trophy." I don't think anyone of us cares a bit. But, man, oh, man, the island buzzes like a swarm of bees around a honey pot. Suddenly almost every Dutch expatriate becomes a hockey player overnight.

The Dutch teams from Taiwan, Hong Kong, Bangkok, The United Emirates, Indonesia and Singapore are all invited and, long before the invitation is received, the captains have said YES. *How can we not*? Big companies like KLM and the ABN Bank sponsor us from start to finish. I can't wait.

Our team practices endless afternoons under the relentlessly hot Singapore sun. The field where we practice is situated between the tall, suntanned buildings in the middle of the sizzling city, which gives us an extra push to do our best. The tourists like to watch us sweat. We work hard to create a winner's mentality and we have faith we can build our muscles. We want to be able to "endure" this three-day tournament in Jakarta; our lazy, tanned bodies can use the exercise. Nothing can prepare me for what Jakarta has in store. The winner's mentality and my Trust muscle are firmly built. I need them for what is to come.

Josh leaves three days earlier for Jakarta than I do. Amazingly, he has a business meeting at the Sahib Yaya Hotel, the place in which we are all staying during the tournament.

Josh is not a hockey fan and assumes it will be boring to watch everyone work their butts off under the tropical sun. He decides to stay for the party during "opening night" and leave the first day of the tournament.

The opening night is like a fairytale; for hours my feet don't touch the ground. I float. The temperature is warm but delightful; the heat of the day is gone and the afterglow that warms us is just fine. The party is held outside in the back yard of the Dutch ambassador of Indonesia. He has an exquisite knack for detail and knows how to make a party rock. Extravagant flowers decorate the scene in the most elegant style. Next to the big green plants in the yard, there are numerous crystal vases with big white lilies and an abundance of more exotic ones I have never seen before. The tables are filled with Asian food and a hip band plays jazz tunes until the moon falls asleep behind the horizon.

I am introduced to a great number of new people. I am having a wonderful time. Josh leaves before the sun comes up and I wake up with Aimee who sleeps in our room, too. She and I will share this room for the next two nights.

This morning we all start with breakfast in the main restaurant on the first floor. It seems if people hardly take time to eat. Everyone is eager to go downstairs to the big hallway.

When I walk into the hallway it is a cacophony of the Dutch language. Old friends meet new friends and the atmosphere is pure excitement for what is to come.

It is great to meet so many Dutch people after being away from Holland for over a year. Together with Aimee, I walk to the bus that brings us to the field. Buses drive up and down from the hotel to the field; they come and go. It is already hot and I wonder how we will play in this temperature. It is eight o'clock in the morning and we haven't even set more than five steps outside the hotel and we are already drip puddles of sweat as if we have done our first rounds on the running tracks.

The bus arrives ten minutes later at the field and, when we get off the bus, Aimee, who is a good captain, searches for the familiar faces of our teammates.

We need to stay together because our game is announced in 15 minutes. I follow her quickly; I better not lose her in this crowd. Then she stops and says, "Hey let me introduce you to our friend." She tugs at my sleeve and pushes me toward him. Obediently I let her move me. I stretch out my hand and look into a freckled male face.

"Hi, I am Syb," he says with a loud voice while he shakes my hand hard. He looks me straight in the eyes. The shake of his hand resonates in my heart and within that split second the familiar voice of my Soul says,

"It's HIM...*the man of your life*...he's THE ONE!"

I blink my eyes and let go of his hand. An instant later, I answer my Soul, "No. I am married to Josh and he is the nicest man in the world. Why would I choose to be with someone else?" I hear no answer; Soul is silent. Deep inside me, I can't argue with the Truth. I know it's HIM.

A second later Syb turns around and runs away. The spell is broken as if this magical moment never happened. My heart pounds like I ran the South East Asia marathon by myself. For a split second, my train of thought skips all the stations in between. I race to the end station named Destiny. *Was that the place I was to go with him?* I trust that if the thoughts I have reflect my heart's desire it is worth taking the risk. No matter how big or how painful; the consequences are mine. I take a breath and shake my head and let go of my thoughts; *where is my hockey stick?* I better hold onto my magic wand to manifest the future I have in mind.

Aimee calls and I run. For a moment I forget the handshake. The tropical heat is relentless and, without my doing anything I bump into Syb again after my first game. Our bright red faces show exhaustion and excitement at the same time. I tell Syb he reminds me of Bart, a good friend of Josh.

Those are the first words I say to Syb. It is like Syb and Bart have the same kind of unlimited bouncy energy. I continue, "Bart was Josh's best man at our wedding." This remark sets the tone: I am a married woman and Syb says no more. He looks at me and says to my stunning surprise that Bart is one of his best friends, too. He shared his desk with him at Philips Electronics in Eindhoven. *How can this be*? I meet the man of my dreams in Indonesia and he lives in Taiwan. I live in Singapore and we both share a Dutch friend we haven't seen for quite a while. In Holland Syb lived in the South and I lived in the West.

Does Destiny have any concern with location?

If we forward or play back the story ... I was already connected to Syb without my knowing it. I had sent him my private travel journal from Guatemala. This journal is already in Syb's possession. Neither of us connects with this amazing fact. Years later Syb discovers *the Saskia* who sent *the intimate and personal* pages copied from her trip diary via his friend Bart was *me*!

Energetically we resonate on the same note, no matter what my marital status is. We drink a lot of Coca-Cola together, every free moment he seems to be standing right next to me.

I love to watch him race behind the ball; he is like quick silver and, without a doubt, he is the most energetic player on the team. Whenever the loudspeaker announces a team needs an extra player, Syb rises and runs. The word exhaustion does not belong in his vocabulary. He plays a double number of games and I can easily say he is literally unstoppable.

I can't share my excitement with Aimee just yet. I don't know what I feel for him. Tonight there is an even bigger party than the night before. All the players are dancing on the field when the last game ends. We don't need to shower and dress to feel that the party has begun.

A few hours later everybody meets in the main hall. I am showered and changed. I feel like my old self again. My hockey outfit doesn't bring out the most feminine in me. The buses are waiting. I hear Syb's voice behind me when I enter the bus. *How could he be right behind me?*

We arrive at a mansion that can't be described with words; the garden is filled with flowers smelling of a mixture of lilies and jasmine. The mingled scent of the Indonesian *kretec* cigarettes and sage reminds me romance is in the air. There are waterfalls; a band is playing and the food is divine. Above our heads, the starlit sky is bright. I lose sight of Syb the minute I enter this "Garden of Eden."

The clock ticks smoothly and I am surprised when I look at my watch and see it is 10.30 PM. We are all mellow; our energy was burned off at the field and our sore muscles most likely are pretending they are asleep.

I feel like dancing, but *where is the man of my dreams*? I have a hard time finding him in the crowd. I walk around and spot him talking intimately with the one and only bachelorette on my team. I know I need *to move fast*. She is a dangerously attractive blond and I better free him from her spell. I can't believe that of all people she has found him or *had he found her*? I walk over to the two chatting birds and pull at Syb's sleeve.

"Come Syb, let's dance," I say in a teasing voice. I invite him with my eyes. He accepts my lead and a minute later we move through the swaying and sweaty crowd. We dance as if our life depends on it. It might be our last. It doesn't take much to keep us going in tune with the fabulous music; our bodies are in complete sync with one another.

Suddenly Syb wants to take a break. I look at him in surprise. "Are you tired *already*?" I ask him in a tone of voice that stirs something in his Soul. "Am I tired *already*?" He stares at me in disbelief. *How dare I say this*? We are both drenched with sweat and out of breath. "No, of course not," is his answer and we dance until morning comes. In this defining moment, I recognize his Soul instantly. He is an extraordinary combination of strong masculine energy combined with a sweet and well developed feminine spirit. He is my *Soul mate* and he doesn't know it yet. Not yet. I want to hold on to our dance forever and I wish the sun would not come up. We dance cheek to cheek; it is a sacred romance that needs no words and exists in a time zone that is not of this earth.

For an evening I forget the world around me and I am only focused on what is happening in the NOW and that fulfills me deeply. We dance to the tune of longtime lovers in an illusion somewhere on the equator lines.

After midnight we are brought back to the Sahib Yaya Hotel. Most people go straight to bed, but a small group of us decide to stay for a last drink and a last dance in the lobby.

Syb and I stay. A pianist plays Billy Joel songs while we sink into deep comfortable leather. We are oblivious to the challenge facing us in the morning. At four o'clock the bar closes; we have no other choice than go to bed. Reluctantly I get up and I am back to reality; my muscles ache, my body is stiff and my heart is wide open. I head for the elevator. Syb and the others join me and ride to the 4th floor. He steps out and waves, "Bye, sleep well."

The door to the elevator closes and he is gone. I still have five floors to go.

In bed my body, mind and Soul are spinning, I feel the rhythm of the dance in accord with my longing. I sleep in my sweaty clothes. I want to hang onto every piece that smells of HIM.

At breakfast I am not hungry for food; I want just a sight of Syb. He is not there and in the bus I sit alone. This is our last day and every team plays at least four games. Our lack of sleep doesn't seem to bother any of us. The night before must have loosened up our aching muscles. I watch Syb play with an enthusiasm and energy I have never seen before. He is *really good.* I admire his endurance, one of an unlimited supply. I feel inadequate in my play. I am an average player and certainly the heat doesn't bring out my running skills. My legs turn to jelly every time I see Syb watching me. I am so aware that my short skirt and blouse don't match my bright red face. But I can't hide. If he can swallow the sight of me like this, there is a bright future on the horizon.

The day goes by and my friends notice Syb and I are hanging out together *a lot.* What amazes me is almost everyone knows Syb. Inge reminds me that I must ask him for his last name otherwise I may never be able to contact him. The end of the day is near and I still have to figure out a way to talk to him; there doesn't seem like there is any chance. The tournament is over in a flash and I find myself watching the award ceremony with an empty heart. It is over; *where is Syb?*

I look around and there is no sign of him. Then I spot him at the back of the shed taking a shower with a hose. I learn later that this is typical of Syb.

While the winning team gets the final handshake, I walk over to him. I am hesitant to say goodbye. *How do you ask someone for his last name without making it too obvious that I want to stay in touch with him*?
The buses arrive and it's a chaos of goodbyes. Everyone is rushed and we all need to get back in time to catch our flights. I don't even know when my plane leaves. My thoughts are focused on something else. I feel that time is going too fast for me to get my act together. I *must* speak with Syb. From behind me I hear, "Hey, can you help me with my stuff?" I blink my eyes and turn around. Syb gives me a big smile and hands me his suitcase. For a moment, I am speechless. The hurry, the buses and the people fade to the background. Time stands still; it is only us.

I tell him about my life in Singapore and share a story about my beloved cats *Yin* and *Yang*. Syb teases me about their names claiming *Yin* is missing a 'g' at the end of hers. I laugh and ask him to bet on it. I know I am right and I can't imagine he seriously thinks he is too. We make a bet and in the few minutes before departure; we enjoy arguing about *the deal.*

I want dinner but Syb says he will send me a big bag of earrings from the Taiwanese night market. I am not interested in earrings, only in Syb. Finally he agrees on dinner; if he wins, I will cook him a dinner in Singapore. Syb is in Singapore often on business trips, so this is an easy promise. If *I* win, he has to cook *me* dinner in Taipei. I joke with him that, since he is a bachelor, he might not have difficulty with including a ticket for me.

Syb gives me his broadest smile and says, "Of course, anything." I guess his pride and manly manner make him wave away the financial consequences of a ticket and, indeed, he looks very cool. I'm impressed!

If I had known him better, I *never* would have dared to make a remark like that; I was feeling free-spirited and care-free. We were in a bubble that floated above the earth. I had no concerns; my worries would come later. The bus horn honks, we exchange addresses and off he goes. He will not be home for the next ten days, which gives me enough time to write him that I won the bet. I wave to him when the bus leaves. I know I will see him again even if I have to swim across the Black Sea to the shores of Taiwan.

Yin and Yang

I fly home and am greeted by a sleepy Josh. It is hard not to share the reason why the tournament was so wonderful *and* the whole story about my winning a ticket to Taipei. I do my best to keep my tone light. Perhaps I am lucky he is half asleep because he hardly reacts. The next morning he asks me about the ticket and the look on my face tells him enough. I am going *no matter what.*

From the first moment Josh and I met, he set some rules about intimacy in our relationship. We are not allowed to tell each other if we fall in love nor confide if we have an affair with someone else. Since I never even considered the possibility, I reluctantly agreed. Truthfully, I never understood the reason behind his rules. Josh was convinced it would do too much harm to the relationship, that it would break the relationship in two if we told each other such things. There would be no mercy in that case, just the end of the marriage.

I wonder what to do. Josh's rule says to keep my mouth shut. It seems like the easiest solution. Josh is the most gentle and sweet person in the world and to hurt him on purpose is too painful to even consider. Although no physical intimacy happened between Syb and me, Soul spoke loud and clear and my heart heard it, too. I tell Josh about the tournament and leave most of the Syb part out.

"When you go to Taipei, I will drive you to the airport," Josh says, "however, I don't want to hear anything about it.

"I am not interested in hearing about this guy Syb or about the countryside either." Josh is firm about this. I just nod my head and silently agree. The days pass by in a daze. My head and heart are in a fuzzy cloud; my body is sick. I am wretched on all levels. My body knows the truth; I am so in love I can hardly walk. This is being *in love* as I have never been before. *Is this what true love feels like?*

My heart knows I might have won the bet, but I will lose my marriage in return. It is a costly exchange.

I take a picture of my cats Yin and Yang. They look triumphantly into the camera. At the store, I buy a balloon sticker with the words "Guess who won the bet?" *Was the Universe playing games?* I stick it next to the proud face of Yin. She knows what her Life Purpose is all about.

I write the letter that will go with the package. The words come straight from my heart. I tell Syb that before my logical mind takes over, I need to tell him how I feel. "You made a deep impression on my heart," I write him. My goal is to sound light with enough feeling to give him a hint. I end with *que sera sera, what will be, will be.* And I mean it. I don't know where Soul is taking us. I attach a little story about the Yin and Yang principles. That bit of education can never hurt. I send the package as soon as I finish the letter.

I don't hear back from him for months. I wait and wait and, after a while, I don't rush to the mailbox anymore. *Will I ever meet him again?* He feels so far away.

One night, while Josh is away, I sit down on our big blue sofa. It is midnight. I am in the sweet company of my cats who purr by my side. Yin gives me a compassionate lick when I tell her I am sad. I've had enough of the unanswered and the too long wait.

It is time to converse with Syb's Soul.

I close my eyes and drift into an altered state. Easily I connect to the energy of his Soul. I ask why he hasn't responded to my letter. *Had I scared him away?* "I cannot," is his first reply. "I am not ready, I need more time…" I feel his genuine energy and I realize he is truly not able to do this visit yet. I let him go. I understand his hesitance.

I lie back on the couch. It is a beautiful, breezy night. Outside the cicadas sing their chirpy song. I swallow mine. I face my lesson of always wanting to speed things up, wanting it NOW. I'd rather go in the fast lane than be one step behind.

An inner peace comes over me and, for a few days, I feel at ease. No hurry, I've got all the time in the world. Maybe in time or over time I was meant to be with Syb. I needed to trust my Soul; only she knew the timing.

A few days after our Souls speak, two months from the time I wrote my first letter, I lose my cool. Syb needs more time; I need an answer. I can't take the silence any longer. I need to know what he thinks of "us." I decide to call him and end all the madness on my side. I'd rather be a good friend than a secret lover who goes crazy in the end.

It was time to get on with my life and set my secret love affair aside. I want to let Syb go and I feel ready to do so. Soul gives me a nudge on my shoulder when the time has come to call him. With a quick step, I walk to the bedroom. I want to get this over with; I can't lose my courage.
I carefully unfold the piece of paper I have guarded all this time. I pick up the phone while my hand trembles. I am nervous but very sure of what I have to say. Slowly I dial Syb's number; each digit counts. I take my time.

"Syb" is what I hear at the other end. In shock I put the receiver down. *Why would someone pick up the phone on the first ring?* I needed some time to bridge the gap from my head to my heart. *Now what?* I dial again and take a big breath. I say my name when he picks up on the first ring. I am ready to take off; my speech is well rehearsed.

He stops me before I can make another single sound. My words stay stuck in my throat. My explanation about why I wrote the letter is lost. I want to rattle off that we can be friends; the deal about the ticket, the bet, we can let it go, in fact, it was all a joke. From now on, we are free, no strings attached. However, I can't say a word because Syb starts *his* well-rehearsed speech.

"I was just holding your letter in my hand when you called," Syb says, "I want to discuss dates."

I am glad he can't see my expression. I am speechless and shake my head. I can't come up with dates off the top of my head; I hadn't thought that far ahead.

"Let me check when the school vacation starts," I say with a back to "normal" voice. I hang up and wonder where this phone call will lead to. In my mind's eye, I imagine how two "strangers" meet in Taipei after only one night, two days and a two-minute phone conversation about a ticket.

I fly downstairs and look for Yin. *Where is my designer of destiny?* I can't find her and I don't have the patience to wait for her return. A minute later, I hop in the car to drive to Inge and Aimee's house; they know how crazy I am about Syb.

The MG starts without a problem. The leather convertible top won't close today but I enjoy the sizzling heat on the top of my head. I maneuver fast through the busy evening traffic. My best friends need to know about my "visit" to Taipei.

In Taipei, Syb shows my letter to Dingenis, his bachelor friend and "partner in crime." Dingenis, a Dutch man with a lot of common sense, says the girl who wrote the letter is in love. He must have a sixth sense. Aimee and Inge are happy for me yet we all wonder if Syb is ready. *What had the Universe written in the stars? What would we do if I went to Taipei? And what would I wear?* Three major questions were posed as if my life depended on them.

In Taipei, Dingenis and Syb discuss the same things. *What will we do*? They make a bet. Syb comes up with a different scenario from Dingenis. In the end they are both wrong.

What is the Universe's game when Bart comes to celebrate New Year's at our house in Singapore? The phone rings and Bart answers our phone. It is Syb. Bart recognizes Syb's voice right away. Syb is calling to make sure it is REALLY okay to send a plane ticket for me to visit.

He asks Bart what Josh will think. His conscience is playing a guilt trip now. Bart reassures him that our marriage allows for a lot of freedom and separate travel. He says it isn't a problem as far as he can see.

However, Syb and I both know Bart can't see and that Josh isn't blind. "See what happens when your plane ticket arrives," Syb tells me. To be honest, I don't want to wait; my waiting was done. I am excited beyond belief.

I count the days till my "visit" in February. The day I leave I don't want to pick up the phone. I am afraid someone might call with the news of a disaster and ruin my trip. Before I leave, Syb asks me to buy a *dhurrie*, a Middle Eastern carpet, for him. "You choose," he says. It is good I don't know how picky he is.

Aimee comes along as my shopping helper and for hours we browse through the store basements. There are hundreds of dhurries to choose from. *How do I pick something to match Syb's taste and what colors are right?* Suddenly, one carpet speaks to me. It is light blue with pink on the sides. I know this is *the one.*

Exhausted yet satisfied, I let the clerk roll the dhurrie into a small parcel which I will carry on as hand luggage. There will be no check-in for me.

At the airport I walk around restlessly; I'd rather go. A bottle of whiskey seems like a good gift. I buy one for Syb. *Did my Soul nudge me to buy this gift and assure the outcome of the trip?*

My plane takes off and instantly I feel relief. *Finally* I am on my way. But now that I am, the future begins to be a bit unnerving.

Who is Syb anyway?

Temptation in Taipei

Syb waits for me with his "*new*" car he bought a few hours before in a ten-minute deal in front of his office. Proudly he shows me his "new" silver Ford. I know nothing about cars and apparently neither does Syb. He said the seller slapped the roof a few times with his hand and walked around the car. This meant the car was old but it was good. No test drive was needed; trust was good enough. Syb has no doubt about the car. The tires aren't flat, the engine runs and the tank is full. *What else is there to worry about?* When he hands the seller the money, the car is his. "We needed a car," he says. And that will be true enough for this visit.

Our meeting is not as awkward as I thought it would be. We hop into the car as if we are old friends. We know nothing about each other. I can only remember our dance. I have to get used to Syb in a suit. *Who is this Syb, the business man?* He looks so different.

We drive off and I have no idea where we are going. It is now the Chinese New Year and everything is closed for a week. The roads are full and so are the hotels. The Chinese warned Syb; I think *who cares*? I am with Syb, we are driving *some*where and the world is ours.

Syb has planned a mini tour of the island. On our way we pass an old temple. Syb stops the car and asks if I would like to go inside. The Gods smile on us as we enter.

Nobody has entered this temple for ages and the statues look very old and dusty. The giant Buddha, however, shines golden in the late afternoon sun; it is magical. The silence is enhanced by dozens of butterflies that soundlessly brush their wings against big Buddha's cheek. Mesmerized, we walk toward the long table and pick up the wooden dice. We know, according to the tradition, we can make a wish if we throw them in a certain order. "First, let's buy some cola from the machine down the street and drink to us," says Syb.

"I have something better," I say as I reach into my tote bag and pull out a bottle of pink champagne from the airport. We stand in front of the altar and take hold of the wooden dice. We both throw and we are lucky; the dice shows the pattern of good fortune. We make a toast with the champagne to celebrate our future. Pink is the color of my bubble.

When we leave the temple, we walk and talk animatedly to the car until Syb announces enthusiastically that we are going to a "dealer dinner" somewhere in the outskirts of Taipei.

Syb has "planned" our trip, which means that the end destiny is open and the road will lead us "door to door" for dinner with several Philips company dealers. The Chinese love Syb and his joyful open manner; he understands the Chinese finger games and uses a few Chinese words mixed with his strong Dutch accent.

I say, "That's cool," not meaning one letter of those words.

I had fantasized about a romantic stroll through the Taipei night market or at least something a bit more exciting than a sit-down dinner with a bunch of Chinese businessmen. Syb means well *but when and where is the romantic part?*

It's fun to drive through the tiny streets of Taipei. Laundry hangs above our heads and I wonder how it can stay clean with the dirty exhaust lingering in the air from the cars passing by underneath. My eyes dart from left to right; there is so much to see that is different from Singapore with her polished buildings and shiny streets. My few hours of flight have dropped me off in a foreign country where nothing resembles my preconceived notion.

When we arrive at the outdoor patio of the house where we are supposed to dine, we are ushered in by six men. Inside, we take our shoes off. After several welcoming slaps on the back, they push us toward a staircase that leads to the "attic."

The way they welcome Syb speaks for itself; he is their big boss and best friend. Syb laughs and shakes hands and imitates their back slaps; he is one of them. I am invisible. The Chinese are good at pretending and I am not sure if I am a welcome guest. All the women sit downstairs. *What did they think of me, hanging onto Syb and going upstairs with him?* With every step, I wonder what will await us.

The upstairs "attic" is an empty room, except for a square table and chairs. Everyone is asked to take a seat. I sit down next to Syb but I am completely invisible even though they occasionally smile at me. A woman is not their choice for their sacred domain.

I feel like telling them I feel as uncomfortable as they do. I don't understand a word of what they are saying but I admire Syb's talent for pretending so well that he does. Sharing the same childlike and playful energy is enough; Syb does that really well.

I am not used to sitting in silence; I am totally out of place. Inside, I laugh at myself and say, "See, here you are at the side of the man of your dreams. *How's the romantic fantasy so far?*"

I think of Inge and Aimee. *What would they think?* I bet they would roll around on the floor laughing. I wished I could show them "this made for TV movie." I hear "someone" whispering in my ear, "Told ya. This is what happens when you follow your dream."

We are served course after course of wonderful Chinese dishes. The women downstairs do their utter best to spoil their men. The men are eager to continue their game and, when the last dish is done, a woman takes my hand and asks me in sign language to come with her. I am too happy to escape this place.

I am quite surprised when she shows me a crisp, clean bed. I look at her and she looks at me. She waits patiently until I climb into bed. She tucks me in and shushes me to go to sleep. I point toward the ceiling and make the same gesture back. "They must shhh," I say to her with a big grin on my face. We both smile and then she nods and closes the door.

I close my eyes and drift off to a fantasy land where life was filled with pink roses and champagne. "Follow your bliss," were the wise words of Joseph Campbell. Instead, here I am in a Chinese bamboo bed in a Chinese bamboo house.

I can hear the loud laughter upstairs. Every now and then, I hear Syb making a joke. They all crack up in their Chinese way by jumping up and down on the floor. The lantern on the ceiling dangles dangerously above my head. I don't know for how long it is that I wait, listen and fall asleep.

A light knock on the bamboo door wakes me up. Syb's head peaks inside the room. He looks at me as if he has done this before with girls I have never met. "Time to go," he says. These words sound like melody to my ears. "Yes, time to go," I think and jump out of bed. We go downstairs and spend half an hour thanking and bowing to everyone. Finally, we leave.

Syb is satisfied with the evening and thinks I am too. I don't say anything; I just focus on helping him navigate the narrow lantern-lit streets. Miraculously, we reach the highway and head toward Tienmou in the north part of Taipei where Syb lives. When he opens the door of his apartment, the spaciousness, the view of the mountains and the river below overwhelm me. I admire the way he so artfully designed the living room; I feel at home right away. The only thing missing is something for the cold tile floor.

I hand him the *dhurrie* with great pride. He rolls it out on the floor; it fits the space exactly. "It is perfect," he exclaims, and it is true. The colors, the design, are tailor-made for him and this room. I get an A+.

"I have something else," I say and hand him the bottle of whiskey.

"I can't believe this," Syb says with a frown. I am surprised by his reaction to my present. "It's really funny," he says; that doesn't explain the frown.

I find out later that Syb and Dingenis talked about my four-day 'visit' *a lot.* According to Syb, one option was that he and I create our own "pleasure island" within his apartment. The second option was Syb will be my tour guide and a gentleman; he will keep his hands behind his back, and perhaps take only a stolen kiss. Syb opts for the second. Dingenis bets on the first. I am not asked. A bottle of Jack Daniels – the same brand I brought – is the prize. Dingenis is confident he will win; so is Syb. *How will accepting my gift seal his fate?*

The next morning before I open my eyes, Syb is up and ready to go. He has packed a backpack filled with wine, crackers, a flashlight and the bottle of Jack Daniels. We choose to go south that day and improvise along the way. As we drive, we chat for hours, exploring each other's lives as we explore the gorgeous countryside. We are in a different world.

At a certain moment, Syb abruptly asks in his typically direct way, "You go along with everything I say. Isn't there anything *you* want to see or do?" I am a little shaken by his approach. I don't answer his question. I don't know what to say. My answer is obvious: I treasure every minute with him no matter where we go.

Everything is exciting. The nature of Taiwan is grand; the mountains and gorges are wild and green. We encounter a place where huge rocks came crashing down a steep mountainside and gorged big ridges in the road. There are signs where buses jumped the side rails and crashed; the number of dead is displayed on each sign. The Chinese are matter-of-fact about their lives.

At night we knock on the doors of small inns or hotels on the side of the road. We set a nightly routine of drinking a shot of whiskey before we go to sleep. We are mindful that I am married and keep certain principles in tact.

On the last night, Syb takes me to the first European-style restaurant of my visit. It's called "Café Passion." Tonight there will be no monkey hair or chicken livers. As soon as we step over the threshold of Café Passion, we trade chopsticks for polished silver knives and forks and a "Champagne Cooler." This drink is so heavenly that, upon the first sip, you believe you have entered the realms of the divine. Years later, Syb and I go to recreate it. We become experts in copying the ingredients and have fun making our own paradise.

Café Passion is a place out of a designer's magazine; the inside is in orange and red hues. Every piece of furniture and the menu radiate a sensual expression. It is fabulous sexy atmosphere in the middle of Taipei. The waiter has fun announcing the specials and, when he mentions the entree "Prelude to Orgasm," we give each other a look and say we'll save it for later.

Who would have his picture taken with a balloon above his head saying "Guess who won the bet?" I have to leave it to Syb, this was his bet. The prize I won was sitting across from me.

The waiter brings in big bubbling bowls of pink champagne coolers. Our trip will soon come to an end and there is one pressing issue I have to discuss with Syb. Every time I think of it, my courage sinks into my shoes. I don't know how to bring it up. Again I choose to save it for later.

Back in Syb's apartment, I know the time has come. I need to tell Syb that I called KLM and changed my ticket. I extended my stay by one more day. I wanted one day when I could surprise him from morning till night.

By now it was midnight and the moment announces itself. Syb lies down on the leather sofa and soft music plays throughout the room. The windows are open and besides the river's loud roar, all is peaceful and still. Syb shares openly how easy life is, how much he loves his life the way it is, the Chinese girls are a lot fun. He is convinced he doesn't need more for now; he will probably marry an Asian girl. He makes it sound like his life is "a beach."

I can't bear to listen to his story; it touches my Soul and breaks my heart. Syb has such a limited vision of who he really is and what his life's purpose is about.

Something inside of me screams to wake him up. A channel in me opens and I start to talk. I speak from a place of pure compassion.

I am detached but passionate in my desire to guide him. I tell him he has so much potential inside of him.

"You'll waste your life if you believe in your fantasy, Syb. " I tell him, " Design your life for all you are capable of. Right now you have no idea what that is. You need a woman who recognizes your greatness and helps you discover all there can be."

My intent is pure and from the place I am speaking I am not inferring I am that woman. Syb listens and, for the first time, I see his deep emotional side; tears stream down his face. He is touched and for once he doesn't say anything.

In this defining moment, the blueprint of Syb's Soul rises up and he knows it. Deep silence fills the room the same moment the outside world comes alive. The Chinese shoot their firecrackers with no stopping in sight.

Bang ratttaaaatttta... The sounds from the park below echo the start of the Chinese New Year. I turn my head to face the window and make a wish when a rainbow of color appears at the dark sky. It seems like the rays bow low to us on their way to the ground.

And then it's time to announce my surprise. When Syb hears I am going to stay and spoil him for one whole day, he just can't *let go and let me.* "I have to go to the office," he mumbles.

I wave it away. Syb looks at me and dries his tears. He says, "Okay, let's do it. It'll be fun."

From the minute we get up to the final moment, the next day is good, more than good. The sun shines, the mountains surrounding Taipei look prettier than before. Love is in the air.

We take Syb's favorite "off-road bike." I climb on the back of the motorcycle and hold on to him tight. The day goes by in a blur. Something has shifted since last night. I know Syb's moment of tears went by as fast as they came but, for the first time on this trip, he takes a picture of me.

When we exchange pictures later, I have 71 pictures of Syb and one of the countryside. Syb has 71 landscape photos and this one of me. On the last day, I am finally "in the picture."

His door is ajar but not for long. He closes the door and locks it securely with my goodbye. Before I leave, I am clearly instructed to NEVER EVER contact him again. *We had a great week and now it's over.* I can send my pictures to him and he will send me his.

I pretend to agree; I am not going to create a last minute scene.

The goodbye is hasty. A taxi picks me up and off I go. The journey ends. *Was the destiny reached?*

Taipei already seems so very far away.

I will write peace on your wings
and you will fly all over the world

—Sadako Sasaki

What's Love Gotta Do With It?

I fly back to Singapore. My heart is full and the rest feels numb. I don't know that Syb's last words to me, "We will never speak again," are really the beginning of a lifelong conversation.

I sit motionless and stare into the empty sky hoping to get a sign from the heavens that all will be well. I can't think of the future. My heart beats loud; a love song pulsates through my veins. I need these hours to come back into sync with who I am at home: wife, teacher, friend, daughter-in-law…and *what else do I pretend*? I feel "off track."

I am dressed in a silver and black top that I bought at the night market in Taipei. It's too tight; if I move, it will rip apart. I need to look hip for the concert with Tina Turner; I adore Tina and for her I sacrifice my comfort. Josh will pick me up at the airport and we'll go straight to the concert with Tina. What perfect timing to be in the presence of my favorite rock star.

Aimee and Gerard join us and it is incredible to watch Tina dance and sing her heart out. "What's love gotta do with it" she sings with all her passion, and with all my passion I shake my Soul until I can dance no more. Taipei is far away. My love for Syb is alive but not in reach. He has not only shaken my heart but my life as well. Everything feels upside down and turned around inside of me. I'm a mess.

I feel like an overflowing bubbling cooler of pink champagne that wants me to dance and celebrate my love for him. Instead, I must swallow it too quickly and choke it down in pain.

After the concert, Josh's parents are home at the dinner table waiting. Our excuse to not immediately converse with them is good; we need to shower and cool off first. At least the attention is not on me and my trip. *How can I explain where I was and why?* I am not sure what Josh told them; fortunately, the subject of my trip is not brought up. With my change of clothes, I change back into my role as Singapore Saskia on the outside. Inside I am not the same. *Who am I now?*

It doesn't take long to develop the photos. I send them and wait for

Syb's promised reply. The last word will be his.

I ignore Syb's demand to end our conversation for good. I keep calling him and he always answers. Our phone conversation helps bridge the physical distance. I long to return to Taipei; my heart aches. I want to sit in Syb's window and stare at the river below.

But time drifts by and the seasons change. The children at the school are my safe haven and I transfer my passion for him into my love for them. I write Syb about my classes and tell him the stories the kids share with me. I describe them in vivid detail. He loves to listen and says he wishes he was one of the kids in my class.

We establish a writing routine that rises to a poetic level. I truly see his strong character and beautiful Soul shine through the way he writes about himself and his life.

We write in metaphors and discover each other and ourselves within the depth of our Souls. Nevertheless, it all leads nowhere.

Over time, I feel Syb's confusion and hesitancy grow stronger. I know he is 'the one' but Syb needs to make up his 'mind', too. Every so often he ends our conversation with the promise to never talk to me again; in the end he always does. To go further than the safe stage we are in seems impossible. The energy is stagnant and can't be moved. His guilt plays a big role and it disconnects him from his feelings. The safe place is his mind and it feels like we have come to a dead end. I have given it my all and I am exhausted. I can't make Syb go against his principles.

Even though I would be the one to give up my husband and life with my kids in Singapore, Syb's part is crucial in making this happen, too. I feel despair deep in my Soul and wonder if I can encourage him to listen to the voice of *his* Soul. I have lost my confidence. I need to go on with my life and let him go. I float in a gap.

I decide to end our platonic relationship and set us both free. I will leave him alone. I cannot make him choose me. If this is not meant to be, I have to face it.

On a rainy afternoon during the monsoon season, I lazily watch the big drops fall on the patio of our porch. Big rivers of muddy water flow effortless in the direction of least resistance; gravity is the magnet. The law of attraction makes the water follow a stream that leads into a big puddle. It grows bigger until it overflows.

My stream of consciousness is as effortless as this water; I am in the flow and think—if our love follows the law of attraction—it must eventually follow the law of gravity which was the love we have for each other. But *was that love strong enough to override the undercurrent of doubt?* I can only speak for myself. And yet, right now, I have to admit there is no flow; the stream has lost her current. The river is now a puddle. A passionate relationship needs more.

I take my golden pen and begin to write. I am ready to embrace the consequences of my deed. My pen moves effortlessly while my heart speaks.

I write a love story about a princess who captured the heart of the prince of the Tower of Taipei. I had always teased Syb with that nickname after he told me he lived in a tower. The princess loved the prince dearly and wanted to share her life with him. However, in order to build their castle on the other side of the river which flowed in front of his Tower, the prince had to leave his safe surroundings. The river was a metaphor for his feelings. The tower represented his guarded heart. Even though the princess was ready, the prince was not. He feared the deep waters of the river.

But *who was she to let him drown?*

I mail the letter and feel at peace for the first time in a long time. My heart is at rest. I let him go. I have pursued my dream to the last thread. I was true to my Soul. I drive to a deserted beach close by.

A turtle walks towards me; she is guarding her eggs but is not afraid to leave her nest and greet me. My mission is completed. I am relieved. I know I have done all I could.

Bye, my love. And life goes on.

Trip to the Maldives

The Creation principles are at work

The yearly lucky drawing is held at the Dutch club. The colonial room with the dark leather chairs is transformed into a place that looks more like an African market than a luxurious lounge where poems are read, cigars are smoked and talk is deep into the corners of your Soul.

For months, the talk of the town is about "who will win a ticket to the Maldives?" The island of coconuts and palm trees in the middle of the Indian Ocean named *Boli Fushi* is at stake. I truly believe I will be one of the lucky crew who wins. My daily visualizations are fun. I picture myself snorkeling with the dolphins and I feel myself touch their cool, slippery backs with my hand. This beautiful resort promises to be the most gorgeous place on earth. I am curious who else will win. When the evening finally comes, my eyes are fixed on the numbers of the wheel. My number is 9.

The wheel spins and spins; my focus is steady and so is my intent. The wheel slows and stops at 9…then suddenly it makes a jump to 10. I have no clue why. There is tremendous excitement in the crowd. The people who have won jump up and down. I stand in wonder when the winners are announced by name. I am not one of them. The winners dance until the club closes. I join in and forget about the ticket. I love to dance.

At home I ask myself *what happened?* I so believed in us being there. I thought the law of attraction always worked. I get my answer a month later. Indeed the law of attraction always worked. I was always too impatient. Patience wasn't a virtue I had learned well.

The divine order throws the trip to the Maldives in my lap; not manifested in the way I thought, the circumstances are even better. I can choose the ones to join me on the trip. One condition of the prize was that the winners must go on a certain date; none were able to. They decide to give their tickets away and I am one of the lucky ones. We have to pay for the change of names which is a small amount of money. Everything is free. Only one night in Sri Lanka is to be paid by us. *Were we willing?* We are more than willing. Marie and husband, Aimee and Gerard, some other friends, and Josh and I go, of course. The Universe handed me the ticket a little later. We were going to *Boli Fushi*!

The most gorgeous place on earth turns out to be a very painful place to be. My heart aches for both Syb and Josh. The incredible beauty of the island, the clear waters and skies magnify my inner turmoil. I am miserable. That was the last thing I had expected to happen. My heart is full of Syb, while my outer world is of extraordinary beauty and luxury. My inner world is restless in her inability to express the love I feel. Josh is here with me, and I so wish him to be THE ONE.

Why does my heart think the grass on the other side is greener? As hard as I try, I can't push away my love. I have to face facts. Syb is not here by my side and he may never be.

The dolphins laugh at me. *Carpe diem.* "Enjoy the day, you over-sensitive blonde," they say. I swim around the whole island without a stop. *Why isn't life a beach?*

There is no try, only do.

—Yoda

You Can Still Love and Leave

My heart is broken and my Soul mends the wound in patience.

My letter finds its way to Taiwan while I lay restless on the sand. Instantly he calls. Something is triggered in Syb and he is open to the possibility of a relationship with me. I am overjoyed with happiness, but *how do I proceed?* I must tell Josh and, when I do, I know I will lose it all. I just don't fully realize what all means. That day when Josh comes home from work, we sit down and talk. He asks for proof and, when I show him the phone bill with my calls to Taiwan, he knows enough.

Within seconds I have no home, no money and the phone is locked in the back of Josh's car. He warned me not to tell him about my side step to Taiwan. *Why did I choose to tell him?* He shakes his head in disbelief. He is furious and refuses to talk to me any further. I need to pack and go. I don't know where to and my worst punishment is to leave my children without their teacher. The thought of leaving Josh for good, as well the children, makes me feel like I want to die. I understand his pain and leave.

Late at night, I call Syb from Inge's phone. "I've left Josh and I'm leaving Singapore," I tell him. Syb is torn, horrified at one point and ecstatic on the other. Suddenly his love can flow; there is a future.

Syb's guilt and responsibility advise me to try and mend the relationship. I don't know what there is to *try*. It will be either deny or fake my love for one or the other. I listen and try to *try*.

I return to Josh and do the TRY; the attempt to do this is too confusing to explain. For a few weeks, life continues as if nothing has happened. Under the surface, my marriage is lost. Josh and I do our best; the undercurrent of being in love continues to pull me toward Syb.

Syb needs this trial perhaps more than I do although his heart is broken as well. His feelings have swung from one side to the other. Finally I was free and unleashed his love, and then I listen to him and am back with Josh. The light was red, then green, and now it is red again. "Keep trying," is all he says. *What is there to try if my body is in Singapore but my heart and Soul have left awhile ago?*

When the try is tried long enough, I decide to leave for good and go home to Holland. I think at least I had the guts to stay true to my Soul. With or without my prince I will go. Josh doesn't want me around for one more minute. OUT is his final word. I can understand his anger. I have to go.

And then my prince says, "COME."

I leave the house and stay with Aimee and Gerard, who welcome me with all their warmth. The Singapore expatriate community is shocked; everyone knows me. I am the teacher of their children.

Here I was running into the arms of someone I knew for only four days. The gossip feeds boring lives; rumors spread like wildfire. I am in no position to explain.

Jeremy who heads the school totally understands but he says, "You need to go." He will find another teacher. I wonder *how will it affect the children if I go without saying a word? Is life so unpredictable people can go in a heartbeat without anyone noticing?* It goes against everything I believe in. *What kind of example do I set for them?*

My ticket is booked. I will leave on the weekend three days after Josh says OUT. It breaks my heart to leave everything behind and go home. But *where is home?*

Josh and I have a "last night" dinner in our beloved place in downtown Singapore. It is the hardest and saddest thing I have ever done in my life. I still love Josh; he is the sweetest person on earth. *How can I pursue my path and cause him an immeasurable amount of pain?* We never had a fight; we were brother and sister.

My Soul, however, keeps nudging me to stay on course and not to waver. I am sad beyond tears.

Josh begs me to stay; he will do anything to make me happy. He tells me I can even leave for a year and come back. He is genuine and sincere in his love. I have never heard him express himself so well; he was a man of very few words. Now he opens his heart completely and I am at a loss. I still love him. He says *anything and everything* he will do for me, *whatever it takes.*

Who gets offered that on a silver platter? How can I turn my head the other way? He tries to persuade me with the words, "You don't know this guy. It's just a fling. It will fade." *Was it so temporary?*

I can't eat a bite of the delicious food on my plate. We sit and look at each other. There is nothing more to say. Large, warm, salty tears stream down my cheeks. *Why am I giving up the perfect life for a promise*? Deep in his heart, Josh knows I am going; he is helpless to do anything. We have everything: the house of our dreams, the life of our dreams. I even have the job of my dreams. Only the passion is missing and for me that is enough. The man of my dreams lives on the other side of the dark sea, whether he wants me or not. My flight will be one with no return.

The memory of Josh sitting and staring at me still brings tears eighteen years later. Josh is one of the few persons who truly loved me for everything I was and for everything I was not.

The day I leave, Yin's babies open their eyes. Four divine kittens look at me for their very first and last time. Both Yin and Yang purr when I kneel down and cry; my belly contracts and I almost choke. I can't go. *Why am I doing this? Why leap? Why follow Soul's lead?*

I am in too much pain for words. My beloved dog Spuds jumps at the sight of me, thinking he will go too. It is not to be so. I will be leaving EVERYTHING and EVERYONE behind when I finally close the door.

I haven't spoken to Syb for some time; the pain overshadows the butterflies of before. The only thing I feel is the determined voice of Soul saying: "Go. GO!" I miss the overwhelming feeling of *being* in love. *Where did that go?*

Josh is not at home when I do my final goodbyes. He chose to say goodbye when the taxi picked me up after our last supper. It is "easier this way," he said while choking on tears. There is nothing easy now. The gate makes too many squeaky noises when I close her. I had hoped my departure would be silent and unheard.

Aimee picks me up in her white Audi. I turn my head when we drive off and catch a glimpse of Yin, who sits like a statue in the window. Her eyes are looking at me, and I sense her saying: "You go, girl." I am so sorry I can't be there to watch her children grow.

"You'll be a great mom, Yin," I whisper back to her. Gone is Yin and Yang and my wonderful, playful life. Chapter "Singapore" is closed. Josh has lost his wife and partner, his best friend. The children have lost the teacher who loves them most. I carry my heart heavily under my arm. My white canvas tote bag is slung over my shoulder. I take nothing but some clothes.

What did I really need for this leap? I was about to find out.

I long, as does every human being,
to be at home wherever I find myself.

—Maya Angelou

Homeless in Holland

The hours in the plane pass by in a blur. I cry a lot. I walk around in Dubai airport as a ghost. I am lonely, so very lonely; no one understands the choice I made. I arrive at Schiphol Airport in Holland. I have no luggage. I travel light. I barely have enough money for the train to Assen, the place my parents live.

I take the intercity train to the north of Holland. I am estranged from the beauty around me. My dried up tears block the view of the pretty meadows. Even the Dutch language seems foreign. My inside is so sad; my decision is still crystal clear.

My parent's home awaits with a warm welcome but I can't shake off my chills. Singapore was warm in every sense of the word. I long for an understanding hug or word. There is nobody who can comfort my pain. *How can I help them understand why I have given up my whole life?*

Their love is unconditional but they are in shock that I have left my marriage. I have exchanged their beloved son-in-law Josh for an unknown man who is supposedly THE ONE after only four days. "Who is Syb?" they ask. *What can I say to them?* I hardly know Syb myself.

In addition to that I have ruined my mom's trip. She had booked her first trip to Asia and now I have left. She is to go and visit with Josh alone. At least Yin and Yang can show off their babies. My decision created a mess for others too. I feel so bad.

After a few days, I leave and go to the place I called home before I left years ago. When I arrive at the Central train station in Amsterdam, I feel like an alien from outer space. The place is swamped with tourists and I feel like one myself. Holland is my birth country but *where do I go?*

I talk to Syb on the phone and he says I need to get a divorce before I come to Taiwan. I am not ready; for me it's too soon. I just got used to the idea I was married and now, *divorce? What does that have to do with my love for him? Why can't I come and handle the legal stuff later?*

Syb has made a decision: I must be totally free before I come to live with him in Taipei. Emotionally, I know I cannot divorce in one day. I need time to adjust. This step is too big for me right now. It's one jump after another. I can't do it. But I do it anyway.

Aimee advises me to call her friend, a lawyer, when I tell her about my dilemma. "Do it," is her brief but wise counsel. I call him assuming he can help me get the divorce. He instructs me instead to go to my bank and make sure I take some cash out of our shared account. I don't understand why but I trust him. He is experienced; he suggests I not wait a day.

In Amsterdam I go to our bank and a friendly clerk helps me at the desk. It takes a while before she comes back. "There must be a misunderstanding," she says.

I don't know what she means and I repeat my name.

"It's not the name. It's the account." I look at her with big eyes. "Yesterday the account was closed," she continues. "I can't help you."

I stand motionless behind the desk. *What in the world happened with our account?* I am not sure if this woman understands what I am asking. When the truth hits me, my anger rises. *How dare he pull this trick on me!*

I have nothing, not a penny in my wallet and Josh knows it. In Singapore, all the money I earned was written out to his name and every month my salary was deposited in his account. I never saw any harm in it; now I am facing the consequences. I was never able to draw money from our account in Singapore either. *How could I have been so gullible, so stupid?* I had always thought, "I'll wait and discuss this later." Now it was later and it was too late.

I leave the bank. On the outside I look okay but my inside screams louder than words can say. I don't have enough money to take a train back to my parents! I am stuck in my self-supporting formula: the daughter who will NOT ask for money from her parents ever. They have other things on their plate. *What shape did I have to be in to call for help?* I walk around the canal streets of Amsterdam. I go in circles. Luckily no one is in my way.

I call some old girlfriends and tell them I'm back. My 'old world' is in shock. They want to know, *how could I leave my wonderful world and marriage?*

"You had *everything*. Why trade it for someone you don't really know?" some ask. "You are crazy!" others decide.

One friend adds, "You always smiled and looked *so* happy." For years I was happy. *How do I explain it was my Soul telling me to go?*

I call my lawyer back and confirm his belief that a cat in the dark makes crazy jumps. He was right; here I am with no money and absolutely not a thing but my white canvas bag and a few pieces of clothing that have traveled the world with me. I can't pay him for his service either. As he said, I've left safe grounds and now I have no landing space. He asks me to come to his office in Amsterdam and meet with him to discuss how we will proceed. He asks me when I have time to come and speak with him. I laugh out loud. "Well, let's look at my schedule," I say jokingly. The truth is I feel far from funny. My calendar is empty.

At his office in Amsterdam he asks me out. I can't believe it. *Just what I need* I think to myself and decline his offer.

He advises me to go to Social Services and apply for a "BEWIJS VAN ONVERMOGEN." This is a *certificate of inability or incompetence to live*. The translation is hard to make in English; basically it's enough to know that many homeless people who live under bridges wouldn't qualify for this certificate.

This certificate is a *ticket to freedom*. It means lifelong care by the Dutch state with support on EVERY level. The key word is FREE, everything for FREE. The lowest of the low in the Dutch population "might" attain this certification . . . but only if they are really lucky. In other words this qualification is very hard to get; impossible might be a better word.

Because no one in Holland wants to be classified as 'incompetent,' some people would rather starve. In my situation, I am proud and feel very lucky if I can get that far in life! For me there is only one way to go . . . UP!

I call Social Services and make an appointment. They ask me to come by to pick up the forms I have to fill out. The paper package is thick; they need a lot of information about me and my life. I must bring back all the paperwork showing my bank account, my spending status, my rent, my insurance and actually every document about me that states my complete financial status.

In a way I have traded my job with the kids for one of filling out forms. I need this certificate badly because I have no money and need to be considered as a pro bono case. If I can show my *certificate of inability to live*, my lawyer's service is for free.

On one hand, my emotions about a divorce is that it is one step too far; however, the only way to any kind of a future is to keep moving ahead.

I walk into a building I've passed a million times before. The street where I lived is only four blocks away. I never showed any interest about what went on inside; now I am optimistic and eager to get my foot in the door. What is very different is that I am on foot; I don't even own a bike. For an "Amsterdammer" that is a most unusual sight. I am like a skier on the slopes who has no skis.

I arrive at the appointed time, 2:50 in the afternoon. My white bag hangs nonchalantly over my shoulder. I push the button on the door and, after a few minutes, they buzz me in. The window is protected by iron-bars. Clearly not everyone leaves satisfied.

Someone signals me to take a ticket from a machine and wait. I have time; there is no hurry, my schedule is wide open. A buzzing sound tells me my number is up and automatically another door opens. I smile, indeed *when one door closes another one opens.*

"Let me check your health insurance papers, your bank statements, your bills…" Their list of requests is longer than the breath I can hold. The woman has another hundred questions. The intent is *not* to make it EASY. I am detached from the outcome; there is nothing I can do to prove one thing or another. The facts are I HAVE NOTHING and I live NOWHERE. I have no where to hide. However, they want to see some papers.

They raise their eyebrows. I point to my white grey canvas bag. "This is all I have," I say. I show them my empty purse, my passport full of colorful stamps and I realize the situation is absurd. "You have traveled the world," she says. Indeed I have. I can hardly stop myself from laughing out loud. I am the *living* proof of what is left of my life – I have no other documentation.

My honesty and genuine answers convince them that I am quite a case; they've never seen anyone like me before. Most people fiddle with falsified papers to prove they need this certificate to *stay alive*; here I am alive and kicking, unconcerned about proof because my state of nothingness says it all.

Within fifteen minutes I am outside; the birth is cathartic but fast. "I am unable to exist" is stamped as a living proof on my "certificate of incompetence." It is an accomplishment that deserves a feast! I had nothing and gained everything with this title. *Abundance* was my word of the day.

I leave the building and skip down the street. In Amsterdam this might be a normal sight but certainly some people thought my certificate only needed to be stamped "crazy." To me this is my ticket for my lawyer to take my case and I can go to Syb. Again the Universe was ever supporting me as long I followed the voice of my Soul.

The time that follows is very difficult though. I have no real place to stay except to live with friends who work during the day. I feel very lonely and don't belong anywhere. During the day, I walk through the city and wander aimlessly through the streets.

I want my friends to understand the love I feel for Syb, but everyone asks the same questions, "Why him? What's so different from Josh?" They are looking for FACTS not feelings and so I have no answers for them.

However, I need support to stay on course. *How long will my trial period be?* Syb wants me to have some time "in between." This makes sense from a logical point of view - it's best not to jump from one life to another. However, this *nowhere land* offers me nothing but questions I can't answer.

I almost call Syb's parents and ask if we can meet. I want to talk with someone who knows how great Syb is.

Soul says, "No, not now. Later." I listen and bite my tongue.

I tread water, barely keeping my head above it. Syb sends money and I have a hard time accepting it. I feel ashamed to be dependent on him. Strangely enough it never occurs to me to take advantage of my *certificate of incompetence*. I completely forget that everything I need is for free. I can sleep in a shelter, receive free meals. The word FREE applies to everything. My world is at my feet. The Universe gave its ALL to me. Abundance was gained from having nothing.

Living a "life without money" is hard to explain to others who have it. Sometimes I phone Syb. I am always supplied with phone booths that are "out of order." When I use them, they always work with no need for money. To my great joy, I can talk for free to keep my love alive. Syb doesn't like my new approach to life. "It's not right," he says. *What is right at this time of my life for me?*

I am at a loss for words. *How can I respond to such principle-based judgment?* I feel sad. I miss Josh's unconditional acceptance of my odd behaviors. I wonder if Syb will be so open to my "other" sides. Perhaps it was my time to grow up and leave my little child behind. I count the days until my departure.

Finally the day arrives. I fly to Taiwan on June 16. My friends accompany me to Schiphol Airport. I am overjoyed to have their love around me. They may not understand where and why I am going but they have come to support me no matter what, even if I am back in a week. I am aware of their concern that things might not work out exactly as I have 'in mind.'

By now I am used to their well meant advice.

Thankfully, Soul never wavers her steady voice. "Go," she says. She sticks with her simple heartfelt message and I rely on her.

I hold onto my heart when the plane takes off. The Chinese people in the plane chatter non-stop. I wave ferociously until my nerves and Amsterdam disappear.

What will the future bring?

When things are closing around you
and you don't know what to do
and you need someone to give you
some other point of view,
and what you fear the most right now
are the things your friends might say,
does someone have the answers to
help you on your way?

—Susan Diamond Lethbridge,
A Kid Out There Today

Following My Heart Song

If I thought my stay in Singapore had "prepared" me for my "new Asian life" in Taiwan, I had another guess coming. The two countries are like night and day.

For my first month in Taiwan, I am lonely. I can't figure out the Chinese people with their continual smile. Connecting with the Chinese is difficult for me. I don't know how to do it and ask myself *is it them or me*? Emotions are never displayed, not even in moments of great pain or great joy.

The country's well known sign of humor is to giggle with their hand in front of their mouth. Even that does not express what they truly feel. My first days in Taiwan are the opposite of the warm welcome I remember in America. This land of Taiwan feels so different and so cold. It takes me longer to adjust here.

After a year in Singapore, I was spoiled by the luxurious lifestyle of an expatriate. The living standard of the whole country breathed wealth. I truly enjoyed my life every minute with heart and Soul; however, I never perceived it as "real." We lived in an artificial bubble, very beautiful and very fancy. That was the way in Singapore.

In Taipei everything is really *real*: the Chinese language, the street signs and the native people. Above all, my feelings are very real, too. I feel gigantic in every sense—too big feelings, too big emotion, too big body and just too much of everything.

In the beginning when Syb leaves for work, he wonders what my daily life will be like. I assure him, I will be busy enough. I have a lot to think about; my marriage and my life in Singapore are over. *Where am I now and how do I go from here?* Brothers Grief and Guilt lean heavily on my shoulders. I want to take time to digest the impact of my leap. I need to let the dust settle to see where I've landed.

It becomes clear to me I have to grieve Josh's pain. I know he will run from it and replace me with someone new too quickly. Little did I know

Josh's wife-to-be was already having sleepovers in my home while I was with Syb in Taipei the first time. I found this out years later and Josh's rule of *no tell* made much more sense to me.

I visualize myself absorbing his and my emotions in order to transform them into a future that serves us both. I have to sit with it and take in the old and new.

Syb has no idea how turbulent my inner world is. It has a deafening roar. I carry the sadness of letting it go alone. *How can I share my pain with the man who has opened his heart and home to me?* I face the consequences of my deed alone.

Amazingly enough life makes it easy for me; there is absolutely nothing to distract me from facing my inner world. For hours I am able to sit in undisturbed silence. I don't have to rearrange the furniture in this new home; only my inner house needs cleaning.

I own nothing and this is now quite familiar to me. Perhaps starting over is easier with just memories without material things weighing us down from the past.

Every day I sit on the window seat and stare out over the park below. I let my life pass by and rewind certain passages a million times. I recall Josh's sincere offer to promise me the stars. I remember my determined decline. Nevertheless I believe that, if he had them, he would have given them to me, not one, all of them.

Why does the ground shake so badly when giving up the old? I am slowly being birthed but not quite yet. I am in need of a shoulder to cry on. I wish I could climb a ladder and reach one of the stars and dance on it, but first I have to free my pain. I sit in it and let my tears come out.

What kept me in Soul's spell was her consistent message, "You can still love and leave but GO." I was steadfast in listening to her counsel and I went. It certainly was a challenge to let the turbulent wind blow in my sails. The shallow waters where my boat was moored in Singapore had been calm. The current underneath sucked me out of the harbor and moved me into the deepest waters of the ocean. My Soul was my only traveling companion and my navigator. I had no choice but to ride the high waves for a time and lose sight of the shore. In this journey I was alone because it was my journey. It was for me and me alone to get to the other side. My companion was Soul. We arrived together. And here I am.

The river below our apartment is dying in front of my eyes. The people of our complex use the river as the moving dump that slowly takes everyone's junk out of sight. Without remorse the Chinese throw their stuff in the once-unpolluted waters. My heart cringes every time I watch someone empty their trash bags over the railing of the bridge. I knock on our window and warn them; my attempt is useless. They always wave back at me and smile. After a few tries, I just let it be; they don't need my "encouragement."

It doesn't take long for me to feel my restless nature rise. I have dumped enough of "my stuff" in the river and day by day I begin to feel cleaner, clearer, freer, lighter. I want to leave the apartment and explore my surroundings. Desire starts to itch; my senses need stimulation with more than the window view. The sitting séances of sadness have become too long, too boring and too dull. I want to feel the heartbeat of Taipei. My energy needs movement forward. Most of my tears are gone. I am ready for some *excitement*.

I find my way around the city in a taxi at first. The taxi drivers race like madmen through the crowded streets. My survival strategy is to hold onto the handle of the car door. I fool myself by the thought that I can always jump out if it gets too crazy.

In my pocket, I carry little notes with addresses scribbled in Chinese. I have many notes and, if I am not careful, I hand the driver the wrong note that brings me to a destination different from the one I have in mind. On the back of most of the notes, I've written the English translation.

When in a hurry, it happens more than once that I arrive downtown instead of on the other side of the mountain. All I had to think about was to keep my notes organized. *Why was that so hard*?

After a while I don't want to depend on taxi drivers anymore and I take our silver bird to town. All the street names are printed in Chinese characters. To me, every street, person and shop looks exactly alike.

Nobody speaks a word of English and everybody nods and answers yes when I ask a question. When I want to know if I need to take a left, the answer is a definite, "Yes, go left." If I repeat my question to the next person and ask them if I should go right, the result is, "Yes, go right." The word "no" doesn't exist here.

After some practice in the neighborhood, I start to enjoy my small trips. With "great skill" I cruise through the streets in our Tienmou area. These are narrow streets filled with bamboo houses and little shops. Clothes are cheap here and sales are everywhere.

When I get the hang of it, I want to go farther. I ask Syb how to get home from the BIG city.

"Go as far north as the road takes you," is his good advice.

Tienmou is a tiny sleepy village at the foot of the mountain. When I reach our complex, I realize Syb is right; going further north than this is dangerous. A bushy jungle with poisonous snakes and monkeys dangling in the trees await you in the backyard. The "Dead End" sign speaks for itself. This time I don't dare go farther. I do as I am told and I go as far as the road north leads me. After a while, I can drive home with my eyes closed.

Syb has no empathy for my fear of getting lost. He is born with a navigation system that never fails; for me it is a skill I have to learn. I am insecure in the traffic and totally rely on the sharply pointed needle on my dashboard. My car compass is my reliable companion to guide me home.

I start my Chinese lessons even though I can now tour around without getting lost. I want to follow Syb's example and taste a bit more of the culture. After a year of lessons, he talks Chinese with confidence; if you didn't know the language and only heard him speak, you'd think he is a native. His use of words and grammar might mean something completely different to the Chinese but luckily they never show their thoughts; their friendly nods make you think they are absolutely in agreement. My confidence in communicating will never reach Syb's level.

I have two delightful teachers who bend like bamboo trees every time I ring the bell of their home. Our welcoming ritual takes fifteen minutes or more. To them, I am from another planet and that fascinates them more than anything else in the world. A blond girl in Taipei is not their regular student profile. I love going to my early morning classes, mostly because I feel their heartfelt and genuine passion to learn more about me. We laugh a lot and, after a while, I discover that their interest in me and the western culture is bigger than in their interest in teaching me Chinese. I learn enough and, eventually, I get rid of my notes and navigate my way through town.

My teachers become the dearest people at my wedding, except for Sandra, my Dutch girlfriend who becomes my teacher, too.

Sandra and I meet at a dinner party; at very first glance we connect. Her knowledge of Buddhism radiates like a golden aura around her; I am thirsty to drink in all her wisdom. Like a hummingbird I flutter around her sweet Buddhist energy. We are Soul mates from long ago.

Sandra works during the day and the easiest way for us to get together is to go for lunch within the beating heart of Taipei. As soon as the wedding date of July 7 is agreed upon by the various readers and astrologers I consult, we use our lunch dates to prepare the 'Chinese bride'.

Why did we ever choose to do our wedding the Chinese way? I learn later it isn't gonna be the easiest day of my life.

I am sure I wouldn't have survived the endless evening dinner at my own wedding if Sandra and my teachers weren't there. Our wedding is Chinese style from beginning to end. From a photo session in front of the *Chiang Kai-shek Memorial Hall* to the ceremonial dinner, the focus is 100% on the *groom*. As the bride, I am to wait, invisible and ignored. The most important day of my life is the strangest. Invisibility is not a skill I am good at. It's too bad I wasn't told what was in store. The "subservient" gene wasn't passed down in my Dutch family line.

According to the Chinese tradition, people only congratulate the groom; the bride is his extension. My attempts to shake people's hands at first go unrewarded. Soon enough I realize I am to stay in the background and look beautiful and I accept that this day is a little different than I thought.

I feel immeasurably lonely; the nausea from my pregnancy isn't helping either. Nobody can see what is going on inside me. My smile is bright; my heart is filled with joy. I keep looking at Syb and fantasize about running away with him to Paradise Island. The day grows long and the end is not in sight.

Out of nowhere, my two wonderful teachers appear in front of me. Giggling and happy, they take me aside. They say nothing but tug on my sleeve and usher me with their eyes to go with them. We are on a secret mission.

Their joy is as big as mine. They take me to another room in the hotel. In Chinese, they ask me to close my eyes. When I do, they place a beautifully-wrapped silk box in my open hands. Inside is a golden necklace. I gasp. Their gift is so beautiful and chosen with so much care. Their excitement is what makes my day. These two women give me what I longed for. My heart is full and now I can handle the friendly, drunken men at the dinner table. For ten years, this necklace never leaves my neck.

We receive many red envelopes with lots of money. All Syb's friends and colleagues admire him; he is deeply loved and that shows in the amount of money inside each envelope. The person who keeps track of the gifts is overjoyed. "We did really well" he says as he reviews the 'take' according to Chinese standards. My necklace is worth more than money can buy.

Finding Buddha

We named her Buddha. How could she be called anything else? She was the golden thread in our life. Her death faced me with the loss of her unlimited downpour of unconditional love. From the moment she arrived until the day she died, her wagging tail was our daily reminder of good karma and blessings in our life together. On this day her life with us was about to begin.

I don't know why we drove up the dirt road of the Yan Ming Shan Mountain. What I do know is that we are in tune with Buddha's call. Indeed she was expecting us at the right time at the right place.

After our morning fruit smoothies, we get on the road. Most Sundays, we take a tour on Syb's "off the road" bike. This day was no different. The bike served his name for it well; definitely the purpose today was to go "off the road."

My five-months-pregnant belly is still small enough to sit "comfortably" on the back of the motorbike. Syb likes the feel of his child kicking behind his back. I am happy to wrap my arms around Syb and relax while we race over the mountain roads. No fear, just fun, we have no fixed plan; we will go with the flow and meet what is on our path today.

It is windy and hot yet worse weather is predicted for the next few days. On this day, we want to grab our chance to be outside as long as possible.

The storm that is coming may bring a lot of rain and keep us homebound for quite a while. When we drive into the lush mountains, we pass small rural villages. People sit in squat positions alongside the road. It seems that everyone is busy selling their overcooked and colorful dishes to whoever comes by.

When we are halfway up the winding mountain road, the head of a little puppy peeks around the bushes. She glances at us with her funny dark-colored eye and runs off. It feels as if she is teasing us and inviting us to follow. *Who is she and what is she doing so far from the village?* In an instant, we both think the same thing: she is an orphan and perhaps we should take her home with us. We pass her by in a flash because the motorbike goes fast. We stop and both voice the same thing: *Was the sight of this puppy a sign we should have a dog?* We feel that it might be.

The road we climb is challenging and steep. The deeper we follow the road into the forest, the darker green it gets. I am afraid of the screams of the monkeys making courageous jumps above our heads. I fear that lots of snakes crawl in every bush. Syb reassures me that all is fine, which I believe until we come to a "dead end." I am exhausted and dehydrated and I am sure it's time to head back. I am not feeling that great anymore.

The problem is we can only drive back the way we came. It took us *hours* and I do not look forward to the drive. Our other option is we go straight down through the forest. I do not look forward to this ride either.

We can see a very old trail with hundreds of steps, a natural staircase which most PROBABLY leads down the mountain. OR *is this only our wishful thinking?*

I can't imagine climbing up again if that unpaved, never-used road leads to nowhere. But *what is our choice?* We decide to go down the path of a *hundred-steps-of-stairs*. I wonder if Syb remembers I am not just one person now but two. It seems like it takes forever as we bump full force down these ancient steps.

I think Syb mastered motor biking in a past life. Flawlessly, he makes steep turns and jumps over unmarked bumps. This path may have been an ancient smugglers' route in the times of the Chinese opposition. However, this path is certainly not used normally to transport pregnant women down the hill. It's a monkey's paradise and road of no return.

I keep my eyes closed as if it will help me ignore the loud animal warnings as we invade their kingdom after eons of peace and seclusion. I picture my baby-to-be, Florian, holding on tight although he is really in his "water bed." After this adventure, he must be a winner for life. Finally, the end of the road comes in sight; it's not the end of our journey quite yet.

Down the mountain, the forest stairs ends in a road and, as if we smell home, Syb races down the spacious empty lane. He goes full speed toward

Tienmou when a car suddenly appears too close from the right. In a split second, we are both flying in the air and land on the asphalt road. In a bit of a shock, I stand up and look at my belly.

I am shaking and so is Syb. We look at each other; we are both okay. The guy from the car comes toward us to shake hands. We "talk" Chinese with our hands and feet; the guy giggles and says, "Yeah, yeah. Accident. Bad, very bad." We all nod in agreement. The bike has a dent and the car has a dent and off we go.

This is the typical Taiwanese way to handle a situation like this. Rules are optional and speed limits are optional above all. Accidents are part of the daily scene. We decide to go eat ice cream at Baskin & Robbins. We are covered with dirt and dust and, by the time we enter the ice cream store, the accident is long forgotten, NOT the dog.

The next day we drive up on the mountain road and look for the place where we last saw "our dog." We want her now but she is not there. There is no sign of her. At exactly the same spot where she stood yesterday, we notice a dark red Buddha statue completely covered with plants.

How come we didn't see the statue yesterday? Slowly it dawns on us that we will find our dog; there is an orphan waiting for us and her name must be Buddha. Now that we had the name, how do we find the dog? We keep looking for her but return home empty-handed. We are filled with trust that our paths will cross.

That night while we are gazing at the stars on the deck terrace of our penthouse, we send her an invitation, "Buddha, you are welcome! Just show us where you are."

Sooner than later, she accepts.

A few days later, a tornado makes her appearance. Everyone is warned to take precautions and I am glad my mom arrives just before the storm hits. We listen to the news and follow the instructions. I have to seal the windows with tape. The bath tub is filled with water in case the water supply is shut off. After securing our home, we leave in the car and go in search for our dog. My mom urges us to go; she knows full well that we will not rest until we do so. She is in concert with our intention to find Buddha before the storm arrives. I must have inherited a love for adventure from my mom. We drive down the winding mountain road while the storm picks up speed. The car can barely stay on course and sways from left to right. We have no fear; we know our little journey will be worth it. When we arrive at the Buddha statue, we discover there is a road running underneath and parallel to ours. On it there is a fire station.

As we pass the fire station, a puppy pokes her head out from one of the big wheels of the fire truck. My heart misses a beat when I see her eyes. The wind blows her almost off her feet.

When we get closer, we see more of these little dogs hidden under the huge wheels of the bright red truck. Because it is very dark and we are parked in a place that is not visible from the station office, the firefighter who comes out doesn't see us. He yells and scolds the little dogs and kicks one that walks too close to him sending it in the air. Apparently, these cute puppies are not welcome in this place. We wait until the man disappears and watch the scene a little longer from a distance.

"If she comes out again," says Syb, "I'll grab her and we'll take her home." There are a lot of orphans that need rescuing but we can only take one. With that said, she pokes out her head with the one black-spotted eye. She peeks around the wheel of the truck and stares at us for a moment. "Take me" is her message. We have no doubt that this white dog is our "Buddha."

Syb gets out the car and walks toward her. While I write this, I still can't believe she didn't run away. For the next fourteen years that she is a part of our family, she was the shyest, most scared dog I have ever known. As if she knows that Syb loves her instantly, she looks at him and allows him to scoop her up in his arms.

She is shaking a little; she probably was never touched by a human other than being kicked. A moment later, she is in my lap. We drive straight to the vet but he is closed. Everything is closed on "tornado night." It is a strange sight because normally the many food stalls make the evening scene colorful and alive; tonight not a single soul is outside. We hurry back home.

At home we put her in the sink. Hardy and Hiker, our cats, gather around the sink to inspect our new house guest. It must be quite a shock for them to watch Buddha's color change from dirty black to white. The cats are going to teach her how to behave; as soon as Buddha is ready to get up and play, she adopts a cat-like manner.

In no time Buddha learns to be as playful as the others. How divinely her arrival was timed is clear. The first night she cries and cries for her brothers and sisters.

My mom is not only an experienced mother of five, she has rescued dozens of orphaned animals. She takes little Buddha into bed with her. Buddha loves hearing the beat of my mother's heart and, just minutes later, she is fast asleep. How deep her gratitude is can never be measured. For all of her life, Buddha treats my mom as her guardian angel.

When Buddha's life comes to an abrupt end after fourteen years, my heart is broken. So deep is the pain in my Soul; I have never experienced a deeper loss in my life. A part of me goes with her.

Buddha's life is a tribute to unconditional love and unwavering acceptance of change. For fourteen years, she accompanies us through every moment of turmoil and expansion. She never wavers in her love. In her heart, she makes a place for five children and the many animals that come and go. In every family photo we take from the moment she arrives, there is a white tail or other body part of Buddha.

In her last days, she is in great pain; her kidneys are failing and I am desperate. I want to relieve her suffering. Syb her savior is not home; he is in South Africa. She hangs on until the Monday morning he arrives back home. The night before, all of the animals - Zoë, Tiger and Simba - form a protective circle around her.

Syb brings her to the vet the following morning; perhaps there is still something they can do. We get a call a few hours later. We need to come right away.

Buddha is already in transition when we arrive. My heart breaks as I hold her in my arms. She shakes fervently; it is her time. We are thankful from the bottom of our hearts for all she gave.

With that she goes to the light. We close her eyes and wrap her in a childhood blanket. The once-dark circle around her eye has turned grey, she is indeed very old.

.

We have her cremated. We receive a beautiful black Chinese urn with her ashes delivered on our doorstep.

Who arranged that so perfectly?

Dear Buddha, we behold you forever as the love that you are . . . please lead us the way.

Baby Steps

Stepping into motherhood – experiencing the ultimate lesson in how to lose myself and find myself at the same time – was the road I was on. Each child revealed more of me.

To be 'used' to the fullest, having lived life to the max, *isn't that the ultimate goal to strive for by the time we reach the end of the ride? Don't we all want to look back in awe and acknowledge our greatness. Isn't it better to express our God-given talents in all that we are and take a chance than live a mediocre life by playing it small?* I knew my self so well.

How arduous was this road to travel? When I became a mother, my journey to grow into a greater version of myself as a woman began. I birthed my first son and my new other self in one BIG breath. My life changed in that subtle moment. Suddenly it wasn't all about ME anymore; I came last. Without preparation, I was rebirthed and welcomed into my brand new world of motherhood without a slap on the rump: sleepless nights, breast infections, and underwear up to my waist. One cliché followed the other and I soon discovered all were true.

My child was my world now and he consumed all of me with utter joy. The umbilical cord of oneness was strongly tied from his heart to mine and, within that bond, I lost myself. I felt used, used up; my sense of Self was gone. *Who was I now?*

For a while, Soul let me do it 'my way'. When she had enough of ME, she stood up and then took care of me. She showed me that to be 'used up' was only to be done *spiritually*. I needed to *mother* my divine essence from the inside out by nourishing my God-given talents as a mother AND a woman as well as a professional. Finally, I listened. I was in for an amazing ride.

Florian

The earthquake begins when Syb is in his office. I am half asleep with

Florian in my arms. My heart stands still when the floor shakes and the glass window breaks. The nurses run around and scream. It's like all hell is breaking loose. Then there is a deadly silence. My whole body trembles.

The world is upside down for one long minute. My life is changed in this one moment of total fear. My belief of 'it's *all about* ME' is shattered in pieces like the window.

Suddenly to be a new mom overwhelms me. From now on, everything will be all about my children. I firmly believe that as a mother I have to save my children *no matter what.* This enormous responsibility now falls around my shoulders like a heavy, hot wrap. I wake up to a new world of motherhood. I am in shock as to what just happened. The room is a mess as I put my child to my breast. My mother instincts are intact but still I tremble.

January 12th—it is almost midnight.

"I am still waiting; no sign of labor yet."

My mom laughs when she hears me talk. Both my mom and my dad are in Spain and Syb and I are in Taiwan; the distance is bridged easily on this lonely night. "Remember Saskia, it's your first and you have all the time in the world." She tries to ease my nerves by reminding me that my due date is January 13th. "It would be quite exceptional to have your first one right on the due date." I guess she is right and hang up.

My mind wanders back to this morning. At the American fitness club I was asked if I wanted to be interviewed tomorrow as "the most committed and fit person of the month." I said *yes* and, with that said, the pedals of the Staircase exercise machine I was on landed with a big bang on the floor. The machine was broken and this stops my exercising right away. To me this was a sign that enough was enough. The Universe was saying that my body didn't need any more 'fitness' right now. However, I made a commitment so I know I will come back tomorrow for the interview. Tonight however, I don't care about tomorrow; I am impatient—I want my child NOW. I am bored with waiting and, this particular night, Syb is partying at a business dinner; he will be home late.

I massage the reflex point on my feet to hasten birth. At least I am actively participating in getting things started. I don't know what to expect. I have a conversation with my unborn child and ask if he or she is willing to come tonight. I shiver because my big belly can't keep me warm.

It is very cold in our house because we have no heating system. We have a little stove but very little heat escapes because our three cats and a dog are cuddled up in front of it.

I look outside and watch the river in its never-ending motion. I can see the Chinese men poking around their small fires in the park, the smell of ginger and pork is faint but enough to make me hungry again. I want Syb to come home.

The moment Syb opens the door I get up. I am ready to go to bed. It is late and I am tired of waiting for both Syb and my child. I walk toward the bedroom and labor starts.

"Syb, the baby is coming," I announce happily and we both stare at the stack of videos that are waiting for this moment. The gynecologists advised us to rent five videos in order to 'kill time.' Our stack of videos mean we are 'well prepared' for our baby's arrival.

In addition to the instruction regarding a video, Syb learned in class how to wash a plastic baby doll. It was quite an 'intensive training' and we know we are fully prepared and up to the task. We passed the test: we rented the videos and the 'baby doll wash class' was a blast.

To offer education and practice in breathing during birth or information about the different stages of labor was never heard of. I'm so glad Syb knows how to wash and hold a plastic baby doll. That will bring him far in life as a parent.

The contractions start as soon as we turn on the TV. They come every five minutes and the movie is hard to watch.

I do my best but the attempt is useless.

"At least we can do two movies," is Syb's optimistic approach. According to him, we still have lots of time; I am feeling not so sure about this. He is tired from being at the party and would rather go to bed instead of pretending to watch a movie and clock the contractions of his wife.

Suddenly I see the ridiculousness of the situation.

What are we doing? I ask myself. *Why are we watching a video?* I am having a baby! "We'd better leave, Syb. It will take us an hour to get to the city."

Syb feeds Buddha and I chase the three sleeping cats out of the baby's bed. No cats are allowed in this basket from this moment on. I get into the car but I can't sit; the contractions are too strong. I want to move my body—*how can I turn and twist inside this small car.* "Syb, please, drive fast . . ." is all I can say. Syb likes to hear that and fearlessly pushes down on the pedal. I can't picture myself giving birth in this car. We race down the bumpy road of 'Chang Chia bei Lu.' The many red traffic lights are ignored; I am happy to know they are optional here anyway. Syb feels carefree; the previous party hours have loosened him up. I am in labor and still have some loosening up to do.

Syb drives fast but we get lost in the downtown area; in the dark, every street looks the same. The Chinese street names don't give much direction either. The downtown is busy with lots of food stalls open at the peak business hour of midnight; no one cares to help us find the Chinese hospital.

Their habit of saying *yes* to everything is hard to work with tonight. I'd rather hear a clear no and clearly know they don't know the way instead of following instructions based upon a big guess of where the hospital might be. We follow some and are more lost; it is late. I switch to the back seat and sit up upside down; I am more uncomfortable than I can stand.

Syb turns left and we both sigh as the contours of the hospital are in sight. We recognize the guy on the corner who sells pork chops. Apparently his business is open 24/7. We park in front of the hospital and Syb helps me out. A Chinese nurse looks at me while I am panting and in the middle of a contraction. She says, "Hospital full, no stay." We must look like Mary and Joseph.

I ignore her comment and sit down. *What was that again she was telling us in her best English?* I can hardly talk because the next wave washes over me. I mumble, "I am getting baby NOW."

She tries to communicate her authority again, "Full hospital, no bed for you." It is 3:00 AM and it's my due date: January 13th.

Another nurse comes along and looks at me. She points at a stretcher behind a curtain of the emergency room. "Lie down," is all she says. I climb on the stretcher and wonder what will happen next.

Syb stays by my side after parking the car. It takes the nurses awhile to figure out what to do with me. Even though I visited this hospital every couple of weeks for the last seven months, they can't find my name; it is easier to send me away at this mighty hour.

Finally, the third nurse asks me to get up and go to the basement for an interview. I can hardly walk but I follow her. I am in a daze and do as I'm told.

Downstairs, I hold my belly and wait. My files are lost; this is not a huge surprise. Chinese hospitals are Chinese and that says it all. However, I know that Chinese women have babies here and, I figure, if they can, I can, too. A Philippine doctor asks me a thousand questions; *what is there to know?* His expert opinion is that I am 'getting a baby' and I suppose he is right. So, *what are we waiting for?* He makes a gesture, "You go up" and Syb and I just nod yes. We are like two docile sheep following directions without protest. A nurse waits for me at the elevator and takes me to the sixth floor.

Indeed the hospital is full, I think, when the nurse opens the door to 'my room.' To my surprise, three of the four beds are taken and five family members are sleeping on the floor. Only one sleeps on top of the flat table in the middle of the room. Heavy breathing worse than mine fills the damp room. It smells like blood everywhere.

Wailing women are on one side and another man wails at the other. No one seems disturbed when I enter; they are too sick to notice. In this hospital, family and friends are the caretakers and there are a lot of them in 'my' room.

My head is spinning; I need someone to support me in this process other than Syb. His alcohol level needs some time to catch up with the fast-paced process of this birth.

I have no idea about breathing or what position to take. What position can soothe my body and my mind? I look around but think I had better close my eyes.

The nurse takes me to the most disgusting, dirty bathroom with poop and blood on the floor. "You need a shave and an enema," she says. I disregard the disgusting bathroom and let her do her work. She leaves and Syb and I are left alone with our sick roommates. I am glad they are not paying attention to me; I am very uncomfortable and I wish I knew what to do. I want to pace up and down but the people lying on the floor cancel out this plan.

Two hours later, another nurse comes in and checks me out. She only speaks Chinese and, without my understanding anything, she leaves. Syb goes to lock the car and bring his camera. I stand there holding my protruding belly. *Is this what giving birth is like?*

The people in the room who are moaning distract me; nobody attends to them. Their family members are all fast asleep. The door opens and a nurse comes in to take me downstairs. This time, I can stay on the bed. It rolls easily to the elevator that brings me to the basement; this must be the delivery department.

I meet Syb in the hallway with camera and video gear strapped around his neck. He takes my hand and holds it until we reach the basement. The nurse rolls the bed against a wall and then she leaves; there is silence all around us. *Where is everybody? What do I do now?* I am not so confident anymore and wish for guidance in how to proceed. The contractions come and go within seconds instead of minutes. *Why has she parked my bed along this wall?*

No doctor is in sight. I wonder if they know how far dilated I am. I can feel the baby dropping down; the pressure is hard to resist. Syb keeps reassuring me I am doing fine and I have all the time in the world. I know I don't.

Suddenly, another nurse comes in and moves me into a room where patients recover after their operations. Again family members are here to help but they have to wait outside. I am so uncomfortable; I can feel my baby coming but I can't allow it. I sit on my leg and push the baby's head up into my belly. Never in my life will I push UP again; with my first child, it's the only way to go. Nobody is there to help me and I really need assistance. The ob/gyn told me over and over never to push if no one was there. He said I could rip open and die. I am not looking forward to that. So I push UP instead of down.

For one divine moment, I sit and pull my legs up; due to this odd movement, an old lady in the hall peeks between my legs. "This woman is getting a baby," she shrieks and stands up from her chair. She runs to find a doctor. Just as this happens, Syb says he needs a cup of coffee. I can't believe what he just said. "No, don't leave me here, don't go!" I beg him to stay. Again I push up not down; it hurts a lot to go against the flow.

The old woman must have been an angel placed to save me because her tone of urgency sets something in motion; within seconds invisible hands roll me into the delivery room. It is dark and everything feels cold and metallic as the nurse straps me onto the small iron table.

My legs are in stirrups. I can't move yet I am afraid I will roll off the table. This table is made for Chinese dolls not for big Dutch girls. Again I am alone after she leaves me. Syb is taken to another room to change his clothes.

I look around. My contractions are gone and I feel very peaceful but confused about what to do next. I hear a loud baby cry. I look between my legs . . . *is that mine?* All the doors are closed and I can't see much.

Dr. Chen steps in and suddenly all is well. I am saved. My favorite doctor with his big round face looks at me with questioning eyes. He thinks I am doing this too fast since this baby is my first. He checks to see how far dilated I am. "You can push," he speaks the magic words, but they are spoken far too late. I have pushed my baby up and tucked him tightly back into the womb. I have no push contractions; my belly has come to rest. Everyone stares at me including Syb.

"You go and push," says Dr. Chen again. I wish he knew he is hours too late with his encouraging words.

I take a breath as if I have a push contraction but there is nothing. I pretend that I feel another one and I reach deep within. With all my power, I connect my body, mind and spirit to this baby's soul. Now everything feels easy and effortless. Whoosh! Florian is born into the world with one beautiful movement.

A moment later, Dr. Chen holds Florian like a trophy in the air. "You have birthed a SON," he says with pride. For the Chinese, it is far better to birth a boy than a girl.

Syb will be celebrated for his *yang* potential. Dr Chen is very happy at this auspicious moment as if he played a major role in creating the gender of our child. He smiles at Syb and shows his thumb. Good work!

I feel as if I am not of this world as I hold my newborn Florian in my arms. "You are *so* beautiful," are the first words I say to him after birth; we have had many conversations before. Before I know it, they take Florian away and roll me out of the room. Again my stretcher is pushed against the wall. Only fifteen minutes have passed since I was in the same spot. The old lady who saved me is fast asleep on the floor.

The nurse hands me a phone and I dial the same number as hours before. "Hi, it's me again. Your first grandchild, Florian, is born," I announce happily. In Spain, my parents uncork another bottle of red wine. Syb and I are overjoyed. A nurse rolls my bed into the elevator. I go back the same way I came.

As a new mom, I am entitled to a room by myself. They move my bed into my new room and leave without saying a word. *What do I do next?* My adrenaline is high and I am very thirsty. Nobody is there to help; I assume a shower is what is best. I am a bit wobbly on my feet but I can manage to stand still. The shower feels good.

I am back in bed when Syb comes in and I ask him where our son has gone; two hours have passed and he has no idea where the nurses took Florian.

I am glad I saw them put a name tag around his ankle; in this hospital, I would not be surprised to find another baby in my arms. *Chinese hospitals . . .*

We wait a few hours before we are rewarded with the sight of our son.

A glass trolley with a sleeping baby is rolled into my room just at the moment I am dozing off. The sound of Chinese voices wake me and a glorious baby Florian enters the room. He looks like a baby prince surrounded by his three nurses. They park his royal trolley next to my bed.

A nurse hands me a bottle and I decline it; I tell her I wish to breastfeed my baby. She tells me I am stupid and I will get an infection. I don't understand her resistance to this idea. I saw my mom feed all of my brothers and my sister this way. However, that was in Holland; in Asia, breastfeeding is considered an option only for the poor. That means every woman in Asia will feed by the bottle. When I ask her how to feed by breast, she shrugs her shoulders and walks away repeating what she said before: I will get a breast infection. On her way out, I ask hesitantly, "Can I take my baby in my arms?"

"Sure. You can do whatever you like; he is yours," she says. With that the green light goes on. I pick up Florian and put him to my chest. His big blue eyes are wide open and he looks adorable.

After that, Florian never leaves my side. The crib is pushed into a far corner and Florian resides permanently in my arms. At night, he lies at my side and usually stares at me, trying to keep his eyes open as long as he can.

I feel he has been away from the earthly realms for a long time and now he is back as the first Röell born to Syb and me. We are very honored by the gift of him. I wonder why he chose us. *What is he willing to learn from us; what will we learn from him?* Long ago, our mutual agreement was made and I am so happy to have him in my arms.

I feed him every two hours and my nipples are sore and broken; I am determined to continue in spite of the Chinese way. It is hard to figure out the best way to breastfeed; I am an inexperienced mother. Syb brings books and we study the different positions as how to breastfeed; it seems like quite a skill.

While in the hospital, I develop the predicted infection. *How could I not?* Syb takes care of me; he follows the Chinese habit. During his lunch break, he rushes back and forth from the office to bring me food. At night he moves his bed next to mine. In this hospital, the family feeds and cares for the patient.

There are robot-like men who bring us food once a day. They sleep in the staircase outside the hospital. I am always shocked when I see mine walk in the door; his mouth is drooling and he looks as if he is in a trance or heavily sedated. His step is very slow; he walks foot by foot. His shuffle gets familiar after a while and I can hear him coming from a mile away.

The food is cold when it reaches my lap but I feel sorry for him; I hardly touch my food. In that way, he can eat mine just like he eats everybody else's.

We leave the hospital after four days.

We not only carry our child out the door; it takes three trips to load all our household items back in the car. Every day, Syb brought more things to entertain mother and child and, by the fourth day, we had accumulated quite a load. I hold Florian in my lap as we drive home.

The experience of going home is the opposite of going to the hospital. We obediently stop at every red light and we are annoyed by the Chinese drivers who appear suicidal in their refusal to stop. We are new parents; we feel our responsibility noticeably from the start.

In Tienmou, we see five Buddhist monks dressed in beautiful orange robes. We park the car and, instead of walking upstairs to our apartment, we walk toward the monks. The oldest monk stretches out his arms when he sees us coming. One by one, they hold Florian and he is blessed by each one.

After two weeks, we take a drive back to the hospital. We have a child who NEVER cries and we are not sure if that is okay. I am confused as a new mom because EVERY book I have read talks about babies crying; mine does not.

In the hospital, they don't know what to tell us. They weigh him with a big wet diaper; he has gained a lot of weight. "He must be happy" is their diagnosis.

Florian sets the tone for all our babies who follow. It is only then, I realize how lucky we are to have babies who never cry. *Is that why we had five?*

Following Florian's birth, everything changes very quickly. Our lives begin to move faster than the river in front of our apartment. Within six weeks, Syb and I move back to Holland. Within a year and a half, I moved from two different continents, got a divorce, remarried, gave birth, and moved back to Holland again. Life is like a rollercoaster.

Sytske

To have more children was a calling I heard long ago but I also knew we had to wait with the next one until we found our new house.

For nine months, we 'camped' in eleven different houses since returning to Holland from Taiwan. After I clean up the last home, I am tired of our search for the perfect town to live in. It is a lot of work to leave each house spotless and it is time to make up our minds and choose a place to settle down. When we came back from Taiwan, we were new parents but our idea about our lifestyle hadn't changed considerably. We thought Amsterdam would be our best bet and, perhaps it was, if we were still a childless couple. When we stay in a friend's home in the middle of the city, I realize I want more space. I am fed up carefully maneuvering my stroller between the white poles called *Amsterdammertjes*. It drives me crazy to carry my baby, the stroller and my heavy bag of goods from shopping to the fourth floor three times a day.

One day, I mistakenly lock myself out when Florian, who is now eight months old, plays with my keys and is parked in his stroller behind the door INSIDE the house. I am locked out and he is locked in. This is NOT good for our future I conclude; we need a kid-friendly town if we want to have more children. Amsterdam is not the place.

We are babysitting Syb's sister's house in Bussum and all of a sudden realize *this* is the town where we want to live. After that decision, I find our new home simply on a morning walk with Florian in the stroller. I peek through the window of this one house that a neighbor mentions is for sale and I know this is it.

The first night we sleep in our new home, Sytske is conceived. I am sure she was waiting for that magic moment; she takes the idea of waiting to be in our new home quite literally. Her timing is divine.

.

It is July 21st. The sun is going down as we drive to Amsterdam. Little do I know I have only a few hours left to enjoy my big belly.

The birth card that will announce our new baby's name must be delivered to the printer *before* the baby is born; Syb and I are delighted to finish this precious task early. For the first time, we feel as if we are "in time." Anyway, that is what we think. Syb has sketched a drawing of our new house with a big stork in the front yard. The card shows where our home is located on a world map from a bird eye point of view. The Angels can see exactly where this little soul had landed. This was symbolic without us knowing it.

The Dutch tradition is to announce a baby's arrival by using the sign of a stork. The story goes that in ancient times storks delivered the baby to your doorstep. In keeping with tradition, Syb rented a wooden version that is as tall as the chimney of our house. When the baby is born, instead of calling all our friends, all we have to do is place this enormous stork outside and the message will be delivered before we even get back inside. Our baby's due date is July 27th and we have five days left to finish all the tasks on our 'to do' list. Since our first baby, Florian, was born on his due date, I am guessing this baby will do the same.

I am looking forward to experiencing birthing at home. In the last week, I have enjoyed every day as a gift; now I am slowly counting down until the final day. Syb does his share by preparing our new nest with endless hours of painting and redecorating. Tons of work awaits; our bedroom is first. It is painted pink; though we have no proof that the baby is a girl, I felt the color had to be pink. Our first attempt we hate; the room looks like a brothel. After the paint dries a day later, we rip off the wallpaper and the pink is gone. In our next attempt, we choose pink again but in a softer tone.

When we get back from Amsterdam, Syb stays up late. He wants to finish painting our bedroom door. I can't bear the smell. The door is on the hallway floor and bottles of paint are everywhere. I can easily break my neck in the dark if I am not careful to watch each step. It's a mess but we have lots of time to clean up. At 2:30 AM, Syb stops. His work isn't finished but he thinks there is always 'tomorrow'.

I wake up at 4:00 AM feeling slightly nauseated. I get up and walk to the bathroom and throw up. I don't feel good at all; I start shaking. I wonder if I am sick and I climb back into bed. *What if this is a sign of birth?* I look at the unfinished door; the paint is still wet. I don't want to wake up Syb; he is sleeping soundly. I don't have contractions and so I conclude I might have the stomach flu. I better follow Syb's example; I close my eyes and doze off.

I wake up half an hour later; I don't recognize the strange sensation I am having. I shiver. The midwife instructed me to call her at the first sign. She thinks the birth will be very fast because the first baby was born quickly. I wake up Syb, who looks at me with sleepy eyes. "I have contractions," I tell him.

"They will go away," he says with his familiar tone of expertise, "You'd better get some sleep." He turns over to the other side.

I roll over and wonder what to do. When the next contraction comes, I know I am in labor. Syb tries to persuade me to go to sleep, "It won't last, don't worry." His approach doesn't work for me. I get up. It is 5:15 AM and I make the call. Marianne, the midwife, arrives fifteen minutes later.

The night is peaceful and I feel confident with her there; she will guide me well in this birthing process. I am told that her innate wisdom and feminine intuition are akin to that of an ancient medicine woman. Syb makes her a cup of tea and she sits down.

The pink curtains in the bedroom are still drawn closed but I peek through them to view the backyard while they chat.

Soon the sun will be up. I hear the distinct chirping that announces a new day. It is still dark as I greet the day and change my regular pajamas into a pair of new pajamas I bought specially to wear during the birthing process.

I talk with Marianne and drink a sip of tea but I really want to move my body. The contractions come and go; still I have no pain. I swirl my hips in circles. I float into a trance-like state. Rhythmically I turn my hips around until Marianne asks me to lie down on the bed. She is curious to see how far dilated I am. Reluctantly I give in. I'd rather stay up and move around rather than lying down.

"You can push," she says. This is too soon I think. My first memory of birthing was a big ordeal, not in pain, but in being moved around. My 'Joseph and Mary memory' of Taipei is still fresh. Half an hour passes since Marianne arrived. The atmosphere is peaceful, silent and safe. It doesn't matter; I am not ready to birth. I look at my huge belly and ask myself how can I push this baby out? Right now, I cannot make the connection from my large belly to a baby being born. Something needs to shift in my mind.

Marianne goes downstairs and comes back with a wooden birthing chair. Gently she takes my hand and asks me to sit on the chair. "Is someone coming to assist us?" she asks, not showing her concern. Hours before, she experienced a home birth in which the umbilical cord broke off and splashed the room with blood.

"No, nobody is coming. Syb is here," I say. "The assistant nurse lives too far away."

I didn't know home births required two women. I am not aware of Marianne's concern about doing this alone.

I sit down and let go. The gravity is all my body needs. This time I know my breath is my power. Sweat seeps out of every cell; my body is drenched but my woman power is stronger than I have ever felt in my life. My breath becomes my anchor and instantly I feel my body's desire to bring my baby out into the outside world. I inhale and feel her, yes! I can now make the connection from my belly to my baby. In one push and a long exhale, I sing her into the world. Sytske Maria makes her entrance on earth at exactly 6:10 AM.

Her coming is announced with a sunrise behind the curtains. "It's a girl," says Marianne in a soft voice as she presses the most beautiful baby girl with dark curly hair and big blue eyes to my heart.

Syb goes downstairs to bury the umbilical cord under the big tree in our backyard. Tradition says it will bring her luck.

Hours later, mother, father and child bask in a pink glow. The sun shines abundantly through the pink curtains. It is July 22nd and an angel has arrived on planet Earth.

Eleven years later, Sytske shows me a page out of her diary:

"Once I wondered what an Angel looked like. I wondered where they live. My friends don't believe in Angels or any ghost stuff. I believe you can become an Angel when you die.

"I knew my great grandma was my guardian Angel but I still didn't know what an Angel looked like. Then one night, my mom walked into my bedroom and asked how I was doing.

"Then I suddenly realized I already knew what an Angel looked like. An Angel looks like my mom. My mom is an Angel because she always looks out for me. She is so special to me. When I grow up, I want to be an Angel just like her."

Funny, I think. When I 'grow up', I'd like to be an Angel just like *her*.

Shaffy

"Make sure you have all the tools we need for the home birth because your pregnancy will soon come to an end." I believe the midwife's words. I rush to the stores three weeks before my due date. I buy everything on the list and, as soon as I tuck the 'birth box' in my closet, I feel safe and breathe a sigh of relief; now the birthing can begin. Every night I am prepared to go into labor. After many weeks, I am wishing the midwife made a better guess. Before I go to bed each night, I clean up the living room as if it's my last for a week. This ritual repeats itself for five more weeks.

My belly is *enormous* and this is noticed by everyone. "When will the baby be born?" they ask me a hundred times a day as if I know exactly when. The weeks pass by and the question changes into an agitated, "Isn't the baby not born *yet*?" *What were they thinking? Did they think I birthed my child and still walked around as if I carried twins?* I start to avoid people; it drives me crazy. Apparently, Shaffy has his own timing and he is not inspired by a midwife's prediction. My due date passes as if it is an ordinary day. Nothing happens; the night turns into another day. My due date is not his.

This baby sits tight and my belly keeps growing. His body becomes too big for me to move around comfortably. My frame is frail and I often sigh from extreme pain when he wiggles his shoulders. I have zero tolerance now for his acrobatic back flips. A week after my due date, I go to meet with my gynecologist for an ultrasound. Proudly I walk into his office. Without looking me in the eye, he points at the table. "Lie down," are his sparse instructions. I haven't met him before, and his distant behavior makes me uncomfortable.

He does his job and takes the ultrasound reading. "This baby is WAY TOO BIG to be born naturally," is his expert conclusion. He almost sings the words out his mouth. He seems very happy with himself. I say nothing. He shakes my hand and lets me out.

Outside the hospital doors, I am upset and allow the tears to stream down my face. My womanhood was insulted by his words; *how can a man say that to a woman who is planning a home birth? Did I really need a C-section?* I decide to dismiss his stupid words. I will birth my baby naturally. I will not allow *his* hands on my body. I know, if I believe him, I will be in fear, tense up, contract my muscles and end up in the hospital.

I refuse to support his righteous attitude that women are better in the hospital. I don't agree. That's not for me.

Syb puts his arm around me and I dry my tears. This baby will be born naturally; the hospital is only a last resort.

The Universe orchestrates her timing according to Shaffy's plan. I am scheduled to have labor induced on Monday if the baby is not born by then. On Saturday I am home alone. Syb has Florian and Sytske at his office and I am sewing another blanket for the baby. My creativity flows abundantly; I can't stop creating new projects. My energy is unstoppable.

The doorbell rings at lunch time and Jose the midwife stands on my doorstep with her suitcase in her hand. This must be mistake.

What is she doing here? I have no new news. I can only think she is a 'Godsend' because I am not happy with the planned induction on Monday. I am terrified about the possibility of being in the hands of a gynecologist who doesn't believe in a natural birth. I have prayed and prayed that the baby will come before Monday. Jose knows my wishes but *why is she here?* I tell her it must be a mistake; I didn't call her.

"I thought I'd come by and see how you are."

I am touched by her concern. "Nothing is happening, no signs yet," I say.

"Come and let me stir that little one up a bit," she says.

We go upstairs and I lay down on the bed. Willingly I allow her to do what she has in mind.

She tells me she is going to try and induce some movement of the uterus muscles by stirring and poking inside.

I can't say I enjoy it but I am open to anything that may start the birthing process. When she is finished, she tells me to lie down for another fifteen minutes because I can expect some mild cramps. It also might induce the birth. If nothing happens by tomorrow, she will come back for a home visit and break my water. I am beside myself with joy. I know that either today or tomorrow the baby will be born; that will avoid a hospital-induced birth if Shaffy decides to join in our plans.

Jose lets herself out while I am resting on my bed. When Syb comes back, I tell him the good news. I call my parents and ask if they can take Florian and Sytske tomorrow because we will be "busy birthing our new baby." To celebrate my last night of pregnancy, Syb and I go out for dinner. Syb suggests we go to Amsterdam; I am more drawn to stay close to home which is very unusual for me. We go by car to our favorite bistro. It is only a three minute walk but that is not an option for me. I do have some mild cramps which I ignore.

At the restaurant they seat us at the best spot in the house. My back is warmed by the fire that burns fiercely. I choose my favorite fish dish. Every now and then I gasp for air. "It must be a cramp," I say to Syb. We eat our dinner without much disturbance except for my taking very deep breaths between each spoonful of tuna tartar. I can handle this pain, I think.

A gifted, young man plays the piano; he plays without a pause. I listen to his music in between my breaths. I inhale and exhale on his beat.

If I knew I was entering the transition stage of labor, I would be in bed by now instead of eating my last supper. "What do we want for dessert?" the waiter asks. My honest answer is that I am full, very full. I glance at the menu; everything is too much. Suddenly I long to go home and watch the movie we rented for tonight. I walk to the car breathing through every contraction thinking they are the mild cramps. We arrive home at 9:45 PM. Syb pays the babysitter and goes to turn on the movie.

As soon as he pushes the START button, I let out a wail. With a big kick, my water breaks and I feel Shaffy is ready to be born.

"Syb, I am having the baby. Open the front door for the midwife and close the kids' bedroom doors," I say in one breath.

I have the phone in one hand and I am dialing the midwife's number as we run to the bedroom. My mind is racing, too. Syb runs after me holding his hands cupped behind my back. *Was he thinking this big nine-pounder would be such an easy catch?*

Syb takes the phone from me and talks to Jose, but she wants to hear my voice. I don't say much; she knows enough. In the meantime Buddha is outside; she needs her evening walk. She is a very independent dog. Later, the neighbors describe the amusing scene: a dog runs out the door and is loose on the street; a midwife races down the street, parks her car in the middle of the pavement and runs like a banshee into the door which is wide open.

In the midst of that, I am doing the 'hip dance' in my room to help the baby descend. Jose runs upstairs and, as soon as she arrives, she has the situation under control.

Syb can't find the birth box that was stored for the last five weeks.

They both ask me where 'the box' is. I tell them but neither is able to find it. I am too busy 'catching my waves' to go and look for the box. The baby is almost here. We will have to improvise; I can't explain where the box is. They are in a hurry; I am at peace. There is very little time now. I squat down against the side of the bed and I pull up my fancy evening dress. My fancy earrings dangle while I pant. I want to use the labor chair but there is no time to go downstairs and get it. The baby is on his way.

I close my eyes, tune into my body and talk to my child. I let him know that I am ready. I ask him *is he, too?* Together, he and I are in another world while Syb and Jose do the thinking. My mind is switched off; my body is in charge and her wisdom is my lead.

There is nothing to hold me back now. While I am leaning in the most uncomfortable way against the side of our bed, my legs begin to shake. I can barely hold the squat position for much longer. I feel the baby's broad shoulders pass on the way out. Within seconds, I sing my third child with the deepest octave of my underbelly into the world.

I put Shaffy Samuel to my chest and pull my evening dress down. My belly is gone and I have my baby in my arms. I am already dressed for his birth day. Shaffy made his entrance into the world at 10:10 PM. It is twenty minutes since dinnertime.

I am ready for dessert now. Let the celebration feast begin.

A joyous, gentle, brilliant soul is now on *earth*.

When we discover that the truth is already in us,
we are all at once our original selves.

—Dogen

Stripped Naked

Today my clothes won't matter. I will be stripped naked—down to the bone—if I believe my friend.

The morning of the first day I stand in front of my closet and ask myself what I should wear. *How should I represent myself? What is my image?* I can pretty much pull out any style; today I am not sure what is best. I decide for something simple.

I'm going to *Landmark Education* in Amsterdam. I've heard a lot about this life-changing, three-day course. One of my friends is wildly enthusiastic about it. Since she came back from the course, something about her changed; she radiates a golden glow of self confidence and inner power. She explains vaguely that it deals with transformation and looking at your 'stuff.'

"You'd better find out for yourself," she says. I don't really understand what 'stuff' I have to face yet I am curious. My Soul is clear. "GO," is her counsel. A part of me is fearful which simply means transformation is going to happen.

I leave the house with butterflies in my stomach. Fortunately the nerves grow less as soon as I enter the train station. I am on my way! I buy a round trip ticket but really don't know if I will be able to catch the last train back. It is said about this training it will take as long as it takes to strip you naked. *How will I get home if the train is gone by the time the class is over?* I can only trust it will work out somehow.

The train arrives in time in Amsterdam. In a daze, I walk over to the Rokin, the famous main street in Amsterdam. The closer I get to the building, the faster my pace. In a way I wish it was already over; however, there is no way back now. I quickly scan the problem areas of my life but I have a hard time finding them. I don't have any specific issues I can think of. My friend said they unravel your story. *What story do I have? Do I even have one?*

Wanda, the course leader said, "The quality of your life depends upon the story you dwell in." I didn't understand what that meant until *after* my birthday.

I can rest easy; it will take only a couple of hours for me to be faced with the real ME. Finding our blind spots . . . that is what Landmark will show us. We learn, when looking at a pie, there is a little piece that represents the area of *what we know*; a slightly bigger piece represents the area of *what we know that we don't know*; and about seventy-five per cent is the part about *what we don't know that we don't know. That* is the most interesting piece. At this point, my blind spots—the "*I don't know that I don't know*" pieces—are hidden like turtle eggs in the sand. I need some nesting time for the "*don't knows*" to crack out of their shells and crawl to the surface.

The morning starts at 9:00 AM *sharp*. The doors are closed less than one minute after the clock hands point to 9 AM. No one is allowed in. Late is late.

Wanda, our program leader, explains the rules of the course. Everyone attending must take full responsibility for being on time; no one can be late; that means no train delays, no accidents, no excuse will be accepted. She tells us we have to BE OUR WORD *no matter what*! This is one of the most repeated phrases in the Landmark training. Everybody hates the program leader instantly; some people want to leave the room.

Wanda's true intent is to impress us with the message that too often we create a world in which we blame others or outer circumstances for our misery. It takes me awhile to get it.

"If you are not your word and screw up, clean up the mess," she instructs us. She tells us to SHOW UP IN OUR TRUTH AT ALL TIMES. If we say something or promise something, do as we said—BE OUR WORD. We can say we are sorry if we do not meet it; just don't come up with excuses. So, in the Landmark training, we need to be here at 9:00 AM sharp or before. If we are worried about the possibility of our train being delayed, hop on the intercity an hour earlier so we are here on the dot.

I never realized before how easily I made up excuses instead of saying a simple "I'm sorry." No one is really interested in the 'why' anyway. Wanda tells us it is much more authentic to speak from this level of truth. Excuses are a story, too. With this discussion of *being on time*, many people in the class have issues that are triggered; a lot of anger rises to the surface. Our leader doesn't waver. "You prefer to blame the circumstances." She tells us we don't know the true meaning of the word '*integrity*.'

With this example, Wanda sets the stage for us to investigate how we deal with life in general. *How often have we blamed our parents, friends and lovers for the loss of our power?* During the next three days, we will investigate the stories we built around ourselves. *How true are they? Have we interpreted certain events in a specific way and concluded how best to live our life based upon those experiences? Have we shrunk our authentic selves and lost our true voices in order to avoid pain again?* The Landmark teaching explains we all have a *winning formula* (WF) that contains a *fixed way* of reacting. We are very predictable beings . . .

It is quite an insight for me to hear this explained in such a simple way. In order to determine our WF – our winning formula, we are asked to find three events at three different stages of our life. Wanda leads us in a guided visualization and, immediately, three significant events pop up for me.

I see an experience when I was three years old, one as a teenager, and one when I was in my early twenties. I am shocked to see my WF – MY WINNING FORMULA – is built around the theme "I can do it all *alone*." I have formed my WF around the NEED to be independent, strong and courageous at all cost; that equates to *I do NOT need help of any kind ever unless I can help it.* To me the need for help is a sign of weakness and, above anything else in the world, I do not want others to see me as weak.

Wanda gives us time to share with each other what we've 'uncovered.'

In a way I like my WF so *why would I change it*? It had served me well up to now. I had accomplished a lot on my own.

It won't take long before the moment of truth shatters my world.

"All of your winning formulas are different in some ways, but they are alike in another way. The truth is that they are everything you are NOT," says Wanda. There is total silence in an audience of one hundred and fifty people . . . we all need time to grasp this inconvenient truth.

Wanda explains, "We build our winning formulas as a survival mechanism based upon an experience in which we feel extremely powerless, unloved or who knows what. We then come to a conclusion about this experience and make a decision to protect ourselves *no matter what* so this will never ever happen again. We all do this and are unaware of the moment this happens or the consequences. From that painful moment onward, our winning formula is in place. We begin to wrap a story around our original, beautiful, magnificent essence—our true self. The older we become, more and more we cover up our shining until one day little or nothing of our original self shines through.

"It is like being a flea in a box. When fleas are born, they feel free to jump to an unlimited height potential until the moment someone puts a lid on the box. The moment they bump their heads, they put their story in place: "We mustn't jump higher than that to avoid bumping our heads; bumping our heads is painful."

After that, these fleas never jump higher than the lid even if the lid is removed immediately after. Their story about how high they can jump is set for life. They will never experience the pain of bumping their heads again; their winning formula is permanently in place.

"Human beings are much like fleas in a box. We don't want to get hurt and we want to avoid the pain of being unloved, abandoned, unseen or unheard.

"To avoid pain, we give up the magnificent part of ourselves that has the potential to reach the sky. We buy into our 'head-bumping' belief at an early age; life, in return, gives us the same kind of experiences over and over to confirm our belief about who we are NOT. Our story stays unchanged. We stay forever trapped in our own box. We become used to being smaller versions of our true self and we think that smaller version *is* our true self."

Wanda's words shine a spot light on me. I truly see myself for the first time. This realization runs deep and cathartic. Up until this moment, I assumed my winning formula was who I really was. Now I am seeing my winning formula only kept me from real fulfillment and love.

I notice that *my* idea of being strong made me refuse help at times I truly needed an extra pair of hands. I realize that, in fact, my WF is very domineering and controlling, too. *Why else would anyone refuse help when someone genuinely offers it?* I had to make all my decisions alone – not out of a love of being strong – rather out of a fear of appearing weak.

The day flies by and I am both shaken and glued to my seat in the back of the room. Everyone is invited to come up to the front to tell their stories. I am shocked to hear all of the stories of abuse, rape, dying, cancer, and so on. One story is worse than the other. I am brought to tears. They have so many more problems than I. *Did I have a right to go on stage and tell my story?* No, I don't think so, and I stay stuck to my chair, far from the stage. My stuff is minor in comparison with their stories.

However, as the day continues, I get more and more irritated with those who come back on stage. I am especially annoyed by all the attention they are getting. Their stories are indeed worth listening to *but why do they have to repeat them again and again? Haven't they had their share of the limelight?* I sit stewing and wondering why our leader is putting up with this; then my questions begin to be directed at myself. *What is going on with me,* I wonder. *Why does this bother me so much? Was I feeling the need for the attention I never asked for?*

Then I see IT; the pattern is very clear: I am *totally* in my winning formula. I don't need attention; other people have bigger problems. I can take care of myself and, on top of that, I will figure it out *all alone*. Bottom line, I am strong and independent. I am fine, *right*?

No, this time I must tell the truth: I am NOT fine. Tears well up in my eyes, and I wrench my hands as I recognize my familiar story: I grew up in a family of five being the second child and oldest daughter.

I always felt the others needed more attention so I made sure not to cause problems for my parents. At an early age I learned to manage life on my own. "Don't worry about me, I am fine," was my favorite response. I felt responsible for everyone's happiness.

Until midnight, the participants continue to come up to the stage and share. The leader asks them questions; her questions lead each one to amazing insights. All who have the courage to come up to the stage walk away blissful; they are ecstatic to have recognized the story they dwell in. I am blown away when I begin to recognize a part of me in every sharing. Even though I didn't have exactly the same experience, our experiences are the same in their essence.

I can now listen with my heart wide open; my judgment is gone and I see myself in everyone's story. Someone shares a story about hiding; I ask myself *when did I find myself hiding?* I go back to a time when I was little. My sister was rushed to the hospital at midnight and I hid in the kitchen closet. I was very scared my sister would die and I didn't want my parents to see that I was feeling *their* fear my sister might die. So I carried my pain into that closet; no, I told myself, I didn't need attention, she did. Of course, I was strong . . . a very strong, six-year-old.

The evening is not over until way past midnight; it is pitch dark when I step outside the big building. My decision is crystal clear: Tomorrow is my birthday. The biggest present I can give myself is my SELF. I will give my true Self to myself.

Even though most of the participants won't get home before 2:00 AM, we have an assignment; it is to write a letter about our winning formula: *how does it work for us and how does it operate in our life.* For me it is time to "come out of the closet." I leave the building at 1:00 AM. By now the last train is gone. Miraculously another participant asks me if he can give me a ride home. Thank you, Universe!

When I arrive home, Buddha is the only one awake. She welcomes me happily by swishing her tail. She is the first to greet me on my birthday. It is March 16th and I sit down on a chair in the cold kitchen. I place my writing pad in front of me. I have no problem writing this. Passionately, my heart pours out on paper; it was waiting for this opportunity for a long time.

I am unstoppable; it is time to show up and tell. I promise myself to be the first on stage the next morning. I will claim my birthright; it will be a birthday present to last a lifetime. I don't know how I will dare do it, however, I will ask for the attention of all one hundred and fifty attendees. I have to. With that I drift into a dreamless sleep.

I wake up with all my children singing around my bed. Their happy faces and self-made drawings make a delightful start to this important day. This day holds promise. Today I have no question of what to wear. I know how to match my clothes with who I am; it is my birthday and I feel the beat of my Soul in my shoes. I choose a frivolous skirt, high heels and big earrings. I look as if I am going to a party and, of course, I am. I have never done anything like this.

However, I have no doubt I will be true to my promise. I can not back down now. Fear of speaking and stage fright won't hold me back today.

When I enter the room, I choose a seat close to the podium; nobody can beat me in getting up there first. I can see the microphone within reach, and my heart pounds. When the session starts, I walk toward the podium.

Before I can reach it, someone grabs the microphone and the first person begins to speak. I walk back to my seat. I ignore my fear. I wait patiently, trembling inside a bit. Then it is my turn . . .

I take the microphone and wait a second. I stay cemented to the floor and take a breath. I will not run and hide. "I am Saskia." Three hundred eyes turn to look at me. In a very clear voice I tell them my idea to be on stage first this morning "because it is my birthday." I continue, "My worst fear is you will sing *Happy Birthday* to me and I won't be able to handle all the attention."

My emotions finally burst and I start crying. The audience begins singing so loud it must be heard outside the building. I have not even started my story. They sing and laugh with joy for me as I cry and laugh between my tears. It is hilarious. I have never had so much attention.

I share my letter about how I traveled all over the world, how I took many courageous leaps, how I birthed my four children in five and a half years, how I studied too much to mention, how I set up a successful practice.

As I go on, it all sounds more and more ridiculous. I stop for a moment and say, "And you know what? I pretend I can do it all alone because I am strong and I don't need that attention. I believed I never needed any help. The fact is, if you want to know the truth, I do need help and I do need attention. I am very vulnerable . . ."

I go on and on and share deeply from my heart while tears stream down my face. I tell them about what I endured: studying during my four pregnancies and taking exams while sneaking to the bathroom to throw up. No one ever knew how sick I was.

Nevertheless, I accomplished a LOT. My intense drive and hunger to learn more created in me a desire to give it my all. Unfortunately, the certificates reflected that effort without pride. I celebrated my successes alone.

My story is entertaining enough to keep everyone's attention and I am encouraged to go on. The crowd laughs and cries. I reveal *everything* I am NOT. I share the pain from dimming my shining light and hiding my talents in a 'practice' behind our house. No one else had to know of my gifts; they were only for the clients who came to me for a treatment.

I cry because it is painful to expose all of what I was hiding for so long in front of all these people; I was used to hiding. However, from listening to *their* stories, I know as I share mine we are ONE. From where I stand, I can see others recognize their own pain in my story. We cry together and I receive the blessing of being truly heard.

I ask *what had this journey been all about? How much more did I need to DO to ultimately approve of myself and BE myself? When was I ever going BE enough just the way I am?*

The words come from my heart; they sparkle like gems; they are very precious to me. When I am at the end, I acknowledge myself for the very first time. Through my tears, I smile from ear to ear; laughter ripples over my face. "Thank you for giving me the opportunity to stand here completely exposed—stripped naked—showing you what I consider to be the worst part of me. For the first time in my life, I acknowledge me. I can't express what it means to be acknowledged by all of you, too."

The audience stands up and gives me a huge applause. Never in my life had I so completely given myself to anyone. Now I did it in front of one hundred and fifty! And as a result, the truly unexpected happened. I received a *standing ovation* for what I assumed was my *weak* side.

I float off stage and back to my seat. My old winning formula is crushed, my identity gone. *Where is the 'I' if there is no story? If I am not my old self, who am I then?* Oh, yes, it is so simple. I am ONE BIG possibility. I feel so free. Is this what is meant to experience bliss? I have a lot of questions. The flea is free to jump as high she likes.

At the break time, strangers come up to me, hug me and wish me happy birthday. They tell me how much my story meant to them and how much they love me.

It is an amazing experience and a surprise to me that, when we show our vulnerable side, we are more likeable and loveable. I am beside myself; I need time to integrate this insight.

Our leader says our WINNING FORMULA has a purpose; that until now it has served us well. However, there are new ways of being that generate *unlimited* possibilities and far more adventures. She tells us we never really lose our winning formula completely; we just need to be aware when we are in it and take a leap.

Then she gives us an assignment to write a story about everything that troubles us. We must read it to our class partner as many times as we need to until we are ready to let it all go. It may take a while and, if necessary, we might end up staying up long after midnight. Our partner is instructed to listen, only listen, and nothing else. The question is *how much longer do we want to listen to our own misery; how addicted are we?*

I write my tale about all I can think of that bugs me; what is in my way of coming to full bloom; my habits that keep me in my own box; the people who have caused unhappiness. It takes me until near midnight to finish it. I read the story over and over to my partner and he listens patiently.

He nods and doesn't say a word. I keep going until I realize the nonsense I am telling myself.

I start to laugh and my partner starts to laugh, too; he is relieved and all too happy to break the long listening spell. In sync, we break out in an unstoppable, freeing laughter. I bend over backward; I feel relieved as never before.

My partner experiences the same; it is far easier to recognize someone else's nonsense than your own blind spots.

It is long past midnight when I take the last train home. When Buddha welcomes me, I stroke her beautiful white fur and tell her about my day, "Buddha, this was the best birthday party ever because so many friends sang for me." She wags her tail, hoping to take an early morning stroll.

Did she understand and approve of what I just said?

When I open my eyes the next morning I feel empty. I look for my old self; she isn't there. I feel unsettled. I bike to the train station and buy my ticket. I go through the motions but I am looking at the world with a different set of eyes; it feels unreal and unfamiliar to my *real* self.

Because I arrive early in Amsterdam, I decide to stop in my favorite store, *de Bijenkorf.* I want to take a quick look at the new fashions for spring and perhaps buy something new. I have no idea what color or style fits me anymore. *What was my style again?* I have left my persona behind in the empty, echoing hall of repetitive stories last night. I haven't had time to take my story back or make a new one. So I buy an orange sweater. I don't know if this new color suits me; I have never worn anything orange, but I put it on without concern.

Back in the front row I change seats with the old Saskia. I left her there yesterday.

"You might feel disconnected, sort of out of control," Wanda, our leader says. I certainly do. It is scary to have complete silence in my head. There is no chatter, no inner dialogue. It is so peaceful. The one talking is finally gone. I feel blissful.

Wanda tells us that soon enough we will pick up the 'old pieces' that can take us back to where we came from if we don't stay aware. I vow to watch myself; I don't want to dive into the next familiar pothole as I always did.

I sit and watch the world around me. The impact of the course hits me. The course is coming to an end. Wanda dims the light in the room.

"Now close your eyes and listen to this." Wanda starts to read.

Our deepest fear is not that we are inadequate.
Our deepest fear is that we are powerful beyond measure.
It is our light, not our darkness that most frightens us.
We ask ourselves,
who am I to be brilliant, gorgeous, talented, fabulous?

Actually, who are you NOT to be? You are a child of God.
Your playing small does not serve the world.
There is nothing enlightened about shrinking
so that other people don't feel insecure around you.
We were born to manifest the glory of God that is within us.
It is not in some of us; it is in everyone.

And as we let our own light shine,
we unconsciously give other people
permission to do the same.
As we are liberated from our own fear,
our presence automatically liberates others.

— Marianne Williamson

From A Return To Love: Reflections on the Principles of A Course in Miracles

We all sit within the power created by these words. One hundred and fifty heads nod in unison.

Who are we NOT to be brilliant, gorgeous, talented, fabulous?

We leave the building late; I am in time to catch the last train.

My head is still; my heart is full and my step is light.

A Ritual of Greatness

The day after Landmark Education, I walk into my office. My certificates and diplomas stare me boldly in the face. *Why was their presence suddenly so obvious?* Almost the whole back wall is covered; before now, they were never worth a glance. I hammered and hung them on the wall for my clients. Burt Goldman, my hypnotherapy teacher, said clients need confidence and trust in their therapist.

The truth hits me hard. I see the ridiculousness. After three days of Landmark Education, the truth is very clear: I never thought I was good enough. That is why I always needed to study something more and more and more. *Where was the end?* I never took the time to acknowledge *myself.* My greatness was hidden in the back studio behind our house. When people commented on my diplomas, I waved their compliments away. Now I stand there in shock. Mandela's speech resonates in my head. *Who am I to be brilliant, gorgeous, talented, fabulous? Fear of my own greatness? Oh boy, how scared was I?*

After Landmark, I'm not blind anymore. I decide to do an acknowledgement ritual, a good start on the path to fearlessly expressing my so-called "greatness." I place a *do not disturb* sign on my office door and close the curtains. For the next two and a half hours, I am in labor.

I sit on a high chair in the middle of the room so I can oversee my whole practice and view all the walls. Music plays an important part. I choose a song of the Dutch singer Marco Borsato. He sings in Dutch, "How would it be to be the King of your own kingdom, just for one day? How would it be to sit on your throne and be as beautiful as you could be; and how would it be to sing your song in full?"

I listen and resonate with his message. Yes, *how would that be?* Tears start rolling down my cheeks. *Why do we cover up and hide from our power?* I look at my diplomas and certificates. The hours and hours of study during my pregnancies while throwing up were hard. I did it anyway. I look at everything hanging on all the walls.

Often friends asked me *why don't you wait until your kids are older?* It never made sense to me to wait; I loved my studies and yet it took a LOT of endurance to show up at all times. Nobody ever knew. "I am fine; I can do everything without help" was my winning formula. It molded me with an iron hand. I had memorized a lot.

With practice I became good at it; my brain became like a sponge. At stolen moments during my babies' naps, I sat with my back against the radiator on the floor of the living room and studied as fast as I could.

Celine, my next door neighbor, was the only one who knew how hard I worked. She sometimes saw me through the window during those moments sitting in my favorite study spot. She told me once that I looked as if I resided in another world; she was right.

I sit on my high chair and the music does her work. My eyes scan the diplomas one by one; I look at all of them. I tell myself to spend at least three minutes per certificate. I am not allowed to go fast. It is difficult; I feel the pain of never giving myself a pat on the shoulder. The music plays the same song over and over. "How would it be . . . "

"Oh, my God, stop it," I think more than once. When I am done with all of them, I sigh. I get up from the chair and walk over to the shelves. I look at all the books I have; not only have I bought them, I have read them all. Then I open my desk drawers and look at the different tests I passed; I delve into memories of what it took me to get to graduation. Despite the hard work, I remember the delight of studying and learning everything I laid my hands on. I had longed to increase my knowledge, and my thirst to learn more was never stilled enough to stop. For years I stacked my books in my babies' strollers. The zoo was my favorite place to "hang out". While the kids played, my nose was in the books.

Now I can't believe how hard I was on myself. I break down and sob. Many times I want to walk away from this painful ritual, but I am relentless; I can't stop until I've faced it all. A deep sense of joy sweeps over me when I am done with part one. I've cleaned up my inner closet.

OK. The first part is completed and I walk back to my high stool in the middle of the room.

I envision my high chair as my throne. I imagine I am wearing the most delicate, velvety dark blue cape around my shoulders.

How would it be to sit on your throne for one day?

I sink into all I am; I sit on my throne and FEEL it. My kingdom is inside, not just for one day.

One of my greatest teachers once said, "Embrace your own magic first." I think I just did.

I close the ceremony by smiling at the back wall, the books and the inside of my drawers. The music stops. After two and a half hours, I am done. I am exhausted but feel euphoric when I open the curtains and walk outside. I am reborn.

It's time to pick up my kids from school. At the school, I chitchat with the other mothers. My velvety cape around my shoulders keeps me warm. I wonder if they notice a difference about me.

Later that afternoon, I buy a card for myself and write the poem of the song I played for my ritual on it as a reminder of this important afternoon. The card says HAPPY BIRTHDAY and only I understand what that really means. I know there is still a long road to unravel but step by step I will learn. At least I know how it feels to sit on my own throne even if it was just for a moment.

The ritual has another effect. Within a month's time, my income, my clientele and my workshops have multiplied times four. In the months that follow, I have a waiting list I can't finish before I leave for America.

Dagpo Rimpoche

His smile touches a memory from a thousand years ago. I burst into tears when I hold his hand.

While I am stirring the red *puttanesca* sauce for our evening dinner, Sandra calls me. Her oldest daughter Louise passed her first swimming test. *Would I like to come and celebrate this with her tomorrow?* She is very proud of her; I am, too. I am the godmother of Sandra and Sander's three children.

I switch off the fire on the stove and place a lid on the pan with the boiling tomatoes. It is 6:00 PM. This is certainly the most convenient time to feed my hungry children; however, I need to go now. It can't wait for tomorrow. I call them to come down from upstairs. "Let's go guys!" I say and load my four kids in the car. We drive through the deserted streets of Bussum. Nobody is on the road; it is dinner time.

I am absorbed in my thoughts and I almost run over a woman who is doing last minute shopping before the stores close. Everyone is in a hurry to get *home*. I am on my way *out*.

When I stop at the red traffic light a voice from the far distance says, "When the student is ready the teacher appears." I turn my head and look around as if I would meet the one who was speaking. To my right I look at the main post office with people running up the steps to drop off their mail and, to the left, I see a woman with two kids on the back and front of her bike.

She doesn't recognize me although we know each other from the pre-school days of our kids. She must be thinking of dinnertime, too. Her kids look crabby.

Mine chat happily in the backseat of the car; they like adventures and are delighted to go somewhere else at the time for baths and getting ready for bed.

A few minutes later, I arrive at Sandra's doorstep. She sees me coming and quickly waves to me to come in. "Come in and meet Dagpo Rimpoche," she says, "You have to stay a while and feel his presence. His incredible energy is *so* healing." Without a word I follow her through the dimly lit hallway; the scent of incense mixed with curry comes to my nostrils and I remember suddenly that I haven't fed my kids.

I float into another world as I step into the living room and look at the two beautiful Buddhist men sitting on the couch. They are Dagpo Rimpoche and his companion who takes care of him. They sit in silence and look at me. Mesmerized as if a magnet draws me toward him, I walk to the couch with my hand stretched out to greet him.

I say politely say, "Hello, Dagpo Rimpoche, I am so happy to meet you." He greets me, too, and looks at me with the biggest smile I have ever seen. With his smile he touches my heart so deeply. I feel his great love transmitted to my Soul.

I take a deep breath and want to hold onto his hand forever.

Then I run to the kitchen. I sit down and tremble from head to toe and burst into tears.

It feels as if an unstoppable flood washes my entire body. I can't stop. I will not stop for the next two weeks. He is a Soul mate who touched *my* heart and Soul before. I cry about our reunion. For the next two weeks, my eyes well up every time I think of him. We must have had a very strong connection in the past.

Sandra watches me and understands. I tell her all I want to do is sit next to him and be in his presence. She looks at me and smiles. She puts an arm around my shoulder and urges me to go back inside and sit next to Dagpo. He is expecting me. I take a seat next to him and try to make conversation. *What is there to say?* He is the most enlightened person I have ever met. I tell him that I cried in the kitchen. "We have met before," is his simple explanation.

I nod *yes*. I see an image of a past life where we lived in a monastery in Tibet. The high mountains surround the monastery. My kids ask if they can eat dinner with Sandra's kids. *Where was I?* Of course, we can stay for dinner. We all move into the kitchen.

Dagpo will be teaching in Amsterdam; when I hear about this, I know

I will go. When the student is ready the teacher appears. Here I am. I understand the message and I clearly see the thread I am to follow.

Two days later I drive to a grey brick building in the outskirts of Amsterdam. Syb takes care of the kids and I am ready for my teacher. Upon arrival, I realize I don't know anyone. Sandra is nowhere in sight.

Most people wear woolen socks and carry a blanket and a pillow under their arms. I had no idea what I was supposed to bring. I brought a notebook. I've never been to a teaching like this. I walk into the room which has a big stage in the front. On the walls hang a colorful Buddhist painting, shawls and all kinds of sacred objects. The smell of incense encircles the room. Slowly the space fills up with people who don't talk and look very serious.

Where should I sit down? The space is still empty. I choose a spot on the floor not far from where Dagpo is to teach. When I sit down I hear, "I am sitting there. This is *my* spot." The high-pitched woman's voice sounds upset. I look around me. I hadn't noticed anyone at that particular spot before.

Wait a minute, I think. Apparently some of the students in this class are still "human." I am so surprised. I thought in the Buddhist community everyone was into love and compassion; perhaps not. Not everyone was ready to alleviate each others' suffering. I feel slightly uncomfortable after this incident. *Was this my karma?* I smile and look for another spot; I am very careful not to step on someone else's toes.

When Dagpo comes into the room, everyone begins chanting as if they are singing a national anthem. I pretend to join in and sing along. Tears start to fall as I look at him. His teaching is beautiful. He talks about the causes of our suffering; our mind is the key. I love every minute though my legs hurt quite a bit. Lotus position is not my favorite; it is a cause of *my* suffering . . .

Meeting the Dalai Lama

Who is more 'holy', Sinterklaas (Saint Nicolas), *Jesus, Buddha or the Dalai Lama?* I think for a moment and I don't know how to answer my kids.

I am at Sandra's house at 10:30 AM sharp; it is *the* Dutch time for coffee. While we chat and drink our *koffie verkeerd* (the Dutch version of *cafe au lait*), she tells me she's going to study with the Dalai Lama in Germany for a week.

Something clicks inside. Without hesitating, I say I want to join her – not only me but my whole family will come along. She stares at me. She knows I will be 37 weeks pregnant when the seminar takes place. I know Syb and the kids will love this experience and our fifth baby will wait; I have no doubt. I bike home and call the booking agency to get the ball rolling. Syb and the kids are as excited as I am. Easily everything falls in place. We will stay in a little cottage close to the site and even Buddha our dog is allowed to come. *How could they refuse her?* Her tail doesn't stop wagging when I tell her she is going to be in the presence of His Holiness the Dalai Lama.

A few weeks later we are ready to go. I don't really know what I am in for; Soul says: "GO." She must know more about Gideon's arrival than I do. He'd better sit tight until his due date.

Syb, the children and Buddha pack our car in the pouring rain. My big belly contracts from the upheaval.

If this baby is an early arrival, I am sure there is a hospital nearby to help. If I can do it in a *Chinese* hospital, this should be a piece of cake; I am an experienced birther by now.

Before we hit the highway, we stop at the pharmacist. My hemorrhoids are *killing* me. I can't sit. *How will I sit with these for seven days listening to the Dalai Lama's teachings?* I figure I will deal with it when I get there. First I need to survive the ride to Germany. We drive on in the worst rainstorm ever, not knowing a tornado is on its way. It is early in the morning and hardly anyone is on the road. The drive is smooth and the roads are wet. When we arrive in Germany, we find our cottage is pretty basic; it consists of a living room and one bedroom. The kitchen and the living room are one. The kids rave about the place, "It's so cozy." Indeed it is.

I look outside and hope the rain will stop. The yard is very small; if the rain stops, at least they can get some fresh air if the place gets too cramped. At that time, we don't know the rain will cause flooding in the whole country and we will almost have to evacuate.

We rush in and out of the house unpacking the car. The rain is so heavy. So far so good; the kids like this wet adventure. They don't know much about the Dalai Lama. They ask me thousands of questions I can't answer. I am surprised by their interest. I share what I know; yet, I don't even know why we are here. What I do know is we are exactly in the right place at the right time.

We settle down and unpack the big box of Lego blocks and stay inside. We have no choice today.

The next morning, we drive to the site where the teachings will take place. The car bumps up and down on the muddy roads as we slowly find our way to the complex. The camp is an old army base located in the woods and hidden from view. Big tents are erected; the many prayer flags announce the Dalai Lama has arrived.

We agree Syb will come back at lunch time and trade places with me. In this way, we both will attend half of the teachings each day and the other one of us will watch the kids.

When I enter the complex, I am impressed, impressed in a huge way, by the ambience. Suddenly I am transported back to Tibet. Monks in orange robes are chanting. Nobody is in a hurry; time stands still. The outside world disappears and I can only hear the rain tapping on the roof of the enormous tent; it sounds like a gigantic fabric drum.

Eleven thousand people from all over the world have gathered to listen to his Holiness the Dalai Lama. I look for a chair to sit in. There is a choice; you can sit on the floor or sit on a chair. In the front of the room, the monks have created the most beautiful and colorful Mandela I have ever seen. The stage is decorated for the Dalai Lama. He will talk to us about the *Lam Rim*, the most basic of the Buddhist teachings.

I look around and conclude of the eleven thousand I am the "most pregnant."

Why am I here? I will find out soon enough. I'll be okay as long I can *sit for four hours in a row* I am thinking to myself.

The Germans are punctual; the teaching starts exactly at 9:00 AM. Every single one of the eleven thousand people is in the room and in readiness; no one is late or asleep.

A deep sound fills the room when his Holiness the Dalai Lama and his followers come in. I glance at his devotees; everyone holds his and her breath. I am cradled in the sacred vibration. I close my eyes and chant, pretending to sing the same prayer many here know by heart. The teaching begins and sentences in Tibetan roll fluidly out of the Dalai Lama's mouth.

In a split second, the cradle dumps me like a fool; I can't understand a word. *How can I learn from what he is saying when I don't know WHAT he is saying?* Of course, it is in Tibetan. *Had I thought he would speak English?* Then I remember something; when I first entered the tent and handed in my ticket at the counter, the event staff gave me a black box that would translate the talk in English. *How could I forget?*

Relief washes over me. I install the black box so I can hear the right language. It will be easy to follow now. I relax and sink into my heart and listen, not always understanding with my mind.

My Soul knows what this is all about. It is beautiful and I am so grateful I am here. My baby doesn't stir. Outside the rain pours without letting up. I am at peace and hope Syb will experience what I am feeling when he attends in the afternoon.

During the bathroom break, I see Sandra in the back row. We smile at each other and wave. I want to explore all of the Buddhist stands of books, clothes, food and statues of smiling Buddha's so I head to the bazaar. The bazaar is a big part of the complex. Every stand is worth a look.

I stop dead in my tracks as soon as I pass a small table of books. A chill runs through my body. Months before I had a dream in which I was shown a book I would buy. The title was something about healing the mind. My dream showed a very vivid image of the cover. I was told I didn't need to search for it; I would find it when I was ready for the information it would provide. And here I am; the book stares me in the face. I can't miss it; there is only one copy. Piles and piles of books are on the table and yet I recognize this one; it stands forlorn at the corner of the table. The book with the blue cover sits waiting for me. It is called *The Healing Power of the Mind* and it's mine. *Was this a message from Dagpo Rimpoche?* I buy the book and walk away thinking *life is a miracle.*

When the morning teaching ends, I follow the crowd outside. *How will I ever find Syb?* I walk outside the tent and, as if he knew when and where I would be, there is Syb. He has a big grin on his face. One child sits on his shoulder; three others are running around. Buddha walks toward me wagging her tail, happy to see me. My eyes follow Buddha as she runs off to the food area. She is without a leash as usual.

We call her back and she doesn't listen. Buddha . . . Buddha . . . Buddhaaaa . . . Buuuddhaa!

The small children's voices sound like angel bells throughout the spacious hall. People turn their heads; we are oblivious to their stares. We don't realize only until later how ridiculous we sounded.

Did these people think we were calling on THE Buddha so he would appear in person around the corner?

Delicious smells of Chinese food ignite our appetite. We sit down at a table next to a group of orange-robed monks. The kids drink in every detail of the scene. Syb and I are transported back in time to our life in Taiwan. After lunch, Syb switches roles with me. Before I leave, I remind him to turn on the translation cassette. I know how Syb thinks: if I survived four hours of Tibetan teachings without translation, he certainly can do that, too.

I drive back with the kids and Buddha in the car. The rain is so heavy now I have to stop the car alongside the road for awhile and wait for the rainstorm to subside. I can't see anything out of the windshield. The woods are starting to flood and the roads are muddy and unpaved. It's not easy for a station wagon loaded with kids.

The kids ask me hundreds of questions such as, *who do I like more ... Jesus or Buddha or Sinterklaas?* The teachings have opened a new door to their world and mine. What amazes me most is that, even at their young age, they have an interest as big as mine. They want to hear everything I learned this morning. I am very glad when I finally find our way back safely to the cottage; usually, I am not very good in following directions.

I can't understand one thing: my hemorrhoids are gone after sitting for four hours straight in a chair.

The pharmacist said they would take a couple of days to heal. Early that morning, I asked Dagpo Rimpoche to heal them when I said my prayers. *Did he hear my request?* They say he hears *everything*.

I had to admit to myself that he granted my prayer once before. Once when I asked him for help while I was working in my healing room, he granted my wish.

I was with a client in a deep hypnotic state when a swarm of wasps decided to enter the room. There was a big nest in the roof of the attic of the building where I had my healing room and, somehow, they must have found their way in. I was very allergic to stings but I was more afraid they would attack my client. I could not wake my client in the midst of regression therapy.

In desperation, I looked at Dagpo's picture on the shelf in the back of the room and asked for his immediate help. As soon as I asked, the wasps made one last circle and disappeared from the room. The client never knew what happened. I never forgot.

During the whole week, the kids are happier then ever, and their questions never stop. Syb and I teach them what we are learning. Our days repeat the same ritual: first they drop me off and return "home" where they play with the Lego blocks for a few hours; then back to the tent to eat lunch and, in the afternoon, the same ritual of returning to the site to pick up Syb.

My days are filled and fulfilling. I love being in the presence of the

Dalai Lama and listen to his teachings.

He invites us into the world of love and compassion with lots of humor. My endurance to sit comfortably is a challenge. My pregnant body wants to move which is absolutely impossible because I am stuck to my plastic chair. I don't want to disturb the devoted audience by walking through the packed crowds of people. I am glad my baby stays still; he doesn't move an inch and, thankfully, there are no signs of labor.

The rain continues to pour and, after a few more days, the woods are flooded and the roads look more like ponds of water. The ground underneath the large tent is muddy and wet. The tents are having a hard time standing erect now; I can see the heavy winds putting stress on the poles; the whole tent begins to move with the wind.

Early in the morning, they announce there is a flood watch; there is a *tornado* on the way. They contemplate evacuating all eleven thousand people at noon; we need to be prepared to get out *fast*. Our peaceful place is not so peaceful anymore.

Being pregnant usually makes me feel strong and powerful but the thought of needing to run for dear life if the tornado strikes was not supporting that. The idea of pushing my way through the massive crowd makes me feel sick to my stomach. However, my mother instinct kicks in; I have no doubt I need to bring my unborn baby to safer grounds. Being part of this mass "survival plan" was not *my* plan.

I call Syb with a cell phone I borrow. It takes a few calls to reach him. I don't want to wait till the final minute.

As usual, Syb is totally at ease and reassures me I will be fine and I shouldn't worry. *Stay* is his advice; he has no idea about the state of mind and emotions of a pregnant woman close to the due date for birthing her baby. "Can you please come here as fast as you can?" I plead, "People are already leaving this place and we will never be able to get out of here by car." I am *so* afraid by now.

People start to leave before the final call. When they finally announce the afternoon sitting is cancelled, there is a lot of hurry and scurry. Even then we don't know for sure if this is an evacuation.

I leave and run to the outskirts of the complex praying Syb will find me. I catch sight of our station wagon, an oasis in the storm, my safe haven. This car had never been this kind of symbol for me. I am grateful to find them so quickly. When I step into the car, now my sanctuary-on-wheels, I finally take a deep breath. My baby and I are *safe*. *Phew*, that was a 'close' call.

The next day, the tornado has passed and the teaching continues; everything proceeds as if nothing happened. It seems that the power of prayer of the Dalai Lama is obvious.

We are told if the kids wish to make a drawing for the Dalai Lama, the staff will hand it to his Holiness and he will bless them. The kids draw their gifts, dedicated to creating something very special for the Dalai Lama. The idea of being blessed is the best gift they can ever imagine.

Our final day becomes a surprise for me and a pre-birthday treat for unborn Gideon.

I am late and have missed the intro speech as I enter the room. The Dalai Lama is already talking about some kind of ceremony as I sit down. He is rattling off things in Buddhist terminology. I have no idea what he is talking about. After an hour of this, it seems that every one of the eleven thousand know exactly what to do; I don't have a clue. I watch the energy of all transform; it appears they are anticipating a sacred initiation.

I really want to know what the Dalai Lama is leading us through. Then it happens; my baby wakes up and, today, Gideon suddenly is alive and kicking. He is moving *all* of his body parts; apparently, he wants me to pay attention. *What did he know about all this that I didn't?*

The ceremony begins and I stand there observing what happens. The Dalai Lama calls forth people who have completed certain initiations already as well as the ones who are ready to receive this specific initiation. The moment he starts calling, I get up from my chair. I have to; I am pushed by the force of my baby. I hear him say, "Stand up now." I stand up, not knowing why. I follow the inner knowing of my unborn child.

In the next half hour, we are both initiated and blessed through a sacred

Buddhist ritual performed with a lot of salutations and bows. I obediently do as instructed and I imitate the movement of those near me.

I notice only a small part of the crowd is participating in the ceremony, but it is too late for me to stop. I keep going and wonder if I am *eating a forbidden fruit.*

Do I cause harm to anyone by participating in this ceremony? Was I "allowed" according to the teachings? It doesn't matter. I can tell my baby Gideon is overjoyed; he moves as if he knows the ceremony and is doing the bows inside me. We are the only two receiving an initiation in one body. I giggle and pat my belly.

On the return trip to Holland, I ask myself what really happened there. It feels as if the Dalai Lama planted a deep seed of Buddhist origin in ALL of us.

At home once again, Gideon is due in two weeks. I am ready to nestle in and stay home until he is born.

Do I know who is the most holy?

Apparently, Gideon is the one who holds the answer for the kids. He is born on December 5. It is the birthday celebration of *Sinterklaas* in Holland.

Illness and disease teach us to embrace the moment
and live the journey to the fullest
for no one is guarenteed of tomorrow

Beth B. DuPree, M.D.,
The Healing Consciousness:
A Doctor's Journey to Healing

What Happens When You Don't Think Anymore?

Years later, I still remember vividly how it feels when you don't think anymore. Bliss is the only word that matches this state of "no mind." If this is the side effect of too much anesthesia, I would go back on the operation table again in a heartbeat.

To be without thoughts...one might ask '*How can a mother of five children function like that*?' There are a million schedules to attend to. I know that for sure. I couldn't have dreamed of how easy life gets when the Universe takes over and the planning is in divine hands. A *Let Go and Let God* attitude should be the new trend for motherhood. If only I knew how to hold onto it a little longer…

My parents give me a facial for a birthday present. It is a year ago since I have had my last one and I am overjoyed to go again. I make my appointment for the day after my birthday. For the second time, Regina alerts me of a spot above my left eyebrow. It is flaky and red but so far I haven't paid much attention to it; I ignored her comment a year ago. "You should ask a dermatologist for a good crème," is her advice again.

And the rollercoaster starts right there.

I make an appointment with a dermatologist. On Monday morning when the kids are off to school, I leave the house.

The hospital is nearby and the drive will only take me fifteen minutes. I pass the local bakery on my way and buy a pastry to treat myself when I come home. The little shops on Huizer Street are always filled with people, even at this early hour. I am not the only one who likes her food fresh. It is more expensive; however, I'd rather support the local people than the big supermarket. I look at my watch and hurry to the hospital; I want to get this over with and get on with my day.

Everything goes smoothly. I don't have to wait long and, when I enter the doctor's office, I feel confident he can solve my minor skin problem right away. He looks at me and, in one glance, makes up his mind. "I'm pretty sure you have skin cancer, so let's take a sample of your skin," he says without looking me in the eye. He jots something on a piece of paper. "Here is the name of a plastic surgeon; you might want to make an appointment with him."

I follow him to another room and lie down. Someone scrapes a piece of my skin to send it to the lab in order to determine what type of cancer I have. I don't say a word—this is going way too fast. *Why would I need a plastic surgeon?* I feel like a robot. I have no feelings; I am numb.

I take the note and make a follow-up appointment. Without cream, I leave his office and walk to my car. I drive back the same way as I came. I am on autopilot. The pastry doesn't appeal to me anymore. I call Syb. He is at work.

"Hi, I got back from the dermatologist and I have cancer…" Silence on the other end.

I can see him frown. "I don't understand. I thought you were getting a cortisone cream."

"I thought so, too, but I have cancer; that can't be solved with a cream."

"Where are you? Shall I come?" he asks.

"No, I am fine," I lie while a tear rolls down my face.

A day later, I have digested the information: I have cancer and I want to be well. If it is denial or not letting the diagnosis ruin my days, I don't know. My life goes on.

My friends hear through the grapevine about my diagnosis. News spreads like wildfire. Everyone is concerned. No one knows what type of cancer I have and neither do I. I don't know much about skin cancer. *Did I have a melanoma or any other type*? I am totally in the dark.

For the first time in my life, I truly understand how important it is when you are sick to have positive people around you. Everyone projects his or her story on you. And whether you like or not, it does affect you. As uninformed as I am, I start to become a little concerned after several warnings and concerns from others. Some tell me it might be deadly. I don't want other people projecting their fear on me yet I don't know how to protect myself either.

I call an intuitive friend and she tells me I will be fine. I forget to ask if she means before or after the operation; I believe her anyway and let go of my concern. I deeply trust I can heal my cancer. I do not fathom how truly horrific the experience is going to be. I am NOT prepared at all.

The operation is scheduled on Thursday morning; it seems perfect because I will be back by the time the kids come home for lunch. The day before, Jet stops to pick up her daughter Lavinia, Sytske's friend. "Can Lavinia come again tomorrow?" Sytske asks.

I hesitate for a moment and say, "I am being operated on tomorrow so perhaps we need to pick another day."

Jet looks at me and says, "You what?" Her mouth drops open when I tell her I am having an operation on my face to remove skin cancer. I reassure her all will be well. She looks at me as if I am from outer space.

Although I realize it sounds weird to take this situation lightly, I truly believe the doctors will easily take the spot away and that's it. End of story.

On the morning of the operation, I am in a good mood. I dress festively; my outfit matches how I feel. This will be just like going to the dentist. No big deal. As Syb and I drive off, I wave happily to my neighbor Monica. (Later, she tells me she thought we were going to a party.) The closer we get to the hospital, however, the more nervous I become. As we enter the hospital ward, I wonder what the staff thinks of my fancy dress. They seem not to notice; the nurse in charge just tells me I have to change into a dark green hospital gown. For them, it is business as usual. It is my turn to be surprised.

The nurse asks me to lie down on a hospital bed and begins to hook me up to an intravenous drip. *Yuck! Why do they do that?*

However, I'll still be in and out; in less than 20 minutes, we'll be back in the car again and headed home. Piece of cake.

The plastic surgeon comes in, looks at my face and my cake falls in. He speaks these forever memorable words, "Well, to be so young and have this big of a spot of cancer on your face is a shame. We'll remove everything today but it's a 100% chance it will come back." *What's a 100%*

"chance"? That doesn't even make sense in any situation. In my mind, the only thing for me to do is to push the DELETE button. The surgeon's conclusion is not allowed to be taken in by me or by my body. I feel truly sorry for all his patients, the ones who don't know about the power of the subconscious mind. If I don't believe him, my body will do the same. This doctor has no idea of the impact of what he has said. *Why does he have this need to install a negative belief?* His "truth" is certainly not mine.

The surgeon goes to work and covers part of my face with a cloth. Syb is there and holds my hand but not for long. The surgeon gives me two shots in my forehead. Suddenly, I know this is *not* going to be a piece of cake. The needle is long and bores down deep into my flesh; it hurts more then words can describe. We wait until the shots numb my head so I won't feel the pain. We all wait.

The surgeon picks up what looks like a razor-sharp electric saw. "We need to make a circle and go deep," he says.

"Yes, of course, go deep," I think silently. I am awake floating in whatever was in that needle. *Go deep?* That's my way of experiencing life. I go beyond myself. I go deep.

At this moment, I don't know how vulnerable my face is. He goes to work and the saw sounds like a saw. My face, my most vulnerable part, is in *this* doctor's hands. I feel not only pain; I am about to be cut to pieces. "Are you okay?" he asks without much interest. *What can I say?* Of course, I am fine. *Isn't that what one is supposed to say? What else should I be?* But I am truly in too much pain to pretend this time even as tough as I am. The doctor can see I need another shot and then another and then another. In all I receive *seven* shots of anesthesia in my forehead; *seven* big needles bore deep down into the bone. To have someone take a saw to my face is the worst emotional and physical pain I have ever experienced. I wish now they had put me to sleep.

Syb passes out; there is too much violence, too much blood. He drops my hand and the nurse settles him in a chair behind a curtain. A second later, he opens the closed curtain; he wants to be fully there for me however, his body refuses to stand up. He tells me later that at first, when he looked on this with the eye of an observer, he was ok; when he switched to imagining how *I* was feeling, he felt sick.

I drift into another world. I feel at a loss. I can't describe my feelings. I don't mind the pain anymore; the empathic-less doctor with the electric saw going in circles boring deeper and deeper into my face is frightening.

When I left home that morning, what had I been thinking?

We both must have underestimated the operation. I look at the big clock. One and a half hours have passed and the surgeon is finished.

Where did my twenty minute in-and-out experience go?

"So, you are done for today," he says, "Make another appointment in two weeks to get the stitches out." Then he simply turns around and walks out. I sit up and take off my bloody, green gown; my colorful dress is again revealed. I get up from the table as if I had a catnap in the afternoon. My feet are wobbly on my high-heeled pumps. Dazed and half-unconscious, I try to shake off my dizziness. As I stand outside the room, I wonder what has just happened to me.

I mumble to the receptionist, "Two weeks." They hand me a note. I squeeze it in my hand. *Thank you.* I walk away, step by step. Syb helps to support me. I breathe heavily but silently. I want to be OUT of there. Here I am slaughtered by a doctor who cut up my face without mercy. *Why do they allow this?*

I don't know how to handle what has happened to me. I cannot tell Syb how I feel. He thinks I am in pain. I have a bandage around my head but my pain is not from the bodily wound. The bandage doesn't show the full impact of the surgery. "Let's go shopping and buy something really nice for you," Syb lovingly suggests. "First we go for coffee and apple pie in your favorite place," he continues.

I nod my head carefully and try to give him a smile. I walk gingerly as if I have just birthed a baby. I feel with every step *I am* NOT FINE.

When I get into the car, I have no feeling of where my head is; I have to protect it when I slide into the passenger's seat. Syb helps me; he is the sweetest person on earth. With a concerned look, he drives off. He is now sensing that I am *not* okay. I am nauseated from the seven shots in my forehead, the intravenous drip, the saw and the doctor. They all contribute to me wanting to throw-up. Somehow we eat apple pie; I can't drink the coffee. Part of me loves to sit there peacefully with Syb; inside I am shaking violently.

We go into an exclusive dress shop next door. It is called *Claudia Straiter.* We choose a purple and green silky dress. The material and design are truly beautiful. Syb drops me off at home and life goes on. Mission completed. The kids come for lunch and, in the afternoon, my parents stop in with flowers. They tell me to take it easy. *How can I do that with a seven-month-old baby on my breast and four more bundles of joy running around?*

I bring the kids to school and lie down for an hour. I am feeling *very* sick. I didn't receive any instructions about the state I am in so I think it will pass. No need to make it into a big deal.

I breastfeed Gideon and he doesn't want my milk. He can taste the shots of medicine circulating throughout my breast milk. My head is completely numb and I bump into everything at head level. Later that afternoon, people come to hang curtains in the living room. They need to cut the wooden valances. I can't tolerate the sound of the saw. My head is too painful.

I wake up feeling sick and sweaty the next morning. I need fresh air and so I take Gideon in his stroller for our daily morning walk. Every morning we walk downtown to buy our groceries. I shop daily. (Even after six years of living in America, I still can't give up this Dutch habit.)

We walk through the park and the closer we get to downtown the sicker and sicker I begin to feel. I am out of breath. I keep on walking because I want to get my shopping done.

People stare at me or turn their heads when I pass by. I pretend not to notice. I know my face doesn't look good. There is a big swelling around my left eye; it looks as if I was in a very bad accident. I wish I was invisible. I walk to Jacqueline's, my best friend who lives downtown. When she opens the door, she is dressed in black; she is going a funeral. This means I can't stay. I am too proud to tell her I need to lie down because I feel so dizzy and sick. I just tell her I'll come back another time and off I go. I wonder *what is wrong with me. Why am I having such a strong reaction from yesterday?*

Later I hear most people stay in bed for a few days and, before the operation, they take precautions to reduce the swelling like taking arnica. My head is badly swollen. *How much worse will my condition get?* The doctor didn't say a word about the do's and don'ts or what to expect.

The following morning, I can't open my left eye. My face is blue and swollen. My head is numb and my mind is blank.

I call the hospital. They say it's normal; it will go away soon. Not to worry. However, my condition gets worse day by day. I look like someone beat me up.

The side effect on others comes slowly to my realization. At the bank, the woman behind the counter asks if I was the one beaten up in the latest robbery. *What was she talking about?* I tell her *no*, I was not beaten up; I had skin cancer. Then I laugh—it's getting kinda funny in a weird way—I hadn't heard of the robbery.

Apparently, I am being told I need to face this now and accept that this is not to be taken lightly by *pretending* life goes on and it is "nothing." *Was the world reflecting back that I needed to take a good look at myself and what I was feeling?*

After this, I become more relaxed, much more relaxed. My scalp is still without any feeling. It's strange because I keep bumping my head.

As if the Universe orchestrated certain events with a higher hand, I find myself alone at a time I need to be completely by myself. My cleaning lady cancels for a month and nobody but Gideon is left with me all morning and afternoon.

There is pure silence and slowly I start drifting into bliss. My mind only functions in moments I need my brain to tie the pieces together. The anticipatory faculty is closed and so is the whole section on planning and control. I have NO thoughts now. No past reflections, no future projections. I am completely in the NOW. There is nothing. I have no concerns because I deal only with what is in THE PRESENT. I float with my feet still on the ground.

At first, I don't realize what is happening. I am so in the moment I don't think about myself either. One day a friend calls and asks if her son can come for a play date. I answer honestly. I didn't know and I have to check my calendar.

She asks, "Is your head so full these days that you don't know what's on your schedule?"

I think for a moment and answer, "No, my head is totally empty; let me look at the calendar." And so, it is decided her son can come over to play.

As soon as my head let go of control, absolutely everything is taken care of. I am in the moment with everyone I meet. It is the true experience of bliss. I don't waste my time by contemplating thoughts of how and when. My time becomes abundant. I play endlessly on the floor with Gideon and we both enjoy each other to the fullest.

One afternoon, my friend Nivine comes along. We lie on the floor of the living room on a big blanket with Gideon in the middle. We chat and, without us noticing, our conversation takes us into another dimension. Then I feel the familiar soft tap of my Soul on my shoulder reminding me it is dinnertime. I need to go to Jet's place and pick up Sytske. "Gosh," I say, "look how late it is already!" We both jump up quickly.

I switch on the lights because it is now completely dark. I see a familiar Volkswagen pull up in front of my house. Jet waves and, as I walk toward her, she says she thought it would be a good idea to drive Sytske home. Again, everything is taken care of.

I am so grateful I did not worry about it earlier and interrupt my conversation with Nivine. Our conversation was very dear and important to me. It seemed the Universe thought so, too. At any time I needed it, the Universe became my helping hand; the examples fill this book.

For two weeks, my life is easy. Then one day, I realize I am not thinking. With that, my mind starts to chatter again. My cleaning lady is back. Gideon weans off my breast and, bit by bit, my blissful state fades with each thought coming in. My unexpected sabbatical with the divine is officially over.

One thing remains: I now know through this experience about the real 'being in the flow' of life. Now I have lived it. The flow comes only when you are 'out' of your mind. Only then is there enough room for the Universe to 'move in' and take over.

PART FIVE

A Suitcase Full of Faith

Which will it be?
Will you be like the man
who found a bag of diamonds
while looking for sugar
and threw it away because
they failed to dissolve in his mouth?
Or having found prayer,
will you make your life
a miracle?

—Orest Bedrij,
Yes It's Love: your life can be a miracle

Flight 037

Our friends ask Syb and me what we want as a "farewell present." The only thing we can think of is a *Pilgrim's Survival Kit.* It is to be an inventive, creative *personal* guide written by all of our Dutch friends and family from *their* perspective on how to survive in America. They knew America is a *big* country where we had no jobs, no guaranteed income, and where our five kids didn't speak more than a word of English. All we knew, all that was so totally familiar and a part of our lives for so many years would be left behind. Until the ship's arrival with all our worldly belongings, we could be sitting in our totally empty house for a month or more with only our suitcase and a few colorful beach towels laid out upon the floor. Our *Pilgrim's Survival Kit* seemed – next to our *suitcase full of faith* – the most practical tool for us.

But *where are the tools when you need them most? Why is it we assume our Pilgrim's Survival Kit will only be needed AFTER we arrive on American soil? Why do we think there won't be a need for a life-line during our leap across an ocean to our destination and our destiny?*

When we pull into the airport, everything suddenly becomes REAL. We are *moving to America*. The full impact of this was not anticipated *at all*.

I look at a departing plane taking off in the sky above my head and I realize the moment we take off, we will say *goodbye* to EVERYONE we love.

How blessed we are to have so many friends and family wishing us well! I wonder if one can ever bid a fond farewell *consciously* and *completely. Was that the answer to the perfect way to die?* As quickly as my thoughts come, they go.

We arrive in time at the check-in counter. Our final goodbye is more unreal now that this moment is here. We are concerned most of all about our dog Buddha, who will be traveling alone in a special cage in the back of the plane. Early in the morning we give her a dose of sleeping medicine to sedate her for the flight. They say this is the ultimate "canine health and safety precaution" for any flight.

She wags her white tail while we stand in line and wait and worry. Buddha is in the NOW and can't be bothered with future concerns. She will travel with us as she did so many times before: Taiwan, Holland, all over Europe. She never wavered from being by our side. Today she thinks *this trip to America is a piece of cake.*

We kiss and wave goodbye to her as they close her cage. My heart cringes when she disappears slowly on the conveyor belt that leads to the underground cargo depot of Schiphol. She looks at us. Above her rich brown eyes I think I spot a questioning frown. *Does she know something we do not?*

While Syb and I check in our luggage, the kids run around as usual. From the outside, it must have looked as if we were going on an ordinary trip on an ordinary day, Friday July 6th.

It is ordinary, yes, except for a circle of teary-eyed friends and family who surround us. We learn that Celine has hit another vehicle in the parking garage when she went to park her car. It is that kind of day; we feel a bit off-guard.

My parents left for Spain a few days ago. It was too difficult and painful to see us leave. Sleepovers, lunches in the woods, too many magic unforgettable memories cause them joy and pain. We take those memories with us; however, I can *feel* their pain. My parents love our children from the bottom of their Souls.

In order to survive today, I can't go into their pain; there are too many things, too many emotions hanging about. I understand deeply how hard this must be for them. It will take my parents most of a month to find the courage to drive down our street past our house.

My dad goes back one day to say his silent goodbye. The house contains only the echoes of our kids; their shrill voices bounce off the warm orange walls. In the hallway, he discovers a stuffed Dalmatian dog. This is a real *find*, forlorn and waiting to be found. My dad grabs it symbolically as a physical string connected to us. *Fleur* my parents real Dalmatian is beyond herself with delight when my dad comes home and hands her his treasure. So are we when we hear about it later.

All of us chat as if we will never leave. But, when the time is announced to pack up and go, we feel we must suddenly be in a hurry.

We hug, tears flow; it doesn't take long. "We better go," we say in unison. *What else can we say that will soothe the sadness?*

We wave until our hands hurt and it feels as if we are invisibly pushed; we move through Customs in a blur. I look back one more time. Then our heads turn, our hearts pound, and we need to keep on walking. I am aware of all the tears – I can feel them wet on the back of my neck – but I can't let this overwhelm me now.

I am filled with a strange a mixture of immense joy and sadness. Both are equal in their exuberance and intensity. Months later I cry my held-back tears, sweet in their aftertaste. Memory Lane is worth a trip. What a marvelous group of family and friends we leave behind.

The departure is delayed; we have a hard time waiting. Every one of us is tired to the bone. Our life has been a month-long party and we need to GO NOW.

A metallic voice announces our plane is defective and is being "fixed." Two hours later we are finally allowed to board. "We think we are ready to fly" is their simple statement. A rush of relief ripples through the waiting crowd of passengers; I am not convinced.

As I step aboard the plane, my stomach churns. I hear the engine run. I sense *something* is not quite right. But *how technically experienced am I to detect a mechanical defect in our plane?* I sigh. I need to trust and let go of my concern. It is nothing. It was an emotionally-draining day and all I am hearing is the sound of my nerves rubbing against each other.

It does not add to my comfort that our seats are divided up throughout different sections of the plane. Gideon, our two year old, sits between Syb and I; Sam is seated in front of us chatting happily with two friendly fellow passengers. Shaffy, Florian and Sytske are sitting somewhere behind us near the right wing. We strap our seatbelts on tight when the stewardess announces our departure.

The engine roars, the plane moves. I close my eyes and turn within.

My hands are folded in my lap. I want to remember and savor this emotional take off. We move down the runway at full speed. I silently sigh as I look for the last time at the flat land that housed my Soul for most of my life. Trembling yet powerful, the plane lifts her wings, points her nose to the sky and her tail to earth. Effortlessly she glides into the limitless sky.

We are on our way to another world. I shiver and then hold my body still; my heart is pounding, my Soul bends over in a bow of acknowledgement. Within every fiber of my being I feel the huge impact of the leap we are taking – a leap over an ocean, a leap of destiny. *Will we ever come back home? Where is home?*

While I keep my eyes closed, the door to Soul's message slides open. A soft breeze light as a paint brush touches my inner ear: "The land of *opportunity* is waiting for each and every one of you." I tremble again slightly and squeeze my folded hands.

Am I the only one who knows we are on a one-way flight? Of course, if things aren't going well for the kids, we would return. According to Soul, that will not be the case.

I breathe deeply through the takeoff moment. I can hear the angels' feet dance above our heads. The roof of the plane must be the perfect platform for their heavenly disco. I grin.

The first few hours pass without much excitement or turbulence. As I am looking at the map on the screen that shows we are now located in the middle of the Atlantic ocean, I smell smoke.

This is a non-smoking flight. I ask Syb, who is immersed in a movie, if he smells something, too. He is startled by my question when he realizes he does, too. We look around. Nobody else seems to notice; many of the passengers are asleep. All of a sudden a blue smoke fills the cabin—the plane is on fire.

All at once, everybody looks around, heads turn, eyes meet. Panic reflects in every face. Our question is how catastrophic can this situation be? I look around. I have only one question: where are my kids? They are totally unaware of the cause of the turmoil around them. Three of them are seated too far away from us to see or reach them; we are not allowed to leave our seats.

My mind goes in all directions. *What if we dive into the ocean?* Only Florian and Sytske can swim; the rest will be helpless in the dark, bottomless sea. The pilot comes on the speaker; he announces *there is a fire in the electrical circuitry and we are not sure where or how it began. Some one will "try" to fix it.* I do not like his word "try." *We all need to stay put* and with that he shuts off the mike and leaves us to our racing imaginations.

My mind is quick to retrieve the memory of a plane that crashed not long ago due to *a fire in its electrical circuitry.* After all we've been through, this *can't* be our fate.

Fear spreads faster than a wildfire in July throughout the plane. I am glad the fire within the plane is not so quick or hungry although even the stewardesses look grim. I ask one of them if she knows what is going on. "No, we don't, and *that* is the problem," she snaps at my question. Her words slip out of her mouth before she knows it; her posture shows panic.

I am beyond myself with fear. *I want to hold my children.* I am tightly strapped in my seat and not allowed to move. I feel Death staring us in the face. I ask God, *"WHY? How can this be after we made all this effort? Is it our karma to perish in the deep waters of the ocean before we set a foot on dry land?"* My silent prayer reaches out to anyone who can help us. "I ask an S.O.S. for all of us," I say.

I am feeling the need to know the reason if our life ends right here. *Did we say goodbye to everyone we love in a final family reunion of sorts only to disappear off the radar screen for good?* This is unacceptable to me after all the hard work we've done and we're only "halfway." I rethink my question: *where is home in the end?*

"We may make an emergency landing," the voice of the captain says. My knowledge of our location is up-to-date. I have a clear picture of where we are. The map I am studying shows endless stretches of blue water, no earth in sight to land our burning plane.

The blue mist inside the plane doesn't clear; the smell is *un*bearable. The engine roars with an undisturbed passion. I can only think "I *knew* it;" *being right* in this case doesn't help a bit.

I unbuckle my seat belt and search for the Australian bush remedy *Waratah* in my backpack. It is the remedy for *extreme* courage and survival. Our other potential remedy – our goodbye present, the *Pilgrim's Survival Kit* – is snugly tucked away in the luggage compartment in the back of the plane. *What advice could we use from its wisdom right now? Was there a rope to hold onto during a skydive jump?*

In the meantime, Syb is orchestrating the survival of our kids. Sam's friendly seat-mate in front of us will keep an eye on Sam if it comes to a plunge. We don't need many words for him to understand our request. He nods; he knows enough.

How much do we really have to know each other when it comes to a survival situation like this? We are all in this together and there is no doubt we will hold each others' hands. Syb plans to get to the older kids if necessary and Gideon will "swim" with me. My prayers are ceaseless. I hope someone is *Home* and picks up my call. Above my head it is too silent for my liking. *Where are the angels when we need them most? Have they left their party on our roof top to sleep it off on some puffy cloud?*

The pilot talks again; he tells us *nobody knows where the fire is coming from*. His people are working hard; we will continue our flight. *Yeah, what else did he have in mind?* The smell of burnt rubber is pungent.

Motherhood is hard and unbearable right now. I am at loss for words to describe the pain I feel when I watch my children wiggling in their chairs, their eyes full of happiness, joyfully anticipating the dream they still share. My mind goes to Buddha and tears come to my eyes. She must be choking in the back of the plane with no idea of what is going on.

My thoughts wander between question and affirmation. *Are we safe?* We are safe. I squeeze my folded hands. My heart beats rapidly; I can't control it. *Is this the ultimate lesson to test my faith?* Finally, I put my head to rest and find my faith. The remedy must be doing her work. I now trust we will survive. I remind myself of my divine thread, the cord that's never cut. *How could I forget?*

For a while we stay in our comfort zone through avoidance; the captain doesn't speak, the cabin personnel avoid questions by being busy in the back. We just sit and wait. My body feels sick. Then magically the smoke disappears; the air conditioning is switched off and that works well enough to give us the impression we have the issue "under control." Without interruption we continue the flight to Boston—as long as we don't smell smoke, we can assume we're fine.

The pilot speaks again when we are close to the Boston airport. It seems we can't communicate with the tower, therefore we cannot land. We have to circle until we get contact. Maybe the circuit is burnt. Everyone turns their heads and looks around. *Are we going to land in Boston or what?* The passengers laugh in disbelief; this can't be true. *Who will navigate us?*

I can handle this I think—if I've survived a fire inside a plane – I can trust in the *unseen Navigator.* This is doable. I am getting very curious what the Pilgrim's Survival Kit would have said.

We fly around for an extra half an hour and rumors spread that the captain isn't telling the *whole* truth. Perhaps we are being told to empty our fuel tanks before we are allowed to land. As far as we know, the "issue" isn't solved yet and, if there *is* a smoldering fire, the plane could explode when we touch the ground. As we discuss and fret, the kids can't wait to arrive. They can see the skyline of Boston. We are *almost* there.

Suddenly, we hear the landing gear go into motion and we have to fasten our seatbelts, sit upright and go for the final dive. Never have I seen "ground safety preparation" like this. From above the ground, we can see the entire fire department of Boston waiting for our plane as well as a full battalion of ambulances. Police cars flash their lights at the side of the runway landing. All are ready to *Rock n' Roll* and so are we. The stewards and stewardesses are strapped in their seats while they give us last instructions for landing. They say we might make use of the landing slides and we have to make sure to depart the plane immediately.

The children are overjoyed for this possible treat, not aware of the emergency measures in place to help us leave this unsafe ship. They are more than willing to leave the plane as fast as they can. No problem; they listen well.

We touch the ground with a loud bang. The pilot must be eager to put this plane to rest.

The landing reignites the fire and smoke enters the cabin. Within seconds, the doors are opened by the fire department; they hold big axes in their hands. The kids are excited. We are rushed out to safety by fairly "normal' means to the enormous disappointment of the kids; there are no slides.

But we have landed safely. I still tremble and swallow hard in my state of shock. Our new life has begun. We've arrived home with a bang.

In the basement of Logan airport, the kids run to find our luggage on the right conveyor belt at "Baggage Claim". Buddha is the first one to greet us with her unstoppable, wagging tail. We all run toward her and free her from her cage. She jumps up and down like the kids, but I can see that her eyes are red and blurry.

I can see she has suffered on our fiery flight. *Has the smoke affected her too much?* One thing I resolve: Buddha's new life in America is going to be her *best*. That much she must know. She doesn't question. America is her home. It will be her last as this journey will be the last journey of her life.

When the doors of the International gate swing open, we float through. We have made it! *Welcome to America!*

Two weeks later, I have a dream. In the dream I am told our plane barely had a chance of survival. Apparently, our karma flew us safely to the other side.

Welcome Home

Frits, Joanna, Nico and TJ are waiting. Their little American flags wave at us. They wrap their arms around us when we step through the gate, finally we are here.

"What took you so long?" is their question. Indeed we were delayed. I would rather save the explanation for later.

A huge surprise awaits us and the kids nearly faint when they lay their eyes on the brightest and biggest white limousine they've ever seen. The Kist family smiles behind our backs. A chauffeur in uniform opens the polished door and lets us in. One by one we crawl into the cozy limo; a few minutes later Frits hands each of us a Coke.

We are home. America and Coca-Cola are like baseball and apple pie. I take a moment to breathe in the enormity of our move but I can't quite grasp it. The limo moves so smoothly, we feel like movie stars in a dream that's just begun.

Because of all the busyness of our emigration, the goodbye parties and the arrangements for moving that needed to be made, I wasn't able to foresee how our arrival and first weeks in America would play out. It was too far ahead and there was simply too much to handle. It forced me to trust that both would unfold effortlessly by themselves. There was no other way.

Our preparation for our coming home to live in Rockport was less than brief. A *letting go and letting God* attitude was all I could manage. How we would eat, sleep, cook, sit, have lights in the house, or buy a car would have to be dealt with when we got there. Now we were *there.*

To bridge the gap between the arrival of the ship with our belongings and now, we brought seven beach towels and some clothes. I thought we could sleep on towels on the floor; we were good and experienced campers after all. If our household arrived a few months later and if the summer in Rockport was as promising as we were told, the beach would compensate for the rest. *How was I to know that where we lacked any real plan for the first few months, the Universe would kindly take over?*

My excitement overruled any concern and, while the limo is finding its way to our new front door, I lean back and watch the excited and expectant faces of the kids. We see Buddha pass by in the back of Joanna's car; no dogs are allowed in a limo here. We wave. Buddha barks hello.

The limo pulls up in front and drops us off at THE HOUSE, OUR HOUSE . . . our new *home*. The sun is setting behind the woods; some rays linger and touch the front porch.

Red geraniums in straw pots dangle in the ocean breeze. They smile in our faces with a "There they are at last."

The House is *so* beautiful. We walk around eager to greet her in her wholeness. She is BIG.

We run up the steps and bounce through the side door just like our first time – no locks, no keys. She is open to our arrival and stay.

I enter, stop and blink. A fairy has worked magic with her wand. *Was it Snow White?* Seven beds with fresh linen sheets are set-up in perfect order. A little portable stove sits waiting in the sun room. The fridge is FULL. Seven little chairs neatly encircle a table and a lamp. Our five little dwarfs are ready to try everything out. Now our beach towels can really be used *for the beach*. Tears well up in my eyes. *Is it really true that dreams can come true?* Clearly our fairies Frits and Joanna worked really hard and provided their magic touch!

Syb and I walk together through the house while the kids do their thing at their own pace. Syb and I go step-by-step savoring each moment; they run at full speed. We want to feel every inch of the ground we touch. I'm not sure that the kids have touched down on firm ground yet. The old Victorian atmosphere and the spaciousness of each room vibrate in their full glory matching all the joy we feel.

Frits and Joanna and a few unknown neighbors have cared for us. They probably wondered how in the world we could survive our first weeks or months living in nothingness? It is not the American way. America is big. It embodies an ambience of abundance. Anticipating our needs, they donated furniture from their own houses and a "swap shop" in order to create a *home*.

Our arrival has aroused the interest of *everyone* close by. Ken, our new next-door neighbor, asks me how I will dry the beach towels, how I will iron and if the kids need some music? My question is *how could I have overlooked these common things?* A towel rack, a radio and an iron will be dropped off by Ken a day later.

For weeks, people will stop by to drop off household items – "necessities" – and food to welcome us. The Universe works overtime; she is abundant in her endless supply. We are cared for to the max. Later I realize that, if we had completely arranged and attempted to control this part of our move, we would never have experienced what happens when you allow the Universe to chip in big time.

We make a moonlit trip through the dark house before we go to bed. Buddha serves as the line leader. We feel safe to have our guardian Angel at our side. The house has no locks; a plastic sheet separates the kitchen from the outside deck. *Who cares?* We already survived a burning plane. There is no fear. We are *home*.

The spare lights from the swap shop are thoughtfully stationed next to our mattresses on the floor. When I tuck in the kids and kiss them goodnight, I can't believe our "luck." But deep down I know there really is no such thing as *luck*. Life is not about luck; it's about creating our own reality. I take a deep, full breath and smile inside anyway.

Syb and I go to nestle down into our new beds but, before I say a word, Syb is sound asleep.

I stare at the ceiling and think *how can I ever express my gratitude in a moment like this?* I am so thankful; my cup runneth over.

We all wake early. Abundant sunshine streams through the huge windows; the morning has broken. "Let's go outside!" is our mutual cry. We walk in line through the kitchen, which is still a work in progress. Syb pull's away the plastic sheet that separates the kitchen from the outside world.

In one motion, the curtain is up and we stand on the outside deck, *What play we are in?* We gasp in unison. Our audience waits in the trees. Two hundred squirrel eyes stare at us from between the branches. The trees of the woods are the chorus line; they wave in a slow-motion dance. The breeze sways the squirrels from left to right in a lazy and leisurely motion. They are not in a hurry. They are ready for the play. In this timeless moment, they simply stare and wait; in return, we stand on our stage mesmerized by their gaze.

"Wow," the kids scream in tune with the tree chorus, "It's *Squirrel Land!*"

Did the squirrels of our trees and forest invite all of their neighbors to come and say hello? How did they know we finally arrived? And who gathered them all together at the exact same time to catch our grand entrance onto the stage of our outer world? They must have had a spy at our window and waited until we woke up.

We wave to them. They begin to leave. The play is over and they are satisfied. Some leave in groups, some on their own.

One more time, the Universe shows us how welcome we are. Abundance is *everywhere.*

The Conference

I am thrilled to be attending the phenomenal Hypnotherapy conference in New Hampshire. While in Holland, my colleagues spoke of this conference for years. Our teacher, Burt Goldman, urged us to go but the distance was too far to travel then. Many years passed and only in my wildest dreams did I think I could attend. I realized that after our move to America, Nashua, New Hampshire, the place of the conference, is only two hours away from our home. Now I can go!

In Holland, as I take a look at the conference brochure, I see it lists over 250 workshops! My mind goes blank but I have to make a choice before the deadline. I feel scattered in my thinking so I randomly pick as many workshops as I can fit in one day.

We are in the middle of moving and basically everything is being taken away at the very moment I have to make a wise choice. *How can I think straight while the movers are rummaging through my house? Why did the brochure have to arrive right now?* I sit in the one and only piece of furniture left in the house: a molded plastic chair that will never make it to the States.

I post my application and forget about it as soon as the paper leaves my hand.

On the morning of the conference, I get an early start. I make sure to be on the road a little after 6 AM.

I am relieved to be away from the mess in our house. The chaos of painting and reconstruction makes me restless. Paint spots all my clothes and my hair. After six weeks of 24/7 noise and turbulence, silence fills the car. It is *heaven*. For the first time in weeks, I have a moment to pause and breathe. Week after week we've worked from dawn to dusk. The sacred moments I savor are not a part of my life right now.

In jail, the trick to make a terrorist confess is to wake him up every couple of hours. For me it is simple: to drive me insane just deprive me of any "alone time." The result is that I become disconnected from my Soul.

So it is that I am suddenly surprised and delighted that the "lonely" car ride is really a blessing in disguise; it nourishes Soul and my need to become myself again. What joy! The road is busy with lots of traffic heading north but I don't care. After two hours of self-indulged, blessed reflection, I am in New Hampshire.

I park the car in the hotel parking lot. I step out and am met by a family of chipmunks. The little creatures are quick and twirl around the pine trees, bringing back memories of vacations in Spain. I sit on a bench under the trees and I feel like I have landed in heaven.

The smell of paint fades and makes room for the fragrance of *Spirit*.

The conference is lively and full of people; everyone is in a good mood.

I go to pick up my schedule. I am curious about what workshops I signed up for during the next three days. I can't remember what I picked and have no idea what to expect.

One of the first workshops I attend is life changing. I meet Marcel, who gives a lecture on the *Stillpoint School*. He is from Holland and is a graduate of the school. He will be a teacher there in the fall. I am startled to meet a Dutch guy here at this conference. What is even more amazing is I don't remember signing up for this workshop. *So how did I get here?*

I sit in the front row for his one hour class so I won't miss a thing. He passionately explains the *Stillpoint Healing Model*. I am fascinated to hear him talk about this model and I ingest every word. I copy what he writes on the chalkboard; I *know* I am onto something *big*. At the end, I ask him where I can find more information.

He quickly wipes everything off the board and says, "There's no book but grab a brochure if you'd like."

So I do as I am told. As I lay my hands on the *Stillpoint School* brochure, Soul speaks loud and clear, "You will be a teacher at this school." *What*? I argue and say I haven't even taken the program yet. "Go and become a teacher, if not for yourself, then for others." And with that the voice is silent; me too. I stare at the cost of the program on the back of the brochure. I don't know what I am going to do but I leave with brochure in hand. I am at the right place at the right time; everything is pointing that way.

The first day deeply nourished my hunger to learn more about the power of the subconscious mind.

I leave home even earlier the next morning. I want to sit a bit longer on the bench and listen to the chipmunk's family talk. I stand in line for coffee when I catch sight of two lazy leather chairs. I know where I will sit after I pay. I pay for my coffee and an elderly nice-looking man sits down in one of the chairs. He has the kindest face. We start talking and joking with each other as if we are old friends. Instantly, we feel a bond between us.

Our conversation is funny and animated but, every so often, we are disturbed by several of the older hypnotherapists who greet 'my new friend' and thank him for his contribution to the world. After a while, I get the uneasy feeling I am joking around with someone of great importance at the conference. I don't know yet that he is one of their most famous key note speakers.

He asks my name and hands me a brochure. It's about his upcoming training program for becoming a past life therapist. The course takes place in Virginia in December.

So was that why I met him? Am I supposed to go?

"I don't think you need it but you might like to take a look," he tells me.

My voice deep within speaks again, "GO."

At first I ignore its advice. Then I bump into Henry Bolduc a few more times that day. By the time I leave to drive home, I *know* I have to listen and *go*.

Now I have two brochures in my hand on programs that cost *a lot* of dollars, time and commitment. My stomach feels funny. *What will Syb say?*

The course of my life has changed again in just three days. *Yes*, I will go to The *Stillpoint School* in October and do Henry's training in December. The look in my eyes speaks the world when I ask Syb.

"Go," is what he says; he knows me well. The 'why' and 'how' can be left for later. I trust my Soul.

Early in September I get a notice; I am approved for both.

Little do I know that two years later in 2003, I am a teacher at the *Stillpoint School* and am listed as a keynote speaker in *Past Life Regression Therapy* at the first *World Congress* in Holland.

What if your awareness
of your connectedness to all things
became an earthshakingly positive experience
of flow of energy in the universe
through your mind, body, and spirit?

—Stephen Lewis,
Sanctuary: The Path to Consciousness

Getting To the Other Side

I wake up with a swelling only a few inches above the ankle of my right leg. I haven't exercised although I should …what bothers me most is that my mobility decreases day by day. I am in *a lot* of pain. I can hardly walk and driving is getting difficult too. We don't have a family doctor yet and, after a week of observing how my leg is deteriorating, I ask my neighbors if they know a good doctor. Mary, who lives down the street, refers me to a local medical center in Manchester. I take her advice and make an appointment.

We are still in a mode in America where we have to rely on a stranger about where to go and who to call. We still don't know our way around. The Yellow Pages doesn't help much. Our fingers walk right through them and then right out again. In America everyone is *the* best; the list of recommendations is endless. I wonder who *not* to call. I trust Mary because the hairdresser she referred me to is good. Hopefully the medical treatment will be as good as my hair. The medical center sounds friendly enough when I call them and they have a space open right away.

Now that I'm here, I am eager to have a doctor look at my leg. After filling out a ton of forms, I am ushered into a small room. The nurse examines me with inexperienced eyes. "I'm not sure," is all she can say. *Thanks, Me neither. That's why I am here.*

Within half an hour at least five doctors gather around my nastily swollen leg. One doctor thinks it might be a bee swelling badly out of control but I know it's not. I haven't been near a bee since I entered the States. Another doctor pushes deeply into my flesh. They take my temperature and listen to my heart. I "sound" okay. The x-ray doesn't show a thing. One-by-one they shake their heads. No one has seen anything like this; their expertise can't touch it.

The diagnosis is that I better come back in a week's time. They send me on my way with a prescription for ibuprofen – 1000 mg, three times a day.

Was the objective to get rid of me for good?

My question remains unanswered. After a day of ibuprofen, I am beside myself physically. My aura walks next to me.

The next day I have a great idea. I look up the number of a Dutch energy worker I've called for help before. If she is able to tune into my body, hopefully she will be able to see what's wrong. I call and get her on the phone with the first ring. I trust her; so far her intuition is always right. I tell her about my right leg.

She is silent for a moment and then says, "You are not completely in Rockport yet. Some part of you is still stuck in Holland."

What? I am stunned. This can't be true. I can understand if Syb or another family member isn't fully here, *but me? How on earth could I not be here?* I launched the American plan and initiated the move.

I hang up the phone and sit with the receiver in my hand. If this is true, it's pretty symbolic. The right side of the body is the past and apparently I haven't crossed the ocean with both legs.

Somehow, I need to step into the future with both legs. Body, mind and spirit are One; that much is obvious. My conscious mind was aware and fully aligned with my choice; apparently I left an unconscious piece of me in Holland. How grateful I am that my body warns me of this imbalance. Suddenly I realize that I never took time to align my body before the giant leap we took. I left my right leg behind in the eagerness of Soul to come and settle down in the US. My body needed time to adjust and become aligned. And here I am.

I sit down and let a flood of information pass through my consciousness. *What shall I do with this insight? How can I help myself?* I go upstairs and close our bedroom door. I know a ritual is called for. I take my time and ask how to create a sacred moment that will heal my body and let go of the part of me that still clings to the past. If I want to step fully into the future, I need *both* legs. My body, mind and spirit have to be aligned with all the choices I make.

I divide the room energetically into America on one side and Holland on the other with the Atlantic Ocean in between. I tell my body, mind and spirit, we will cross the Atlantic Ocean. I take a deep breath and mentally rehearse the step. Then with one huge step as if I wear seven-mile boots, I step with my right leg from Holland to America. I affirm that I fully accept my arrival in this country. Then with my other leg, I do the same.

The moment I cross the ocean, I deliberately tune into each leg, giving each one time to absorb the ocean and the space we cross. Now I have arrived in America with *both* legs *and* my feet.

It feels good. I vibrate at a new level of energy that streams throughout my body.

A knock on the door makes me come back to motherhood again.

The kids want to go downtown. Within seconds I place my "mom" hat on and am looking for the keys to the jeep. I've already forgotten what I did.

A moment later the kids and I are racing down the hill with the wind blowing in my hair. Back again, I jump out the jeep.

I realize I no longer have a problem walking. The swelling is completely gone; my leg is healed.

I am on the other side, *all* of me *finally* HOME in *Rockport*.

Nine One One

Peace at last. Syb and I will take a break and climb to the top of our Victorian home today. We will enjoy the spectacular view of the New England foliage from the widow's walk. This is the day. For the last three months, we painted, scrubbed, waxed and polished the floors and walls until we had blisters on our hands and knees.

Today is the day we treat ourselves. We've fantasized about it; I am looking forward to "doing" *nothing.* Syb and I walk back from the school bus stop in a cheerful mood. Everything is perfect. The phone rings at ten minutes after 9 AM.

I can't think of anyone I know who would call our number at this time of the day. *Could it be the school? No*, that was impossible. My kids were saluting the American flag; no teacher would have any good reason to interrupt this sacred moment with a phone call.

It's Frits on the line, telling me to turn on the TV. He says a plane flew into the World Trade Center. We think it is an accident. I run upstairs because Gideon is enthralled in the world of Bambi downstairs. I switch on the news. On every channel I see the same scene of the same plane crashing into the Tower again and again. I am glued to the TV and watch this horrific "movie" over and over. Gone is our morning on the widow's walk. My heart goes out to the widows in New York.

Guilt overwhelms me as I anticipate a war that can't be stopped. *Why had I dragged my family to America? Were we supposed to be involved in this?* As the World Trade Center towers are smashed to pieces, so is my world. I want to bury my head in Bambi with my youngest son; his world and mine are the exact opposite now. My DNA carries the WTC disaster on every level. My heart bleeds along with the victims. I am them. I feel the fear and my survival instinct says RUN. Past life memories of earthquakes, landslides and natural disasters trigger panic inside; in the middle of all the massive catastrophes when the world came to her end, I am there. I know

I have not survived any one of them.

And yet I can't run *this* time. My guilt is HUGE and I want to crawl back to Holland on my knees. There is no way back. For some reason, I can't stop myself from watching the news -- perhaps it gives me a sense of control.

No wonder Soul urged us to leave Holland before 9/11; otherwise, we would not have left. The Universe knew she had to get us to the other side in time but *what for?*

Back at the bus stop I am changed. The person so joyful in the morning now walks with a heavy step. *What do I tell my kids?*

The moms and dads are waiting to pick up their kids; most are crying. Everyone's face carries the signs of misery and shock.

Americans haven't experienced this kind of disaster for some time. Just like Pearl Harbor, this attack sweeps them off their feet unaware. I am one of them.

I hear lots of stories about friends who just missed that plane or beloved ones who were not so lucky. It is cruel and yet I listen to all the stories.

At school the kids are told but they have no idea what it is all about. I don't want to raise their fear too much so I don't say much more. They saw their teachers cry at school, so it is obvious something bad happened. Perhaps due to the language barrier or because they were so young, their life goes on largely as before.

Syb is less distracted and concerned about our future; with his usual optimistic attitude, he believes this worldwide disaster will be resolved. The radio and TV news anchors announce the highest level of alert, much like the state I'm in. I want to help save the world but I feel more helpless than I've ever been. *Why am I here?* We pray for all involved. *What else can we do?*

I stand in shock and disbelief when Syb announces he will leave for Italy on the next available flight out of Boston. He's planned this trip to Italy long in advance and he is going no matter what. I fall apart. I should know better; there is nothing that will stop him. He is going and that is that. He will not give in to terrorists and allow them to destroy his plans. I am a mess; I can't believe he will leave his family alone and unprotected.

Syb is full of trust that all is well; I am not. I beg him to stay but I know I can't make him. "It will never be safer to travel," he says. Maybe so, but *what will happen if there is another attack?*

We have nowhere to go. We barely know our way around Rockport. Besides, *what is our escape plan?*

I feel vulnerable in this new country. *Who do I call for help?* I ask Syb where I should go and what I should do with the kids. *Do I drive North, South or West?* We conclude Canada is the answer. *What about money? Do we still have some?*

I have more question than answers and I feel so alone. Syb will fly out on the first international flight leaving Boston since the attack. The flight is confirmed on Saturday. My prayers did not help one bit. I don't care about *my* life; my fear is how to protect my five children; THAT is enough to break my heart.

So where oh where is my little faith now? How can it be that I lost it?

Syb leaves in a taxi with a driver who patiently waits through my long goodbye. He doesn't know I begin to cry as soon as the cab is out of sight. Through my tears, I think *well here I am in America; indeed my dream came true*. It tastes bittersweet.

It doesn't take me long to figure out my options. I want our passports ready in case all hell breaks loose. I walk through our nearly empty house and review the stuff we'll have to pack. It won't take long because we won't take much. The box that contains the passport is in the green living room and I am happy the box is closed and is still in the same place as I put it. I open the box and count five passports, mine is gone. I count again; it makes no difference. *Where is mine?*

To search for a passport in an empty house sounds easy. Perhaps the search is but it's extremely difficult to face the realization that mine isn't there. I feel I can't look for something when emptiness sits all around me. It's just *not* here.

I walk around and feel like a fool. There is no where to look but UP. I ask God who is playing this hide-and-seek game with me. I hear nothing back and search again. I long for a big pile of mess to browse through and find it.

After a long search, I finally give up and say, "Okay, I get the message. I will stay. I promise I won't run away." I stop my search and whisper, "P.S. However long you need to hold on to that passport, please put it back very soon. Thanks." My request is answered three weeks later. One morning when I glance inside the box, my passport is back on top of the stack. They must have trusted I wasn't going anywhere.

The first night Syb is gone I feel like a lioness wanting to protect her cubs. I walk around the house as if that will help lock the danger out. I imagine terrorists in the backyard. Perhaps our squirrel army will face them with ground-to-air nuts.

My challenge is a house with no locks. There are countless windows that can be opened from the outside and there is a huge dog entrance in the basement wall. We don't have keys for the front or back door and the kitchen is separated from the outdoor deck with a plastic sheet. I am confronted with a fear that is bigger than me, bigger than all of Holland. In Holland I always put a chair behind the front door when Syb was away at night.

In this house, that would be ridiculous, even hilarious. I had better invite my fear in; that seems the only way to go.

I go to work and count thirty-four places where you can access the house without any force. My purpose is let my eyes deliberately shine over *every* place someone could enter. When I am done, I have blown my fear up to the maximum and I am terrified. And with that…I let go of control and effortlessly the big balloon of fear sails out of sight. I walk around like a zombie. I don't recognize myself. My fear is GONE.

I place a photo of Sai Baba next to my bed and I pray to him with four simple words: "Let us be safe." What I would never have believed is that I fall in a deep, dreamless sleep. My fear of being alone at night is taken away by the wind that blows through the cracked windows with no lock.

The next few weeks while Syb is away, the radio announces high alerts: code orange or code red. The country is in deep fear; me too, but I don't want to invoke fear in the children. I play it "light." I keep reassuring them *we are safe. How can we not be?* Actually I am not 100% sure. A chemical attack is anticipated. The nuclear power plant in Massachusetts is close by. I don't even want to think of the consequences. The scare level is too high. Bush does his job; the media spreads his message. Shaffy, our 6 year old, declares he will not *wear any clothing with war prints anymore.* The GAP shirts and shorts go to the Salvation Army. We take the American flag down from the porch.

Despite the turmoil, we all love the serene atmosphere of the fall; in the middle of impending chaos, it feels so peaceful. Often on our walk to the bus stop, the kids say we live in a "fairytale." And no wonder, the scenery is magical with the colorful foliage and sight of the ocean all around us, not to forget *Squirrel Land* in our back yard.

I must admit it is absolutely a fairytale if I am oblivious to the outside world of war and threats. I admire the courage of my parents who do not cancel their trip to visit us. It is their first time. I am grateful they will come. There is nothing that will stop them from coming; even the airlines offer to exchange their tickets free of charge but they stand firm. They want to see us. *Who cares if it is only twelve days since the attack?*

"I can understand what you love about this life," my parents say one night. They understand what we have found and they have the guts to speak out. I realize what it costs them to admit this. Above all it is important for me to hear.

Now that they are here, the circle is complete, especially since they've acknowledged my decision to come to America. Their support feels like a HUGE, PROTECTIVE MANTLE. I love them for their honesty; I know how much they've missed seeing the seven of us. The *quality time* they spend with our kids is not forgotten. It is sealed like a gemstone in our hearts.

To have them as guests in our home is an honor and we have fun improvising. We still have very little furniture and no water downstairs but it doesn't bother them in the least.

They are experienced campers; for them, this is even better. I see how their skills come into full bloom watered by their love for us.

After dinner we put the dishes in a plastic tub and my dad volunteers to carry them upstairs and wash them in the shower. When it's time for them to fly back, it's very hard to let them go; they go back to the world to which we no longer belong. I want to hold onto them forever but instead I wave harder until they disappear through the gate at Northwest.

Time flies and life goes on. Syb returns, yet the pain of 9/11 is still *so* alive. The children adapt easily to school even though they speak so little English.

For hours Syb and I read with the kids. We are not used to the mandatory regiment of the American school system of a half an hour per child. The kids don't complain; in fact, they LOVE all the extra attention.

Syb and I are exhausted to the bone. We paint until midnight every night after the kids are done with their homework and then we fall asleep.

Their drive to master the English language is amazing. I deeply admire their fierce determination. In two months they speak American English like I never will; no accent and fluent like they have been here all their lives. In class at first they pretend to understand it all and somehow that works. However they do it, they are straight A students within a few months.

They are driven to do every single homework assignment. Some parts Syb and I do not understand so I go outside and stop a neighbor to ask for help. Amazingly it works every time. I feel a bit embarrassed but people are so helpful.

It is only later that I realize what a tremendous effort it took for my children to fit in this completely different culture, not only the language, but also the peer group pressure. I especially admire Florian, who started as a middle school student. When I imagine how he walked around by himself the first weeks, how he had to figure out where to go and what to do in school where no one spoke his native language, it makes my stomach churn.

Sytske and Shaffy tell me later that, when they first arrived on the playground at school, they huddled together in a corner of the yard but, after two weeks of that, they got pretty bored. They decided to venture out and each make his and her own friends.

The following morning, they put their plan in action; they split up and walk away from each other, each standing on their own two feet. They watch each other from the corner of their eyes. I never realized how inventive and courageous they were and capable to adjust themselves to this brand new life.

Sam who starts kindergarten goes from being the class clown in Holland to being the "silent kid." At first English to him sounds much like Chinese. However by Christmas, Sam speaks like a native and he is able to get his new friends to laugh at his jokes, too.

Gideon learns the two languages simultaneously. When I bring him to his playgroup, he speaks Dutch in the car.

When he arrives at Tracey's house, he mixes the two languages as soon as he steps in the door. On the way back in the car, he speaks English. Eventually he learns how to separate the two.

Never ever does any one of them complain about how difficult it is to adjust. Their teachers love their enthusiasm, courage and diligence. At the end of the year, each one receives an award for "the most improved student." I am not surprised.

For me, it takes *five years* of living in the US again to learn much of the slang and acronyms which make the American English language so rich and colorful. For example, I learn my five children are truly an All-Star Team; even as their mom, I know they each deserve an MVP – *most valuable player* – award for having played the game *Survivor: Kids vs. the American Jungle* so well and won.

Syb and I work tirelessly with much the same spirit. Our focus is the kids, the house and then our businesses, in that order. We figure the foundation must be solid for us to stand on and reach for the stars. I start putting out abundance prayers and affirm daily that good fortune falls into our laps. We need to start bringing in some money and the Universe can help.

The living proof of my prayers is found on the floor of every path I walk. As long as I pray, the coins are everywhere. I buy a little purse to save them.

One day I ask the Universe to give me a sign if I am ready to open my practice and to show me my life's work. The sign I ask for is a dollar. "Please put a dollar in front of me," I state. I find pennies, dimes but never enough quarters to make a dollar.

Soon I start to regret my request. I can't take it back; it is said and done. I hope the Universe heard me. I become impatient and set a date; I feel I can't wait forever until I get my sign. October 16th is the day I set to open my practice with or without a sign. I create a ritual in my orange-walled office and send my intention out to the Universe. My practice opens on October 16th; I decide to figure out my life's work later.

Nobody knows I have a practice. I have no flyers, no name cards and no American friends besides Frits and Joanna. A week later the phone rings and the one and only woman I told at the hypnotherapy conference what I do wants a session for a birthday present. "I have an opening on October 16th," I say pretending to be serious. I am jubilant when I put down the phone. I jump up and down. I am supported by the Universe and I can't wait to start.

The only thing that still bugs me is I haven't found my dollar yet. *What is the Universe waiting for?* I start looking at the floor every day, day after day. I am determined to find my dollar. After another week of pennies, I give it up and let go. What the heck . . . let the dollar be.

After that, I never look down, only UP.

All You Need Is Love.

— The Beatles

Come To the Edge

"Let's sing our *uni*-verse," I say. *All You Need Is Love* from the Beatles starts playing softly in the background. Everyone stands up and the wave begins. I signal to Dawn to turn up the volume. "Let's get loud from the inside out," Soul says.

I glance over the audience of soon-to-be-graduates of The Stillpoint School and wait a moment before I start my speech. We are all ready for the next step.

Two months before the course ends, Meredith asks me and all the other teachers to give a speech at this year's graduation ceremony. I'm excited to have the opportunity to give the students my final words of encouragement as a goodbye, fully trusting they will spread their wings and fly, each in their own way. It will be the last push to make them jump and soar.

We as teachers guide our own group of students through the four modules of the nine-month program. I am blessed with watching tremendous change and transformation. I am in love with all of my students. However, I am particularly aware of the inner journey of my own small group. In the first group meeting, I urge them to go ALL the way in this process of self discovery.

"Let's all lean IN and not lean back. We want to be players on the field, NOT spectators in the bleachers," I say.

We form a circle with our bodies and lean in; bending toward the middle of the circle with the intention to go DEEP.

It is worth all the effort; with that we laugh and our journey begins. During the next nine months, the birth and enjoyment of a new *Self* for each begins.

The night before the graduation, around twelve o'clock when Susan my fellow teacher and I are ready to go to sleep, there is a soft knock on the door. I open the door and see one of my students on the doorstep. She is in big trouble. "Hold me, heal me, treat me," she says and then cries unceasingly. She is scared to death about the ceremony.

As exhausted as Susan and I are, we take her in our arms; our tiredness disappears as soon we hold her. She seems in another world, far away. When I walk her back to her room, she is in a trance. I am not sure if she knows where she is and if she is aware what has happened in our room.

I whisper in her ear that she is ready for the next day. I don't think she hears me consciously. She says nothing. I feel like the mother she never had. I help her undress and tuck her in bed; she smiles but she is dreaming. I sit with her and wait until I am sure she is fast asleep. I feel honored.

As I walk back to my room, I realize that no matter our age we all need the reassurance of a mother at the moment we leave the nest and spread our wings. A mother's love and trust is the glue that keeps our wings attached on our backs.

The next morning I watch her enter the dining room for breakfast. She looks radiant and in good spirits. I overhear her tell the other students that last night she had a dream that an Angel came to her room and tucked her in. I think she really thought this was what happened. She continues her story and says that the Angel asked her what she needed and that she replied, "I need to learn to receive."

It is silent at the table and all the other women are listening intently. *What did she just say?* For all the women at the table *learning to ask and receive* is a huge issue. It is part of becoming whole; to become whole is a life journey.

I realize that for the very first time in her life, she dared to ask something for herself; at midnight, this was an especially difficult thing to do. After living a life of being in service as a nun, this woman in her last moment before "take off" experienced a tremendous break through simply by asking to be held. She is free now.

The ceremony is held in the main room of a building situated near a wooded area. Meredith and Pat are dressed beautifully. At this early hour they run around doing the final preparations. There are fresh flowers on the tables and the whole room vibrates with an exquisite presence of spiritual energy.

The students wait and welcome their friends and family in the downstairs area. A bell rings when the ceremony begins. Meredith welcomes everyone; the ones who can't be there are welcomed in spirit.

I sit with the teachers at the opposite side of the audience and look at Sai Baba's picture on the back wall. As an Indian Master who walks the earth in full presence of his divinity, he keeps an eye on everyone and on me, too. I look at the faces in the audience and sense their mixed emotions of joy, sadness and anxiety. In three hours they will each go their own way, free, unleashed and with no fear of flying . . . I hope.

When I was preparing my speech, I felt resistance in writing the words down. I like to be able to speak from my heart and not stumble over my words while reading. I want the students to remember the *message*; the words are not important. I know what I want to say and I also know I want to accompany my words with a Beatles song.

Because my speech is not typical, I am not sure if Meredith is okay with what I have in mind. I ask Meredith if I can play music as part of my talk. My feelings of concern are reflected in her answer. She says I may use music if it is *appropriate* in the context of the ceremonial atmosphere. I shrink inside and say, "Of course."

Now I am in doubt if I ought to change my speech and use different music or no music at all. *Should I tone it down?* If I am being true to myself, I have to do it *my way*, which may be louder and more flamboyant than "normal." *Should I shrink my Self down to the expected size by doing 'as expected' and reveal only the smaller version of me? What example would I be for the students?* This is exactly what they have "worked" on the whole year.

It was a good reminder for me of an important choice I had to make: be true to myself. I must stay "steady, steady, steady" just like Meredith said to us each day. "AND be LOUD," Soul adds with an impish grin. I find a way to compromise; I will say what I have to say – the speech is fine. The music will be played at the end but just the first few lines of the song. I will adjust the volume and play the music softly. Dawn, my helper, is instructed when and how to play the music.

When it is my turn to speak, I see Sai Baba's presence in the back of the room. He invites me to stand up. I hesitate. "Saskia, it is your birthright to speak," he says. I need no more encouragement; I take my place behind the podium while Sai Baba looks on.

I start my speech and the words fall easily out of my mouth; my paper stays in my pocket untouched. I tell the students (almost *graduates* now) how I saw my role as a teacher. I was a spiritual midwife. I was to assist at their birth. After being nourished for nine months in the school's womb and being fed the highest spiritual qualities and DNA, they were ready to be born; the course had come to an end simply because today was *Due Day*.

I talk about how everyone of us is a precious gem at birth and how, through the course of our life, we cover up our shining pearl. That all of our "not so good" experiences cling like sticky tape around the essence of our being; slowly we forget the brilliant gem we truly are. We lose our gem Self. If we are lucky, there comes a day when we catch a glimmer of the shining being we really are. We discover that our pure essence was *never* lost; it was *always* there.

No matter what happened in the past, our radiant, magnificent gem has *always* existed; it is up to us to uncover it. It's not about how covered up we are; it's about how to unravel the tape and reveal our true essence.

I share that what we don't know in Western cultures, they already know in certain tribes in Africa: "When a woman is pregnant she goes out into the woods with several other women and together they tune into the heart song of the unborn baby. When they know the song, they sing it to all the members of the tribe. From then until birth and throughout this baby's life, the elders sing to the child and remind her of her song. If the child grows older and commits a crime, instead of punishment, they put the child in the middle of the circle and sing the song again in order to help the child remember her true essence.

"The heart song holds all of the notes of our unique talents and gifts. It is about how we come to love and express our life's purpose." I go on with my story. When I look into the audience I see their hearts go wide open. They resonate with what is true for them, each recognizing something different. I wait another moment and say, "It is for all of us to sing our song to the fullest and bring forth our shining pearl. Listen to the whispers of your Soul to guide you home and never never give up on them." Heads nod, eyes tear.

"Remember that, when we choose to GO after our highest dreams, we need to take extraordinary action and leaps. We also need to be willing to live in the gap between action and results. The gestation period before birth can be tough.

"Nevertheless all of you have gone through all the stages of birthing and here you are to claim your birthright today!

"This year you nourished your essence and built the courage to bring forth the song that expresses the uniqueness that is you. You are almost ready to step outside this school's door and leave the nest…what a precious moment before birth. All that is left is for you to take the final jump."

I read a poem:

'Come to the edge', he said.
'We can't, Master, we're scared'
'Come to the edge', he said.
'We can't, Master, we're scared'
They came
He pushed them ...
They flew."

– Peter McWilliams

Silence. I can hear a pin drop in the audience. I continue. "Let yourself be carried into the greatness of your being. We do not live in Africa but here at the school, each of you have come to know your heart song. After listening to this story I imagine all of you are curious to discover your own heart song. Since we all have the same ingredients in our song, let's listen to the one basic ingredient we all share." I signal to Dawn to turn on the music.

All You Need Is Love begins to play softly at first; I signal Dawn to slowly turn up the volume.

I step back and lean toward the wall. One person stands up from her chair and sways from left to right, then the next person follows and so on, as if rehearsed: one after the other starts to move. A moment later we are all in a dance where everyone is harmoniously in tune with each other. The whole audience holds hands and sings like we are a gospel group in Africa.

I nod to Dawn to turn up the volume. I look at Meredith, not sure if she had this in mind at this ceremony, but there is no stopping it now. I see she is part of the wave, too. She embraces what happened spontaneously. She is smiling from deep within. A surge of joy goes through my heart. This is exactly what I intended, only *better*.

An hour later, they close the door behind us; the students leave as graduates. My job as a "midwife" is done; I feel satiated. They came to the edge and flew…

In the back of the room, Sai Baba smiles knowingly at me. *Sai Ram*

Facing Sai Baba

Why is it so hard to answer his question of four simple words?

For the third time I am joining The Stillpoint School. This time I am not a student or a teacher; I have the honor to be a member of the Graduate Faculty.

After three years I've climbed the ladder and today I am back in the presence of my great teachers, Meredith and Pat. I love them dearly.

My 'job' is to guide and grade the students in their final exam. From what I remember as a student, this exam was my most dreaded moment of the year. I didn't trust myself enough if I would receive accurate 'information' when I read my client's energy field. My fear was I would go blank and not 'get' anything. But Sai Baba's guidance came to me loud and clear. His whisper touched my inner ear; my reading turned into an amazingly powerful experience.

When I walk into the hotel lobby in Vermont and meet Meredith, I know I am home again. Every time I am in this school I have a deep spiritual experience and this time is no different.

As usual we start the morning with a meditation. Indian music plays softly; it helps us to drift even further into the still waters of our hearts. I feel very much at peace. The group breathes in deep silence and, when the time comes to close my eyes, I have watched every student sink into an altered state. Now it's my turn.

Before the meditation, Meredith talks about how our "false" beliefs make us think we have to play "small" instead of living the grandest expression of who we are. We'd rather hide our greatness. It is my favorite topic. It fascinates me that our fixed conclusions about who we are make up the storybook of our life.

To me it is sad when we function according to a "false" sense of self. If only we were aware that we live a limited version of our true potential, perhaps we would dare to dream big about what we wanted to be, do or have. We need to get out of our box and let go of our limiting beliefs.

What is my story; where is the quicksand? I drift deeper and let go.

Sai Baba shows up in the distance. His appearance is vague at first; however, I can't deny it's him when he lifts his veil. His presence is pure love, he smiles and waves at me. I don't know what to say. I wave back. *What does he want?*

"Sit down by the fire with me," Sai Baba points to a spot opposite of where he is seated. I kneel down and have a closer look. It looks like a very cozy fire but I feel naked and uncomfortable. I know he can see right through me. I don't want him to sense my hesitance.

"Give me your 'story' book," he says. He comes straight to the point. He wants to have the book that holds the story of my life. He looks at me and his Soulful eyes radiate an understanding and compassion that pierce my Soul. I can tell he is not taking *no* for an answer; he stands firm in his request.

He holds out his hand to receive my book; I refuse like a little girl who wants to guard her precious toy. *What is he thinking? Did he assume I would give him my book? Let him read the enthralling soap opera about me and my small self?* NO!

"You can throw your book in the fire, Saskia. Imagine how free you will be without your limiting story."

I sigh and cling to my book. I can't give him my story. I feel helpless and confused. *How can he ask me to burn my book; who will I be without my story?* I need some time and I am very uncomfortable. I'd like to run from this conversation; I can't escape.

Sai Baba repeats, "Throw your book in the fire, Saskia. Just imagine how free you will be when you let go of your limited story and release your limiting beliefs. Only then you will find the inspiration to tap into the story of who you really are."

I gather the courage to speak and say, "I cannot give you my book." I am surprised at how stubborn I am. *Why would I NOT give my book to the person who embodies true love?* I feel like I am drowning in my own quicksand.

I long to be free and float in bliss but *what if…?* My memory travels back to the first time I experienced bliss when I came back from Landmark Education in Amsterdam. That last night I left my story about who I was at the table in the big hall. I then floated on cloud nine for days. My mind was "turned off." I had no thoughts; there was no I, and neither did I have a limiting story. I was simply one BIG possibility.

The second time I was in the realms of the divine was when I had an operation on my head. For a few weeks I couldn't think anymore; my mind was numb. There were no beliefs or stories about myself. My life was organized by the hand of the divine. The ease and flow were more blissful than I can ever explain. Now those two times seem far away.

I shiver at the heat of the fire. I can't let go just yet. *What was I hanging onto and why? How well did my story serve me?*

How often do we have to hammer a boulder to cut it in half? Are all twenty-one hits needed to reach the breaking point? What about in my case? Yes, I must admit; I am a tough rock to crack.

Sai Baba takes his time. No hurry; he knows his way.

I cry big salty tears and sit like a log. I can't move. My body is locked in Baba's spell. I am at the breaking point but the hammer needs to come down one more time.

"Look at this fire and imagine it represents the Light of your Soul!"

I listen and stare at the fire; it is BIG and so luminous. It's mine; it is my Soul. *Was that what he said?* My knees hurt from kneeling.

"Give me some time Baba," I beg. Together we watch my fire. *Why is it so scary and difficult to let go of my story?* It fits like a comfortable piece of clothing around my body. Although I've delved into my story many times, apparently there is still more to explore.

I stand up, resisting the urge to stay in his presence forever. I look him deep in the eye. It makes me humble to stand in front of him.

"Give it to me." He is patient yet firm. Like a boxer he makes his unexpected move. He speaks slowly. Sai Baba's voice holds love and encouragement as he asks four life-changing words: "WHO ARE YOU NOT?"

My boulder cracks; this final blow hits me hard. I throw my book in the flames. I need no help. Sai nods and says nothing. The fire gets higher; its flames touch the sky. The book is burning; the fire gets bigger and my light does too. My whole body arches. I suddenly tremble from the cold of letting go while a fierce passion runs up my spine.

WHO AM I NOT? Oh, my God. I feel unlimited and free and my Soul dances around the fire in utter joy. The book is burned and my Light grows bigger. As soon as I shed the luggage of my past, my Light isn't dimmed anymore. *How incredible is Sai Baba for showing me what I needed to learn?* My cheeks are wet, my chin drips and my Soul soars. I have no words to express my gratitude for his lesson.

He doesn't let me leave before he has his final say, "You are *unlimited, creative* and *unique potentia*l, Saskia."

When I come back to the room, I am shaken to the bone. I share my journey with the students and we all cry. *Who are we not?*

Is this question too big for us to answer?

Indeed we need to bring our 'old' story to the fire and light the fire of our Soul to shine in full.

Perhaps he wants me to write my own enlightening story. *Why not*?

Dealing with the Devil

A seed is planted and the germination process begins.

"At least give him a call; he is expecting to hear from you," writes Sharon.

But why on earth would I go to a Writer's Workshop in Sedona? I pull two divination cards for counsel. "Wait" says my Devil. "Ready Set Go" says my Soul.

Her email starts with "Hello my dear friend" and from there on the letter raves about Tom and his workshop. Sharon promises I will learn how to write a book in a short amount of time and go home with a query letter in my hand. I have never heard of a query letter for a book. It doesn't ring a bell and I am not inspired at all by her email.

I dismiss Sharon's invitation and start my day a little agitated. I always get annoyed by the number of solicitation phone calls we get living in the States. It seems that sales people have permission to disturb you anytime and sell you something you are not interested in. This is a completely American phenomenon to us.

The Dutch don't like being pushed into ANYTHING. We have the "well if you really feel like it, you think about it first" attitude, and I am very Dutch in that way.

That is why I could hardly read through the whole letter. *Why was she doing this?* I thought she knew me better.

How little do I know that by opening her email a germination process has already begun. The whole day her message keeps coming back to me and some sort of curiosity about Tom stirs my imagination. *Who is he and why did she include my address in her group email?*

A day later I reread the email. To my stunning surprise, I understand that the email is personally addressed to ME. In the mood I was in, I had skipped the following: *"I know it sounds like I am trying to sell this seminar. I have no idea why I am in this frame of mind today. It's just that I keep waking up and feeling like I need to tell you about it. It is your time to write..."*

I trust Sharon's gut feeling and now my mind races a hundred miles an hour trying to combine the pieces of the puzzle. *Oh, how could I have missed the most important sentence?* I get the chills. I better check out his website, I think, but the truth is I don't need to do that anymore. *What do I need to know about Tom if deep inside I already know the answer?*

Yes, I am to write a book. I've heard that before, not once but many times. However, up until now, THE BOOK had something of a "one day" quality. My life is busy enough. This is NOT a priority on my "to do" list. *Above all, is it my time?*

When I pull two Angel and Dolphin cards from the divination deck, the duality in me is obvious. The first card says:" Wait, don't rush into action right now, bide your time for better results."

The second card says: "Ready, Set, Go! Now is the perfect moment to dive in and embrace your heart's desire."

Again I am confronted with my two sides—*who will win this time?* I am tired of the debate: Devil vs. Soul. *Wouldn't it be easier if I had only one side?* My shadow side or Devil is the part of me that is so fearful of change; it loves to keep me chained. It will always resist any action that moves me toward growth and expansion. My Soul or Higher Self, the fearless and free part, will do anything to move me into my grandest potential, no matter what.

In this case I need to make a choice. *Whose counsel do I follow?* I think of Sai Baba's four rock-busting words: WHO ARE YOU NOT? *Am I being asked to let go of the smaller version of myself, to take another leap and follow my heart's desire? If I choose to go to Sedona, how will the Universe orchestrate this?*

In the confused state I am in, it doesn't cross my mind I don't have to worry about the *how* if this is meant to be. And, of course, as it turns out this "plan" was "in the works" much longer. I have an unused ticket in my desk with an expiration date of May 17th. This means I have to use it in the next few weeks otherwise I lose $450 dollars.

In addition, Sharon owes me money for sessions; she wants to pay what she owes me by paying the class fee. I know she will smile from ear to ear when I ask her to. So basically my ticket and workshop costs are already paid for.

Why did everything fall so easily into place? The last thing I have to do is ask Syb what he thinks.

"Syb, what do you think about me going to a writers' workshop in Sedona?" I ask.

He doesn't hesitate and immediately wants to join me. "Let's go together," he replies.

Facing practicality in this peak season of soccer, baseball and cheerleading makes it hard to leave five kids and eight animals to someone else's care for a week. We decide Syb will go later.

And so it happens I give Sharon a call and tell her I am flying in on Thursday, the day the workshop starts. She is delighted and not surprised. She knows me well.

From the moment I book my flight, the key lesson is to be flexible and open to change. Sharon tries to arrange for the two of us to meet before the workshop starts while arranging that I carpool with her friends. There are so many hurdles on the road to make this happen I start wondering why we even tried it in the first place.

Until I arrive in Tom's basement, things change about every hour: the flight schedules, the pick up times, the car pool, the people who will attend, the hotel, how the rooms are divided up, you name it. The day's motto is: *The only thing that is constant is change.*

In Tom's basement a new part of Self emerges.

It takes three big steps to enter Tom's basement. It is pretty symbolic to me why the workshop happens down there.

When I come in, I step into the battlefield where my Devil reigns. I descend into the deep caverns of my subconscious mind and meet my shadow.

A feeling of being totally out of place sweeps over me. The many leaps I took before seem to disappear in a flash. *Where is my courage today?* I am no longer confident and my Soul's connection is nowhere to be found. I feel lost among the experienced writers. This is definitely one of the very few times in my life that I am in the wrong place at the wrong time. What an agonizing mistake.

The basement is very simple: two couches, a few tables and chairs, no windows to distract us, and only water for break time. We are to concentrate on *ourselves*, I conclude.

An enormous headache settles in as soon as I walk into the underground room. My whole body aches and my bottle of ibuprofen is in my bedside drawer in Rockport. My doubt is enormous. I am the only participant who never wrote.

When it is my turn, I share that my Higher Self, my Soul, is very excited about being here but my small self, my personality, thinks this is a kamikaze action. I have a strong feeling I will die and not make it through. They think what I say is funny but I don't. I am dead serious.

Tom confidently reassures me I am the most advantaged student here. No screwed up background or "skills" to silence or get in the way of my real writer's voice. His words sound like honey to my ears; they don't soothe my nerves.

Before we start we do a deep breathing exercise; we need to be very loud and expressive and make sure to let out ALL our stress. To me this seems more like a tantric breathing or birthing workshop. *Was this what I came all the way here for?* According to Tom, we are a group with too much experience, too much left brain from the East Coast and, with that, too much resistance. That is why we need to do A LOT of breath work.

I wish my headache would go away. I can't even think in this state of pain; it makes me very uncomfortable. "Pain is resistance," says Tom. *What am I resisting after all the effort I made to get here?* "Breathe through," he keeps saying. I do my best and my head keeps pounding. *To give birth was much simpler* I am thinking.

If pain is resistance and we apply this principle to birthing, I suddenly understand why I didn't experience pain in the birthing of my five children. In those moments I surrendered and completely gave over to my body's wisdom. I let my mind go to sleep and instead I watched my body perform the miracle, just like nature intended. My attitude was of letting go. So simple that was…

My mind is digesting this simple sentence from Tom. It makes me understand birthing, and why fear installs so much resistance resulting in pain.

But what was my fear of writing about? What would happen if I let go and surrendered? Would I be able to birth a book? That would be a miracle.

Tom introduces his writer's technique in between our breath work. We have to write at a very fast speed.

He says that, if we don't reach that speed, we are still writing from our ego or left brain. We are meant to write from our heart and Soul and that is very fast if we do it right.

"Let's count the words after an hour of writing and see if you are really connected to the author within" is Tom's assignment. And there we go as if we are in a race. I really try to write as fast as I can. My only problem is I don't know what to write about. When the hour is up, the group starts counting and most are in the range between 1800-2400. The lowest number is somewhere around 1300. I count 947. I cringe when it is my turn to share my answer.

"You must have counted wrong," says Tom. He is very sure of himself. Only I know I sneaked a few more words into my count.

I feel embarrassed and the silent voice of my Devil takes advantage and speaks very loud, "See, you are NOT an author and you should have stayed home." I agree and think I should have listened earlier. *Yes* perhaps *you* are right.

I feel a strong sense of intimidation begin to rise and with that my anger rises, too. I am not putting up with my victim mode anymore. I decide to give up whatever limited story I have about myself. I don't want to be a failure and stay stuck in some sort of crazy belief I cannot write. *How can I not write?* I have many stories to tell. I am the only one to free my Self into the world of my unlimited potential. It is MY call.

There is more breath work for us. I'm not the only one who lets go of some heavy *STUFF*.

"Okay. Now let's do another hour of writing," says Tom. This time I am off and running. In fact, I race. It pays off; at the next stopping point, I count 1950 words. Now I *am* the one who thinks I counted wrong; but it is right. Relief comes over me. Maybe I am in the right place at the right time after all. I am now in my right brain and Soul is in control.

After lunch we do a visualization that makes an enormous impact on me.

"Go back to the time six months before you were born," says Tom. I close my eyes and drift back in time and space. Since I am a very visual person, I just allow myself to follow Tom's instruction without any resistance.

Almost instantly I feel the essence of my Soul arise. The joy and light become present in its purest form. I tingle; the feeling is so intense. I overflow with joy to be able to live my purpose to the fullest. I am in harmony with the divine. I float breathless and I am lost in this timeless place where God is.

I look down. The earth seems very far away. Nevertheless I trust that life is waiting and I decide I am ready to leave the cosmic nest. I travel down the umbilical cord of the Divine and enter into the moment of my physical birth.

Suddenly I am born and, even though I am overjoyed to be in the company of my parents again, I don't recognize anything in my earthly surroundings.

I smell the heavy odor of disinfectant and I turn my head in disgust as if I am really back in the bedroom of my parents. I hear faint noises in the background but the vibration is so different and so dense from what I was used to.

And then it happens: I tone down my high-spirited energy to match the heavier earthly notes. I decide to 'adjust.' I will adapt, not be *too* much, *too* loud or *too* exuberant. I tone myself down. In this split-second, I lose an important part of myself. It becomes part of my life's journey to tune-up to my heart song again.

An original piece I hold on to throughout the course of my life and adventures. The love I feel for my parents remains deeply anchored in my heart.

Tom keeps talking while insights flash like light bulbs in my head.

"Ask your purpose" is Tom's next direction.

I am meant to connect completely to the presence of the divine and to help myself and others learn to trust in the voice of our Soul. The voice is crystal clear. I not only know but feel the truth of what I hear. My eagerness to follow my purpose makes me forget the challenges that are a part of earthly life.

When God's voice asked, "Are you sure you want to go to earth and be your promise?" I know I am ready to dive into my Soul's desire. I am ready, set and here I go!

"Ask for the title of your book and write down what you see, hear or feel." Tom is very straightforward with his directions.

I guess the process works best in this way. No endless brainstorming, just a heartfelt answer straight from your Soul is what he is seeking for us. I suddenly see the words "A Suitcase Full of Faith" as if it is that easy.

I write down my answer. Only later do I come to understand what this book is all about. For now I have enough to work with. Tom is satisfied and not at all surprised.

After dinner, Sharon, Christine and I go to our bedroom. As soon as the three of us sit on my bed, Sharon says as I was expecting, "Let's do some cards." We each pull a few cards from the divination deck I brought with me. I draw the card "Divine Magic" and I can't be happier and encouraged.

The atmosphere starts to lighten up and the room is full of laughter. I am teasing Sharon about *The Devil* card in the tarot deck; he is our shadow, the part we'd rather hide I tell her. He loves to play hide and seek.

When I ask the cards with what kind of energy I should write this book,

I pull *The Devil.* A heavy silence falls and then we burst out in laughter. We almost roll off the bed. This is what I get from teasing others and talking about the Devil behind his back.

Truthfully I am stunned. *What do I think of this?* I definitely don't like it. I understand my Devil doesn't want me to be here; he doesn't want change. No daring adventures for him . . . or me. But I can't entertain his presence while I am in this workshop.

Or should I?

Sharon pulls one more card and gets *The Star*, my favorite card in the deck. It is all about trust. I still stare at *The Devil.* He is my least favorite card of the deck. I will sleep on my Devil's counsel when I go to bed. How little do I know that this card was the most powerful and insightful card I could have pulled.

When I switch off the light and put my head to rest on the pillow. I envision *Divine Magic* surrounding me. I push *The Devil* to the background. I sleep deep and can't remember my dream when I wake early. Christine is still asleep. When I look outside, I see the pink and orange reflection of the Red Rock Mountains at this hour of sunrise.

Something has shifted during my sleep and I don't know what it is. I feel the need to go into meditation and write. When I go to the bathroom, blood falls. *Why now?* I thought it was not quite my time to get my period. Overnight, my body becomes attuned with the flow of my writing process. I feel an enormous surge of energy from head to toe. The game of hide and seek is over. *WHO AM I and WHO AM I NOT? Was I a writer or what?*

My resistance is gone; so is my headache. I can now look the Devil in the face. I have become friends with him overnight. Instead of pushing him away, I will include him in my query letter and in my book. He is a key person in the process of transformation and in birthing my Self anew. Each and every time I wanted change, my Devil would pop up. I was "warned" and shouldn't be surprised. My pen starts flowing and I can't wait to join the other writers in Tom's basement this morning.

When I go down to breakfast, I begin to feel spaced out and can't decide what to eat. The coffee tastes like dish water. Tom has strongly advised us not to drink stimulants but, of course, I have to go against his rule. I am strongly feeling the need for some routine that reminds me of my good old self.

The bagel is not what it seems to be either. I suddenly feel confused. *Where is my life going?* Apparently, change takes constant vigilance.

Deep down I must have known now that my body, mind and Soul were all in tune, change was going to happen no matter what. This was not going to be a little change but a *big* change. In one thing I was sure: It would not always be easy. In what other ways it would affect me, I didn't know. I just knew I was not in control of the process anymore; I had no choice. *Letting go* was the special order of the day.

Following the workshop, I fly back to Boston. I am deeply satisfied. I promise myself I will write this book *no matter what.*

Had I left my Devil in Sedona? I was in for a surprise.

The Devil Wears Prada

Day ONE: 4:00 AM. The high-pitched beep of the alarm wakes me at this ungodly hour. I have no choice. My time is up. I turn around and feel the softness of the blankets wrapped around me. I feel so safe but not for long.

I wiggle my toes and stir my body. The Devil purrs at my side, attempting to arouse me with his teasing presence while showing me his magnetic, satiny smile.

"Don't go," he whispers. I *shhhh* at him, roll out of bed and stumble out into the hallway. A meowing cat brushes against my bare leg. I shriek and almost lose my courage.

I quickly run across the hallway as if I can't be late. When my hand touches the doorknob I feel his warm breath on my neck. A shiver runs up my spine; he wants me to listen one last time. The endless list of obstacles to stop me from writing rattles staccato in my ear: the schedules, the five kids, their practice, my practice, eight animals and my husband far away… The Devil makes his point.

How dare I say *here I AM no matter what?* I hold my breath.

Without my pushing, the door swings open and there I am face to face with Soul. Her broad smile welcomes me and warms my trembling body. Divine blue eyes look at me intently; she needs an answer now. I nod my head yes.

Gently she takes my hand and leads me to my desk. A streak of moonlight peeks through the curtains, curiously watching if I will put my pen to paper.

Within my breath, the in… the out… the roles are changed. At this hour of cracking dawn, surrender was the key to open the door. If I wanted to write, I needed to let Soul speak and not myself.

Instead of pushing to achieve, I had to listen and receive. I had to move out of my comfort zone into my heart, the place where the voice of my Soul resides.

I reminded myself to reduce my speed and be in the presence of the here and now.

I was *so* green.

Opening Heaven's Gate

Sa Ta Na Ma . . .

Day TWENTY-TWO: 9:00 AM.

The key fits and effortlessly I unlock Heaven's gate. I walk in on my tiptoes, carrying a stack of handwritten words on paper. When I lock the gate a few hours later, I am carrying a book under my arm.

With one last sweep I clean the wooden kitchen table, I am done. Gideon and Sam are backpacked and ready to go. Mentally I do the check list: the lunch bags are filled, the homework papers signed, the books back to the library in time, soccer shoes and socks for practice, and off we go…

When I kiss them goodbye at the bus stop, Gideon asks me where I am going. "I am going to Heaven," I say matter-of-factly. I smile and wave at their happy faces pressed against the dirty windows until the bus disappears around the corner of Pigeon Cove.

I hope they know me well enough not to take my words too literally.

Thursday is my *Heaven Day*, and this particular morning my stomach is filled with butterflies and a giddy sense of anticipation that something BIG is gonna happen. An important cycle in my writing is coming to an end. I am ready for its spinning turn to go around in the circle of completion and begin a new phase, not only for my book but for my life as well.

When I started the first page, I had no clue how many pages needed to follow to complete the birthing process and deliver a book.

I just wrote. Tom told me I would know absolutely 100% when there was nothing more to say. I found that hard to believe and I singled myself out as an exception to the rule. I was not as predictable as his other students. Now I knew Tom was right; the flow of inspiration diminished all of a sudden, and the finishing line, the last line, was to be written this Thursday.

It will take me about an hour to get to HEAVEN. The drive along the winding road is smooth and easy. The familiarity of the first part amuses me; for a year I've passed the antique shops with their junk displayed along the side of the road, from iron strollers to rocking chairs that creak when you look at them. They sit untouched and I feel sorry for them. My trained eye spots the rust of neglect. I still check them out, time after time.

The last part of the drive takes me through bountiful yellow fields of sunflowers; their open faces encourage me to keep my pace. I can't hurry in any way. The timing is divine.

A year before, a friend of mine hands me an article. "You need to check this out," she says. Karen knows that for quite a while I was longing to find place to teach, so far to no avail.

When I read about HEAVEN, *Healing Arts and Educational Revenue*, in Newburyport, I know I have found my place. I call and set up a time to meet. A week later my workshops and classes are announced on HEAVEN's website.

Amy invites me in with the words, "Saskia, you may teach any class you want, HEAVEN awaits you." These words caress my Soul. Yes, to be a teacher in HEAVEN, of course, *where else?*

I've never felt more welcome.

And here I am a year later, same date, the golden key clutched in my hand. Carefully I unlock HEAVEN's gate and tiptoe through the peaceful, sleeping place. The Buddha statue at the entrance looks at me and giggles. *How can I pretend to be invisible and escape the piercing eyes of the angels and goddesses displayed on the shelves?* I am careful and quiet as if they would stop me on my way to the blue room. I am too preoccupied to really notice their stares; only on my way out do I hear their cheers.

Just like the birthing of my children, this moment requires a diligent patience. I am going to *allow* and *receive* instead of *push to achieve*. I set the stage and close the curtains, light the candles and settle down into the furry pillows of the *sink-in* sofa. I deeply want to savor this sacred moment of birth with every fiber of my being.

With one deep breath, I start my hum and write down my last words in a tempo that is not mine. Within minutes not hours, I am finished. The book is born. I willingly receive it cradled in my arms.

When I am done, I just sit there and a stream of tears I don't bother to dry roll down my cheeks. I don't know myself.

Who AM I? What have I done? I WROTE A BOOK! *Do I dance? Do I sing? Do I cartwheel on the table? Or do I get out of this holy place and plant my feet on the asphalt earth outside the door?*

It's very unsettling now that *The Manifest is Reality. Gosh, how little did I know what I was about to birth!*

I can't remember how long I sit there and wait until I am ready to get up and leave. It seems like light years later; I open the curtains, blow out the candles and step over the threshold of the blue room, facing the angelic chorus outside the door.

With a skip and a jump, I am outside the gate, my golden key locks HEAVEN, and joyfully I carry *A Suitcase Full of Faith* to my car.

It's now 3:30 PM. I am back at the bus stop in time.

"How was HEAVEN, Mom?" they ask.

I just smile as if nothing happened.

PART SIX

Epilogue

Spinning Full Circle

The room is barely lit. The people next to me breathe heavily. Our drenched bodies are whipped by the teacher's words to fire up the speed and cross the Finish line. The last hill is in sight. It's almost over. Soon we will be Home.

"Give it your all, don't save anything for last. What are you saving it for? Make sure you are USED UP at the end of the race."

Nobody seems to notice but my ride ain't over yet. In one swift motion I find myself on top of the hill. Abiding my courage, I gaze over the edge of the majestic mountain I have climbed. Far below me the earth is moist, the rivers wild; in front of me the horizon rolls wide open. My arms stretch out to the sky. *Why don't I leap? What am I waiting for?*

In one flash the weaving of my web unfolds. I catch a glimpse of how my life unravels in a trail of golden strands; showing my thread in a step with Soul's courageous lead, the unpaved road I followed no matter what.

In this sacred moment of contemplation I long to lay back and nestle in the velvety lining of Mother Earth's womb. But I am called to jump, the beat of passion and purpose pulsates through my veins, igniting my Soul's desire to raise myself to the highest octave and sing my heart song in full.

However before I go, I need to check my luggage, gather my tools and fill my rucksack with Faith and Trust. *What else do I need to survive this earthly call?*

With one big leap, I birth myself anew into the land of the unknown using God's bungee cord as the jumping rope from which I soar. The gravity pulls me up instead of down. For a split second I dangle above the earth, but I have no fear my divine thread is of eternal strength. I am safe in God's embrace no matter where I land.

The music stops and the light goes on.

I look around me. I am alone. *Where have I been?* I have been nowhere. I am here, HOME.

I have to call Gloria Gaynor and tell her she will survive.

My heart fills up with Joy. I've reached the finish line. Before my spinning wheel comes to a halt, I owe my spinning teacher an answer.

"Yes, here I am. I will live my life on the bare feet of my Soul, fearless and free, no matter what!

SASKIA RÖELL

Saskia sees through masks. She knows how to lure you to your truth, the point of no return, where deep change is based on deep trust and you welcome the leap into a new life.

As a Transformational Life Coach, Saskia guides with compassion, humor, wisdom, and commitment at the level of the Soul. The most powerful tool she offers is the example she sets in her life through the revelation of her own stories. She empowers others to live from the heart, find the courage to follow their dreams, and reinvent their lives.

Saskia found her passion for empowering others while teaching at the Rijksuniversiteit of Groningen, in The Netherlands, as a member of the Faculty of Behavioral and Social Sciences in the Department of Experimental Psychology. She has extensively studied the conscious mind, the subconscious mind, and the superconscious mind and how our unhealed emotions effect our destiny.

In 2001 Saskia, her husband, and their five young children took a daring leap of faith, sold their house in Holland, and gave up their thriving businesses to explore new possibilities in the United States. With little money, no job prospects, no contacts and five kids who didn't speak a word of English, they landed in a small town by the sea. It was a challenge of a lifetime. Saskia, however, trusted they could reinvent their lives at that moment.

She has written a book, A Suitcase Full of Faith, about the grand adventure of that move and the example she set of trusting in the face of great challenges.

In 2007, Saskia was initiated into the 9th Rite, the Creator Rite, of the Munay Ki in the south central Andes of Peru. She also uses the powerful tools of the Law of Attraction and the Toltec Wisdom teachings of Miguel Ruiz as an integral part of her work.

Saskia's clients live all over the world and come from all walks of life. She travels internationally, presenting seminars, conducting workshops and facilitating sessions for individuals.

A NOTE FROM SASKIA:

Within the stories there are several tools I describe and use for amazing results in my life and for others in my healing practice. These are real techniques from my toolbox that work and can work for you, too. An online downloadable Suitcase Full of Faith Workbook is due out soon and will support what you learned in the book in a fun yet practical way. For more information on this workbook please write to me at DIVINETHREAD@VERIZON.NET.

Many Many Blessings and Abundance to You and Your Soul!

Saskia

WWW.SUITCASEFULLOFFAITH.COM

Workshops and Personal Coaching with Saskia

The programs are available as in-person workshops and teleclasses for groups; individual sessions tailored to a client's personal needs are available over the phone or in the office. Pricing depends upon the size of the group, format and travel. Please ask for a quote and for more info by email to DIVINETHREAD@VERIZON.NET. New workshop listings and a program calendar are available upon request. Ask Saskia to tailor a program to fit your business or personal needs.

What's in Your Suitcase?

A five-week program of personal empowerment

For groups or individuals

Join me on a tailor-made transformational adventure for individuals ready to explore uncharted territory. Go on a deep transformational journey beginning with the question "Who am I?" and resulting in "I am____." At the end of this program you receive your Soul Compass Statement which illuminates your talents, gifts, and life purpose.

What's in Your Briefcase?

A five-week program of personal empowerment for businesspeople

For groups or individuals

What's in Your Briefcase? tailors the What's in Your Suitcase? program to the special needs of businesspeople. I'll guide you to evaluate your personal values and visions and learn how to express them in congruence with your business life. You'll learn how to make your work a reflection of your greatest passion and create balance between business and personal life.

Finding Your Heart Song

A five-session program for tuning up your soul

For individuals

Our heart is the key to our soul. If we tune in to our heart, we can express our essence in all aspects of our life and claim our birthright of full self-expression. When we're in harmony with our song, we're happy and fulfilled.

The Fascinating Journey of a Woman's Soul

Programs supporting the powerful journey of motherhood

Each program is designed to optimize the most important moments in a woman's life. Saskia, the mother of five children experienced the joy of natural birthing and how motherhood leads to a greater expression of Self and what that means to you. Based upon her extensive life-experience combined with her unparalleled professional expertise, Saskia is now offering these three life-enhancing programs:

The Fertility Intensive:

Supporting Women on Their Journeys to Conception

The Fertility Intensive helps women to release blocks and tap into their natural capacities to become pregnant.

The Joy of Birthing:

Setting the Stage for the Biggest Celebration of All

Saskia will teach you birthing the natural way, trusting and tuning into the innate wisdom of your body.

The Joy of Motherhood:

Preparing for a Life-Changing Experience

Saskia will provide tools and support to help you manage the change and transition into motherhood.

Munay Ki and the 9th Rite

This evolutionary program will both include the energetic transmission of the Nine Rites of the Munay Ki and provide the necessary tools and exercises to empower you to become all that you are. Why wait?

SASKIA RÖELL

BELIEF COACH TRANFORMATIONAL LIFE COACH SOUL COACH

Sign up for Saskia's teleclasses and book study at

WWW.SUITCASEFULLOFFAITH.COM

For more info on Saskia's workshops and coaching, go to

WWW.ILLUMINATEDTRANSFORMATION.COM

DIVINETHREAD@VERIZON.NET

Cover Design by Colin Miller

www.OneGraphic.com